P9-ARN-227

The Human Tradition in America

CHARLES W. CALHOUN
Series Editor
Department of History, East Carolina University

The nineteenth-century English author Thomas Carlyle once remarked that "the history of the world is but the biography of great men." This approach to the study of the human past had existed for centuries before Carlyle wrote, and it continued to hold sway among many scholars well into the twentieth century. In more recent times, however, historians have recognized and examined the impact of large, seemingly impersonal forces in the evolution of human history—social and economic developments such as industrialization and urbanization as well as political movements such as nationalism, militarism, and socialism. Yet even as modern scholars seek to explain these wider currents, they have come more and more to realize that such phenomena represent the composite result of countless actions and decisions by untold numbers of individual actors. On another occasion, Carlyle said that "history is the essence of innumerable biographies." In this conception of the past, Carlyle came closer to modern notions that see the lives of all kinds of people, high and low, powerful and weak, known and unknown, as part of the mosaic of human history, each contributing in a large or small way to the unfolding of the human tradition.

This latter idea forms the foundation for this series of books on the human tradition in America. Each volume is devoted to a particular period or topic in American history and each consists of minibiographies of persons whose lives shed light on that period or topic. Well-known figures are not altogether absent, but more often the chapters explore a variety of individuals who may be less conspicuous but whose stories, nonetheless, offer us a window on some aspect of the nation's past.

By bringing the study of history down to the level of the individual, these sketches reveal not only the diversity of the American people and the complexity of their interaction but also some of the commonalities of sentiment and experience that Americans have shared in the evolution of their culture. Our hope is that these explorations of the lives of "real people" will give readers a deeper understanding of the human tradition in America.

Volumes in the Human Tradition in America series:

Ian K. Steele and Nancy L. Rhoden, eds., *The Human Tradition in Colonial America* (1999). Cloth ISBN 0-8420-2697-6
Paper ISBN 0-8420-2700-9
Nancy L. Rhoden and Ian K. Steele, eds., *The Human Tradition in the American Revolution* (2000). Cloth ISBN 0-8420-2747-5
Paper ISBN 0-8420-2748-3
Ballard C. Campbell, ed., *The Human Tradition in the Gilded Age and Progressive Era* (2000). Cloth ISBN 0-8420-2734-3
Paper ISBN 0-8420-2735-1
Steven E. Woodworth, ed., *The Human Tradition in the Civil War and Reconstruction* (2000). Cloth ISBN 0-8420-2726-2
Paper ISBN 0-8420-2727-0
David L. Anderson, ed., *The Human Tradition in the Vietnam Era* (2000). Cloth ISBN 0-8420-2762-9   Paper ISBN 0-8420-2763-7
Kriste Lindenmeyer, ed., *Ordinary Women, Extraordinary Lives: Women in American History* (2000). Cloth ISBN 0-8420-2752-1
Paper ISBN 0-8420-2754-8
Michael A. Morrison, ed., *The Human Tradition in Antebellum America* (2000). Cloth ISBN 0-8420-2834-X
Paper ISBN 0-8420-2835-8
Malcolm Muir Jr., ed., *The Human Tradition in the World War II Era* (2001). Cloth ISBN 0-8420-2785-8   Paper ISBN 0-8420-2786-6

THE HUMAN TRADITION IN
THE VIETNAM ERA

THE HUMAN TRADITION IN
THE VIETNAM ERA

No. 5
The Human Tradition in America

Edited by
David L. Anderson

A Scholarly Resources Inc. Imprint
Wilmington, Delaware

© 2000 by Scholarly Resources Inc.
All rights reserved
First published 2000
Printed and bound in the United States of America

Scholarly Resources Inc.
104 Greenhill Avenue
Wilmington, DE 19805-1897
www.scholarly.com

Library of Congress Cataloging-in-Publication Data

The Human tradition in the Vietnam era / edited by
David L. Anderson.
   p. cm. — (Human tradition in America ; no. 5)
   Includes bibliographical references and index.
   ISBN 0-8420-2762-9 (cl. : alk. paper). — ISBN 0-8420-2763-7 (pa. :
alk. paper)
   1. Vietnamese Conflict, 1961–1975—United States. 2. United
States—History—1945– I. Series. II. Anderson, David L., 1946–

DS558.H83 2000
959.704'3373 21—dc21

                                                99-045345

∞ The paper used in this publication meets the minimum require-
ments of the American National Standard for permanence of
paper for printed library materials, Z39.48, 1984.

For Billy Terry, Bill Weber, and the more than fifty-eight thousand other Americans who paid the ultimate human price in Vietnam

About the Editor

DAVID L. ANDERSON is professor of history, chair of the Department of History and Political Science, and associate dean of arts and sciences at the University of Indianapolis. His book *Trapped by Success: The Eisenhower Administration and Vietnam, 1953–1961* (1991) won the Robert H. Ferrell Book Prize from the Society for Historians of American Foreign Relations. He also is the author of *Imperialism and Idealism: American Diplomats in China, 1861–1898* (1985) and the editor of *Shadow on the White House: Presidents and the Vietnam War, 1945–1975* (1993) and *Facing My Lai: Moving beyond the Massacre* (1998). He earned a Ph.D. from the University of Virginia, Charlottesville, and served in Vietnam in the U.S. Army.

Contents

Introduction

David L. Anderson

In April 1975, President Gerald R. Ford declared in a speech to college students at Tulane University that the Vietnam War was "finished as far as America is concerned."[1] Momentarily stunned, the audience then erupted with thunderous applause. The ovation was not for Ford himself, although many of his listeners appreciated his frank admission of a fact that had long been apparent. Nor was it a celebration of victory, for the government that the United States had long supported in South Vietnam had already collapsed. Its communist-led enemies were rapidly completing their final military assault on the Southern capital of Saigon. Indeed, the audience was demonstrating approval of a statement that was not historically true. Ford and the students could not know it at that time, but the war was far from over. The guns were falling silent and twenty-five years of direct U.S. intervention in Southeast Asia were ending, but the pain and divisiveness that the war had generated in America would long remain.

The loud applause in response to Ford's simple announcement was an emotional release reflecting a widespread desire among Americans to put the lengthy Vietnam nightmare in the past. The war had tested and tormented Americans collectively and individually in ways few other historical events had. Wars usually begin as calculations of global strategy by political leaders, and they are usually remembered and analyzed as intellectual abstractions of national power and interest. Like nations, however, wars are about people. They are begun, fought, and ended by individuals who are members of families and local communities as well as nations. War is part of the human tradition. It is a big story, like frontier settlement or economic depression, that is composed of thousands of smaller stories. The applause from that Tulane audience was a collective sigh of relief, a human response to a human experience.

In 1975 the United States was beginning to move out of the Vietnam era, but the starting date of that era is more difficult to mark. In the early 1950s U.S. leaders began to consider Vietnam a vital area in the global Cold War against the Soviet Union, the People's Republic of China (PRC), and other communist states. The Eisenhower administration moved to bolster the fledgling government of South Vietnam against possible attack from communist North Vietnam and armed insurrection from communist-led guerrillas in the South. During the 1950s, however, the number of Americans actually in Vietnam as soldiers or civilian officials was less than one thousand. In the early 1960s the insurgency in South Vietnam increased in intensity, and the number of U.S. military personnel jumped to several thousand. U.S. financial aid to the Saigon government multiplied. Despite this American support of the South Vietnamese regime and in part because the aid made the government appear to be a puppet of Washington, internal resistance increased. The usually passive Buddhist clergy charged President Ngo Dinh Diem, a Roman Catholic, with political repression and religious persecution; some monks even burned themselves to death in protest. Discontented South Vietnamese military officers overthrew the Diem government in November 1963 and killed the president and his brother in the process. As political chaos deepened in Vietnam, it appeared that a decade of U.S. efforts to build a noncommunist nation in the South was about to end in failure.

In 1964 and 1965, President Lyndon Johnson moved reluctantly toward the fateful decision that direct U.S. military force would be necessary to sustain South Vietnam. U.S. aircraft began bombing North Vietnam, and full combat divisions launched offensive ground operations in the South. By the end of 1965, there were 184,300 American troops in South Vietnam, and that number grew to a peak of 543,400 in April 1969. The total of Americans killed in Southeast Asia also edged steadily upward, reaching 39,964 by the end of 1969, with no end in sight. As the size and cost of the U.S. commitment escalated, public dissatisfaction and protest also grew. Thousands of Americans took to the streets to express their opposition to the war. Other citizens felt that the protesters were aiding America's enemies. Deep social and intellectual rifts ran through the population.

The Vietnam War forced Americans to make some intensely personal choices. This challenge was not unique in American history. Colonial Americans in the 1770s took enormous individual risks in siding with or against the anti-British insurrection, and Americans in both the North and the South during the Civil War era faced similar choices. Like the Revolution, Civil War, and Great Depression, the Vietnam era marked a historical divide that brought lasting changes in the way Americans thought about themselves, their country, and their country's future. Unlike some of those other watershed events, however, the Vietnam War itself was something in which many Americans, perhaps even a majority, were able to avoid direct involvement. Yet no citizen could escape the conflict's sweeping impact on the nation's attitudes. A visible example emerged during the 1992 presidential election. The legal (and for many, the acceptable) ways in which Vice President Dan Quayle and presidential candidate Bill Clinton had avoided military service in Vietnam evoked questions over twenty years later about each man's character and patriotism. Quayle had found a way to fill one of the rare vacancies in the National Guard that virtually assured he would not be assigned to Vietnam. Clinton benefited from a draft system that allowed not only educational deferments but also local determination of who would serve. Millions of others during the Vietnam era had to choose from an array of options, including whether to serve, resist, protest the war, remain quiet, support the war, go to jail, or alienate family members. Americans made their individual and collective choices, and many continue to live with those choices today.

Young men of the Vietnam generation, those who reached their nineteenth birthdays between 1964 and 1973 and thus were eligible to be drafted and potentially sent to Vietnam, faced obvious personal dilemmas about this controversial war. They were not alone. Their families and communities shared directly in their experience, and many other Americans became Vietnam veterans of other sorts without ever putting on a uniform. Obscure as well as prominent government officials struggled with their own values and perceptions as they labored to fashion U.S. policies. Journalists, intellectuals, ministers, and other reporters and molders of public opinion agonized over the war. College students, construction workers, nurses, teachers, and citizens in all areas of American life found themselves caught up in the mounting internal tension created by the conflict. Some of these individuals steadfastly supported and joined in the war effort, and others either quietly or vociferously attacked the U.S. participation in Vietnam. Other citizens remained ambivalent, with their own feelings pulled back and forth by the swirl of conflicting views.

Why did the Vietnam War become so divisive for Americans? At the time, many citizens who remembered the World War II era thought of that earlier struggle as "the Good War." The costs and sacrifices of World War II were much greater than those of Vietnam, yet that war had united the country while this war divided it. In the 1950s and early 1960s public and congressional opinion generally agreed with the assertion of national leaders that the United States had vital interests in Vietnam. Even as the war escalated in the mid-1960s, the majority of Americans remained prepared to shoulder the burden of the military involvement.

The year 1968 is generally acknowledged as the turning point in public attitudes. It was a year of shocking events. It began with the enemy's Tet Offensive in Vietnam, which, although countered by U.S. and South Vietnamese forces, raised serious doubts about Washington's official claims of progress in the war. American casualties continued to mount at an alarming rate. Johnson withdrew as a candidate for reelection because of the controversy over the war, and civil rights leader Martin Luther King Jr. and charismatic presidential candidate Sen. Robert Kennedy were assassinated. The city of Chicago erupted in an orgy of street violence and ugly confrontations between police and youthful war protesters during the Democratic National Convention in August. American society seemed to be coming apart at the seams, and many citizens of varying backgrounds blamed the war and wanted it to end. Some people thought the United States should simply leave Vietnam, but others hoped their government would unleash the full fury of American military power and end the conflict by the total destruction of the North.

The country was experiencing the breakdown of what scholars have termed the "Cold War consensus." This shared body of beliefs, which had existed in the country since the end of World War II, was not just a policy consensus; it also incorporated the widespread conviction that America and American principles were noble and worth defending. In terms of policy, the Truman Doctrine of 1947 had declared that the United States would assist people anywhere across the globe who were threatened by authoritarianism. Translated into action, this pledge became the containment policy designed to oppose the creation and spread of communist regimes in any corner of the world. Despite the altruistic ring to this commitment, a defense of U.S. interests in global stability and in an open international economic and political order was inherent in the policy, as well. In the flush of America's success in World War II, the potential costs of these ambitious goals were largely ignored.

The Cold War policy consensus also merged with the belief that America was a model of democracy, prosperity, and domestic harmony. In the 1950s and early 1960s the new medium of television popularized and reinforced this image in such programs as *Father Knows Best, The Adventures of Ozzie and Harriet, Leave It to Beaver,* and *The Donna Reed Show*. The depiction of domestic bliss in these shows was idyllic and mythical, and it ignored the economic, racial, gender, and other inequities that existed in the country. Still, the powerful myth led many Americans to accept the notion of a unique "American way of life"—which they would defend even by ruthless force, if necessary. The tougher aspect of this self-image was also reflected in popular television dramas—including Westerns such as *Gunsmoke* or *Have Gun Will Travel*—that portrayed a violent conflict between good and evil in which the good hero used his fists or gun to prevail over the heartless villain.

In the early 1960s on the eve of the Vietnam War, there was, then, a broad acceptance among Americans of the notions of inter-

nationalism, global interests, sacrifice, firmness, and moral rectitude. The nation's commitment to such ideals was eloquently
captured in John F. Kennedy's famous pledge in his 1961 inaugural
address: "Let every nation know, whether it wishes us well or ill,
that we shall pay any price, bear any burden, meet any hardship,
support any friend, oppose any foe to assure the survival and the
success of liberty."[2]

By the end of the 1960s and the beginning of the 1970s,
Kennedy's noble phrases were beginning to ring hollow. Kennedy
himself and then his brother were brutally murdered. Many
Americans still clung to the image of their nation as a bastion of
good in a world of evil, but the violence of Vietnam and the domestic turbulence of antiwar protest, civil rights confrontations, and
urban revolts tempered their expectations. There was a growing
awareness that America was not invincible, that it was not as pure
as its cultural myths suggested, and that it needed a good dose of
humility. Some citizens felt that they had been purposefully misled
by leaders such as Kennedy and Johnson. Others retained their
faith that American officials meant well but had made tragic mis-
judgments. Regardless of the specific individual reactions, the political and cultural consensus that had existed before the war was in
disarray by the end of the Vietnam era.

This national upheaval reshaped life for many Americans, and it
also provided them opportunities to make their own contributions to
the process of change. Early in the Vietnam era—that is, through
the early 1960s—many people defended the Cold War consensus.
Others simply accepted the notion that the United States was a
world leader, and they were willing to assume the burdens of that
role. There were always critics, to be sure, but even they often
assumed that the United States had the power and goodness to promote progress if it could muster the political will to address problems of racism, poverty, tyranny, and injustice at home and abroad.

During the 1960s, however, this confidence dissolved into open
doubt. Although many Americans continued to go about the normal
routine of work and family, the historical imprint of the decade is
one of revolt. Even if most citizens were not in the streets protesting
the war, the lack of civil rights, campus paternalism, discrimination
against women, or other perceived wrongs, the entire domestic society was influenced by this activism. Federal law, foreign policy,
education, entertainment, and institutions of all types were transformed. Some of the new realities forged by the agitation of the
1960s were racial integration of public facilities, greater student
rights on campuses, enhanced legal opportunities for women, and
greater restraint in the use of military intervention as an instru-
ment of U.S. foreign policy.

These changes came literally through the work and sacrifice of individual citizens. Thousands of personal chronicles, both dramatic and mundane, accompanied these fundamental shifts in U.S. society during the Vietnam era. For the soldiers who went to Vietnam, these chronicles are true war stories; for the men and women who remained in America in that era, they are tales from the domestic wars.

When telling and hearing individual stories of personal experiences in the midst of momentous events, there is a need for caution. One of the best tellers of tales of the Vietnam generation is novelist Tim O'Brien. In a piece entitled "How to Tell a True War Story," he offered advice to the returned warrior recounting his experiences, but his cautions could apply to most efforts to relate individual experiences and interpret them for others. "A true war story is never moral," O'Brien wrote. "It does not instruct, nor encourage virtue, nor suggest models of proper human behavior, nor restrain men from doing the things men have always done."[3] The true war story does not uplift and is not even literally true. It does not make a clear distinction between what actually happened and what seemed to happen. The story has a deeper meaning but not one that is explicitly stated. It does not generalize, but it evokes a recognition in the listener. As O'Brien concluded, "A true war story, if truly told, makes the stomach believe."[4]

Some of the biographical accounts of the Vietnam era that appear in this book are this kind of war story. None of them are entirely autobiographical, but some allow the individual's own words and experiences or those of family members to speak for themselves. Several other essays included here are of the type described by one scholar as "fighting stories." These are accounts of the fundamental impact of war; they may or may not be autobiographical, but they form the "political culture of memory." Unlike O'Brien's stories, which avoid explicit lessons, these accounts integrate political communities, shape cultural narratives, and construct self-images. Like O'Brien's stories, however, such fighting tales seek to present "an emotional substance and a higher level of truth than just the objective accounts of historians."[5]

Historical accounts are not necessarily objective, as many literary critics in recent years have argued. If all language is mediated through culture, as deconstructionist literary theory posits, then there is no straight path to or expression of truth. The implication is that there may be multiple versions of truth or that truth is different for different observers. If this theoretical challenge exists for even the simplest of narratives, then the prospect of generalizing from war stories or fighting stories to overarching interpretations of an era is daunting.

In the history of the Vietnam era, however, such deconstructionist musings are as much symptom as obstacle. The Cold War consensus had rested on a firm and largely unreflective faith in the
truth and goodness of the American way of life. During the Vietnam
War that faith was tested to the point of breaking, as U.S. aircraft
dropping bombs and U.S. soldiers and marines firing automatic
weapons laid waste to the population of Vietnam and the bordering
regions of Laos and Cambodia. Painful questions were raised: What
was the United States fighting for? What was the war doing to
American values and traditions? What were the definitions of truth
and goodness?

As the Vietnam era drew to a close in the mid-1970s, these questions had not been answered, but there was a sense among Americans that answers did exist. In the years after the war a multitude
of alternative prescriptions emerged. Although a minority of Americans favored isolationism, most citizens continued to believe that
there was an international role for the United States consistent
with the domestic values of the country. Some advocated a new in-
ternationalism premised on respect for human rights. Others noted
that Soviet military power remained strong and that new economic
dangers, such as an interruption in the flow of the world oil supply,
required a continued global defense of U.S. security. The Vietnam
experience has chastened Americans but not defeated them.

The primary rationale for the U.S. involvement in Vietnam was
an abstract conception of grand strategy. The containment policy
required leaders to try to convince America's most dangerous adversaries in Moscow and Beijing of the credibility of U.S. defense commitments around the world. But for those Americans who made the
policies, who actually served in the combat zone, or who dared to
resist or criticize the nation's participation in the conflict, the
Vietnam War was anything but abstract. The biographical essays in
this volume examine a cross section of American life. Some of the
subjects, such as presidential aide Walt Rostow and Gen. David
Shoup, held positions of influence in the government, although each
took very different views of the war. Others were obscure but brave
citizens, such as Cpl. Bill Henry Terry Jr. and military wife
Seawillow Chambers. Some, such as Francis Cardinal Spellman,
were controversial figures. Ambassador William Trimble was a
career diplomat who faithfully tried to do his duty, and Daniel
Ellsberg was a public official who came to believe that his own complicity in misbegotten policies required him to redefine his duty.
Bernard Fall, Otto Feinstein, and Peter Arnett were careful
observers who developed thoughtful critiques of the war. Bill Weber
and Nancy Randolph were good citizens who got caught up in
Vietnam and became, in different ways, casualties of the war.

Some of the biographies that follow offer generalizations and others do not, but all reveal something of the individuals behind the larger events. None of these individuals is either typical or atypical of the American experience in Vietnam or of any particular part of that experience, yet each has a special story that is worth telling for its own intrinsic worth. At the same time, each contributes a thread to the tapestry that was the American experience in the Vietnam era. There are, of course, many other threads to this tapestry, and there is also an entirely separate Vietnamese tapestry.

As Tim O'Brien so well said: "In a true war story, if there's a moral at all, it's like the thread that makes the cloth. You can't tease it out. You can't extract the meaning without unraveling the deeper meaning."[6] By exploring the very diversity and multiplicity of the individual lives of Americans in the Vietnam era, we can learn much about the tensions and meaning of that entire period of U.S. history.

Notes

1. Quoted in David L. Anderson, "Gerald R. Ford and the Presidents' War in Vietnam," in *Shadow on the White House: Presidents and the Vietnam War, 1945–1975,* ed. David L. Anderson (Lawrence: University Press of Kansas, 1993), 199.

2. *Public Papers of the Presidents of the United States: John F. Kennedy, 1961* (Washington, D.C.: Government Printing Office, 1962), 1. See also Richard A. Melanson, *American Foreign Policy since the Vietnam War: The Search for Consensus from Nixon to Clinton* (Armonk, N.Y.: M. E. Sharpe, 1996).

3. Tim O'Brien, *The Things They Carried* (New York: Penguin Books, 1991), 76.

4. Ibid., 84.

5. Philip West, Stephen I. Levine, and Jackie Hiltz, "Sounding the Human Dimensions of War," in *America's Wars in Asia: A Cultural Approach to History and Memory,* ed. Philip West, Stephen I. Levine, and Jackie Hiltz (Armonk, N.Y.: M. E. Sharpe, 1998), 4.

6. O'Brien, *The Things They Carried,* 84.

I

Americans Enter the Vietnam Quagmire

Some of the early writings on the American involvement in the Vietnam War likened the conflict to a quagmire. This analogy suggested that, in a series of small and seemingly cautious steps, the United States entered into the struggle in Southeast Asia before fully realizing the danger it presented. By the middle of the 1960s, the United States found itself bogged down and in a position that made it difficult to go either forward or backward. Retreat was not easy because, after more than a decade of U.S. support for Saigon, a withdrawal would damage the credibility and deterrent value of America's security commitments to other nations. Yet to move ahead meant to wage a much larger, costlier, and riskier war than any American strategist had contemplated.

One of the proponents of the quagmire theory, historian Arthur Schlesinger Jr., argued that the story of America's war in Vietnam is a history without villains. The saga is certainly a tragedy that ends with enormous casualties, psychological trauma, social tension, and political cynicism. The quagmire concept implies, however, that these were unforeseen consequences of good intentions. There was a genuine desire among American leaders and other citizens to help the peoples of Southeast Asia resist communist tyranny and build prosperous and democratic lives. There was also an underestimation of the political and military strength of America's Vietnamese adversaries.

The quagmire theory has not gone unchallenged. From the very beginning of the U.S. involvement with Vietnam, certain Americans questioned the wisdom and even the morality of Washington's actions. Some early critics were troubled, for example, by the association with French colonialism, and after the French left, there was still concern about interfering in the internal politics of Southeast Asian states. In addition, there were strategic questions about the importance of Vietnam to U.S. security and doubts about the applicability to Asia of containment, a policy developed for Europe to counter perceived Soviet military and political threats there. Some observers even came to believe that national leaders understood fairly quickly that there was no American solution to Indochina's political struggles but refused to acknowledge limits to U.S. power. These critics contended that presidents and their advisers continued a war they knew was unwinnable simply to save political face. In other words, they held that the course of the Vietnam War was not necessarily unforeseen and that American decision makers were not blameless victims of their own good intentions and limited knowledge.

Although there is evidence to support each of these arguments, the quagmire image remains useful. Individual Americans did become trapped into ways of thinking about Vietnam, and various choices they made along the way increasingly narrowed U.S. policy options. The essays in this section examine the responses of four Americans to the issues of Vietnam in the days before the full magnitude and cost of the war became apparent. Francis Cardinal Spellman, the archbishop of New York, exhibited the deep-seated abhorrence of communist dictatorship that permeated American political culture in the 1950s and early 1960s (Chapter 1). As U.S. ambassador to Cambodia, William C. Trimble experienced the conflicts between America's Cold War image of the world and the historical environment peculiar to Indochina (Chapter 2). Walt Rostow was a brilliant American academic whose militant policy recommendations as a key adviser to Presidents John F. Kennedy (JFK) and Lyndon B. Johnson (LBJ) epitomized the widely shared belief that there was an American solution to every problem (Chapter 3). None of these three men had any particular knowledge about Southeast Asia that prepared them to articulate effective approaches to the region. Scholar and journalist Bernard Fall, by contrast, was a bona fide expert on the history and culture of the region (Chapter 4). He tried to caution Americans about the complexities of Vietnam and its neighbors, but he, too, failed to predict how resistant the region would remain to American pressure.

How did the United States become so deeply engulfed in the tragic quagmire of the Vietnam War? How could that great nation have gone so wrong? The accounts of these four prominent Americans provide some insights into such questions.

1

Francis Cardinal Spellman and "Spellman's War"

Wilson D. Miscamble, C.S.C.

The origins of U.S. involvement in the Vietnam War were deeply rooted in the Cold War. Although historians continue to debate how the Cold War started and why it lasted so long, there is no question that many Americans fervently believed that an aggressive, worldwide threat to the United States emanated from the Soviet Union and its communist allies. This so-called Cold War consensus led many prudent policymakers and opinion leaders to consider communist-led North Vietnam as part of this global danger. One of the most visible non-governmental advocates of U.S. involvement in Vietnam as a defense of the nation and of democracy itself was Francis Cardinal Spellman, the Roman Catholic archbishop of New York.

Wilson D. Miscamble explores the life of Spellman and his role as a spokesman for that deeply felt anticommunist sentiment in American Cold War culture. He reflects on the merits of some observers' claims that Spellman played an inordinate role in pushing the United States into Vietnam. He also examines Spellman's connection with Ngo Dinh Diem, the president of South Vietnam, who was also a devout Roman Catholic. Even after Diem's death in 1963, Spellman continued in his unofficial role as the "chief chaplain of the Vietnam War." And until his death in 1967, the archbishop steadfastly defended the justness of U.S. intervention in Vietnam, even as antiwar feeling increased. Spellman's sincere, if often controversial, opinions help us understand how the U.S. war in Vietnam came to be.

Wilson D. Miscamble, C.S.C., is an associate professor of history at the University of Notre Dame in Notre Dame, Indiana, where he received his Ph.D. degree. He is a specialist in postwar American diplomatic history, and his book *George F. Kennan and the Making of American Foreign Policy, 1947–1950* (1992) received the Harry S. Truman Book Award. Presently, he is engaged in research for a book on Catholics and American foreign policy from 1890 to 1990.

In his haunting and intimate memoir, *An American Requiem,* the novelist James Carroll argued that the "Vietnam War began as Spellman's."[1] Carroll presented America's participation in the Vietnam conflict as the product of the obsessive anticommunism and behind-the-scenes maneuvering of New York's Francis Cardinal

Courtesy of the University of Notre Dame Archives

Spellman. His portrayal of Spellman's supposedly major role in influencing American policy in Vietnam reiterated the line first offered in "The 'Vietnam Lobby,'" the celebrated exposé article published in *Ramparts* in 1965 in which journalists Robert Scheer and Warren Hinckle described Spellman as part of a veritable cabal that orchestrated the Eisenhower administration's support for Ngo Dinh Diem.[2] The Scheer-Hinckle allegations "proved highly durable," as one careful observer has noted, and, indeed, they have found their way into the work of a number of historians who link Spellman closely to Diem's rise to power.[3] This view of the cardinal as a key sponsor of South Vietnam's first leader exaggerates his responsibility for American decision making, and, at the same time, it clouds an understanding of his true role during the Vietnam War. He was not so much an influential policymaker as a public champion of the U.S. commitment to the South and the undisputed chief chaplain to the eventual U.S. military effort there. Comprehending the roots and basis of his wholehearted support for American participation in the Vietnam War allows for a richer appreciation of the beliefs and convictions that underlay the broad American endeavor in Indochina.

Francis Joseph Spellman was born in Whitman, Massachusetts, on May 4, 1889. He graduated from Fordham University in 1911 and proceeded from there to the North American College in Rome, where he was ordained a priest in 1916. After service in his home diocese of Boston, he returned to Rome in 1925 to take up an appointment in the Vatican Secretariat of State, where he came to know Eugenio Cardinal Pacelli. It was Pacelli, now the newly elected Pope Pius XII, who appointed his friend and protégé as archbishop of New York on April 15, 1939. From this base as the spiritual leader of two million Roman Catholics in the country's wealthiest and most important archdiocese, Spellman quickly emerged as America's best known and most powerful Catholic prelate. After he was named a cardinal in 1946, his formal authority combined with his personal and public influence to make him a prominent figure not only among American Catholics but also in the country as a whole. His additional service as military vicar for Roman Catholics in the U.S. armed forces, through which he bore responsibility for Catholic chaplains and the military personnel and families to whom they ministered, only added to his public eminence. Beginning in World War II and continuing thereafter, the cardinal made a special effort to visit American troops stationed overseas, and he aimed especially to spend Christmas each year with forces stationed far from home.

World War II provided the occasion for Spellman's emergence as the preeminent Catholic leader and afforded him the opportunity to demonstrate the intense patriotism that remained with him until his death in 1967. Even before America's intervention in that great conflagration, Franklin Delano Roosevelt (FDR) had called on Spellman to act as a mediator of sorts in his dealings with Pius XII. Spellman relished the role, quickly developed a good relationship with the American president, and visited the White House regularly. He left little doubt of his high regard for FDR, proved a vigorous supporter of Roosevelt's policies, and came to be labeled as the president's "favorite bishop." In 1940, he called openly for a stronger national defense, and when Pearl Harbor was attacked, he extolled the righteousness of the American cause and rallied to it with deep fervor. Indeed, Spellman identified his nation and his church as one. "Our President and our Holy Father [the pope]," he declared, "have combined the forces of our great country and the forces of religion in a battle for peace."[4] For him American democracy and Catholicism were linked in a holy struggle against atheistic aggressors.

Spellman's deep disillusionment with Franklin Roosevelt—the president with whom he had the closest relationship and to whom he had the easiest access—came after FDR's death in April 1945 as he gradually learned all the details of the Yalta accords and as he saw the capitals of Eastern Europe fall behind what Winston Churchill would soon call the Iron Curtain. The archbishop wasted no time wallowing in dismay and disappointment at what he deemed Roosevelt's mistakes but instead worked to rouse his fellow Americans to the danger represented by Soviet expansion. His fusion of "the themes of Catholicism and Americanism" only intensified as he faced a new and dangerous threat to his religion and nation.[5]

For him, communism was not simply "an enemy of Catholicism" but also a "challenge to *all* men who believe in America and in God."[6] He warned against the communist threat at home but directed his fiercest protests against communist repression in Yugoslavia, Hungary, Czechoslovakia, and Poland. He railed against the mistreatment and torture of such prominent religious figures as Yugoslavia's archbishop Aloysius Stepinac and Hungary's Josef Cardinal Mindszenty.[7] The graphic accounts of torture, imprisonment, and religious repression—"on a scale," the writer Wilfred Sheed once noted, "that the secular mind never seemed to grasp or care about"—disturbed Spellman greatly.[8] They deepened the visceral antipathy he felt toward communism in all its manifestations. He emerged as the unmistakable "political leader" of Catholic anticommunism in America, possessed of "a simple faith: Communism was evil, Catholicism and America were good, therefore Catholicism and America must join together in combating atheistic Communism."[9] The cardinal spoke with sincerity of a contest between civilizations, and as the 1940s came to a close, he feared that communism was winning.

Spellman's fears only increased as communist forces took the offensive in Asia. The communist triumph in China in 1949, followed quickly by stories on the torture of Western missionaries and the persecution of Chinese Christians, confirmed his deep convictions that communism was the mortal foe of religion and democracy. He readily endorsed the Truman administration's military response to the North Korean invasion of South Korea and soon visited the battlefields, saying mass for the troops at places such as Pork Chop Hill and Heartbreak Ridge. Spellman clearly reveled in his role as military vicar, for it allowed him to play something of a direct part in what he saw as the great and essential struggle between the forces of freedom and tyranny.

The cardinal also vigorously pursued his anticommunist campaign at home, even to the extent of providing limited support for the activities of Sen. Joseph McCarthy. Spellman had, by this point, honed his skills at offending American liberals to a high degree. His heated exchange with Eleanor Roosevelt over the issue of federal aid to parochial schools in 1949, his use of seminarians to help break a gravediggers' strike that same year, and his embrace of Gen. Douglas MacArthur on the latter's recall from Korea, combined with his efforts in the 1950s to ban certain films he deemed salacious or sacrilegious, made him a bête noire for those of a more liberal persuasion. Spellman rarely ducked controversy and was the target for much criticism and caricature. He no doubt deserved his reputation as a social and political conservative, but his motives were sincere, and his actions evolved from a worldview shaped by his Catholic beliefs and love for America. Wilfred Sheed assuredly was correct in suggesting that for Spellman "anti-communism rallied his flock into a Church militant and gave a fighting edge to their faith, while it also made him seem nationally important, a quasi-statesman," but these achievements were essentially by-products of his deep conviction that communism was a lethal threat to his faith and nation. Such a threat, he believed, had to be opposed throughout the world, including in such relatively obscure places as Indochina.[10]

When many Americans first considered policy on Vietnam in the 1950s, they had to check the country's location on a map. Spellman required no such geography lesson. He had passed through a number of Southeast Asian cities on his way home from a visit to Australia in 1948. He stopped at Singapore and Bangkok, flew over Angkor Wat in Cambodia, and made a brief visit to Saigon before heading on to Canton and Hong Kong. This visit seems to have been mainly a friendly call on the fellow religious, and he took the opportunity to pay tribute to the courage of the Catholic missionaries working in the area. He also met members of the local clergy, including, it appears, Bishop Ngo Dinh Thuc, the brother of a Vietnamese nationalist named Ngo Dinh Diem. No evidence exists that they had any further communication until Thuc reestablished contact with Spellman in the United States in 1950.

At odds with both the communist Vietminh regime and the French colonial administration that had Bao Dai as a figurehead emperor, Diem left Vietnam in 1950 in Thuc's company and traveled to the United States and then to Europe. Through the intervention of Fr. Fred McGuire, a Vincentian priest and former missionary in Asia, Thuc and Diem met Spellman.[11] Much has been made of their acquaintanceship, but little seems to have come of it in the early 1950s. Spellman probably helped make arrangements for Diem to stay at the Maryknoll Mission Society's seminaries in Ossining, New York, and Lakewood, New Jersey, but whether they had any other association is unclear. Joseph Morgan noted that "the correspondence of Diem's American supporters in the early 1950s contains no references to Spellman," which suggests that the allegations that the cardinal essentially sponsored Diem and introduced him to influential Americans should be met with some skepticism.[12] There is certainly little evidence for this scenario, and it appears that Diem had quite limited contact with Spellman during the two and one half years that he lived in the United States. Diem dealt directly with the State Department and found other sponsors in Washington, D.C., such as Supreme Court justice William O. Douglas, who, in 1953, introduced the future Vietnamese leader to supporters such as Sen. Mike Mansfield and Sen. John F. Kennedy.[13] Diem appeared to such men to represent a "third force"—he seemed to be a true nationalist and democrat opposed to both the communists and French colonialism.

The role of Diem's American friends in his coming to power has been exaggerated. He left the United States in 1953 and spent most of the next year in France. As the French position in Indochina worsened and reached a crisis point after the fall of Dien Bien Phu in May 1954, Bao Dai and the French turned to Diem almost by default. Perhaps it is true, as Gregory Olson has suggested, that they selected him "because he was the most probable candidate to attract Vietnamese nationalists and receive U.S. support."[14] There certainly were American expressions of support for Diem, perhaps even conveyed to Bao Dai by Secretary of State John Foster Dulles. But it is problematic to suggest that "a Vietnam lobby composed of prominent Catholics, including Mansfield, Spellman, and Joseph Kennedy, worked through John Foster Dulles and the CIA [Central Intelligence Agency] to bring Diem to power in order to squeeze France out."[15] Diem rose to power because of his own nationalist credentials and through the actions of Bao Dai, who was eager to salvage something from the wreckage of the French military defeat and from the respite provided him by the Geneva accords, signed in May 1954. Whether Diem could maintain himself in power depended more directly on the United States.

Ngo Dinh Diem returned to Saigon on June 25, 1954, intent on saving his homeland. Although much attention has been given to his Catholic religion, his Confucian background and his mandarin training gave him the sense that he knew what was right and good for his people and led him constantly to seek to exercise "authority without power."[16] The challenges he faced were enormous, and some Americans in Saigon, especially the U.S. special representative in Vietnam, Gen. J. Lawton Collins, lacked confidence in his ability to overcome them. Yet, against the odds and with the guidance of the CIA's Edward Lansdale, Diem survived 1954 and secured himself in power over the following two years.

As Diem and Lansdale worked together to execute the South Vietnamese "miracle," Cardinal Spellman tried to generate support for the new state.[17] For him the war in Indochina was part of one great conflict that pitted free peoples against communist tyranny. On a May 1954 visit to France to make a financial contribution to the construction of an American church in Paris, he paid tribute to the French heroism at Dien Bien Phu and warned that no one could "maintain an air of detachment about what now transpires in the Far East. Sooner or later we who are free have been marked down for slavery and will be drawn into the line of the Communist juggernaut."[18] Spellman greeted the terms of the Geneva accords with dismay and saw Ho Chi Minh's triumph in the North as "taps for the buried hopes of freedom in Southeast Asia! Taps for the newly betrayed millions of Indochinese who must now learn the awful facts of slavery from their eager Communist masters."[19]

The cardinal's genuine anxiety concerning the fate of those eager to escape Ho's rule in the North prompted him to practical action. In August 1954, after receiving information from "his brother bishops in Vietnam of the massed flight of civilians from North to South Vietnam to escape from the Communist-led Vietminh," he drafted a pastoral letter that was read at all Sunday masses in the archdiocese. In it, he outlined the situation, called for prayers for the refugees, paid tribute to the swift efforts of the American government to assist in their evacuation and resettlement, and informed New York's Catholics that he was supplementing the governmental efforts by sending shipments of food and clothing.[20] With Spellman's support the Catholic Relief Services (CRS) established a program in the South designed to assist in refugee resettlement. Those responsible for the implementation of this program saw the situation in 1954 as "so dismal that we question ourselves as to whether we are doing the right thing or not in encouraging refugees from the North to leave there to come to a South that, according to every imaginable calculation, will be communist itself within the not too distant future."[21] But by year's end one-half million (mainly Catholic) refugees had made their way south, providing Diem with a group of truly loyal supporters, which he used effectively to strengthen his tenuous hold on power.

Early in 1955, after making a Christmas call on American troops in Korea, Japan, and Formosa, Cardinal Spellman visited Vietnam to lend support to the CRS refugee program and, no doubt, also to the Diem regime. Charles Morris's suggestion that the cardinal "was a master of the photo opportunity and the grand gesture, with the politician's talent of leveraging maximum exposure from a minimum event" was amply confirmed by the reception he received during his three-day visit to South Vietnam.[22] The intensely loyal Catholic refugees who had abandoned their homes and fields in their exodus from the North greeted the visiting American prelate as if he were a conquering hero returned home. A cheering crowd of over five thousand met him at the airport on January 5, and people holding welcome banners greeted him all along his drive to the center of Saigon.

Over the next few days, Spellman had a full program of events. Msgr. Joseph Harnett, who headed the CRS mission in Saigon, estimated that during his short visit, he was seen by at least two hundred thousand people. On January 7, he celebrated a mass for refugees that was attended by over thirty thousand people. He visited the Shrine of the Blessed Mother at La-Vang and prayed with pilgrims there. He toured the resettlement areas by helicopter and inspected the housing facilities set up for refugees in their newly established villages. On his final day in Vietnam, he celebrated mass in the Saigon cathedral for the Catholics of the city and later visited an American ship that arrived from the North loaded with refugees. In a typically benevolent and showy gesture, he promised a gift of $100,000 to assist the CRS refugee program in Vietnam. Obviously thrilled by the enthusiastic reception for Spellman, Monsignor Harnett claimed that "the people here, both Catholic, Buddhists, and those who practice no religion at all, have become very devoted to him and certainly regard him as one of Vietnam's most important and devoted friends."[23]

Spellman's visit had a primarily religious and humanitarian focus rather than a political one, and yet, it was riddled with political implications. His mere presence in the South gave his imprimatur to the American effort to sustain Diem's shaky government and to build an independent, noncommunist South Vietnam. Not all Americans gushed over Spellman's presence, however. When his visit was soon followed by that of an Australian cardinal,

Gen. J. Lawton Collins suggested "a moratorium on visits by Catholic cardinals or bishops" to Diem's brother, Bishop Thuc. He feared that the presence of members of the Catholic hierarchy only drew greater attention to Diem's Catholicism, which was "a detriment to him in the minds of many Buddhists and other non-Christian Vietnamese."[24] The CIA's Lansdale also had reservations about establishing too close an identification between Diem and Spellman. He feared that the considerable number of Americans who were "habitually suspicious of 'Catholic power' [might] discern a plot afoot to install a Vatican puppet in Saigon." As James T. Fisher brilliantly revealed, the CIA operative went so far as to construct "an American Catholic *alternative* to Spellman" in the person of a young navy medical officer named Thomas A. Dooley, whom Lansdale orchestrated as "the unofficial spokesman for the [Passage to Freedom] refugee campaign." Unlike Spellman, as Fisher explained, "Dooley was non-controversial, non-ideological and most importantly, non-clerical."[25]

Spellman's public support for Diem's Vietnam has attracted much less scholarly attention than his supposed role as godfather to the pro-Diem Vietnam lobby and as a crucial figure in the Eisenhower administration's decision to maintain support for Diem in 1955. Although it would be more dramatic for purposes of this chapter to have Spellman playing such a central role, if only from the shadows, there is little evidence to support this casting. All the claims about his crucial intervention rely on the suggestion made by Joseph Buttinger of the International Rescue Committee that Spellman and Joseph P. Kennedy lined up support for Diem and endorsed his efforts to forge a pro-Diem lobby in the United States.[26] Buttinger's suggestion lacks persuasive force. First, in 1955 the Eisenhower administration did not need persuasion by either Spellman or the Kennedy family patriarch to support Diem. Some Americans were troubled by "Diem's Messiah-like complex," but they recoiled at the alternatives. Secretary Dulles remained committed to him, encouraged by a range of individuals such as Sen. Mike Mansfield, Edward Lansdale, Prof. Wesley Fishel of Michigan State University, and his own assistant for Far Eastern affairs, Kenneth Young. Moreover, the Vietnam lobby was essentially "a paper coalition orchestrated by Diem's New York publicist, Harold Oram," who created the American Friends of Vietnam (AFV) in 1955.[27] Cardinal Spellman neither formally joined this organization nor participated in any extensive way in its operation or activities, which were, for the most part, inconsequential in shaping American policy in Vietnam in the mid-1950s.[28] Nonetheless, he assuredly would have supported fully its efforts to generate American assistance for South Vietnam and would have endorsed the view expressed by Sen. John

Kennedy at the AFV's inaugural national conference: "Vietnam represents the cornerstone of the Free World in Southeast Asia, the keystone to the arch, the finger in the dike."[29]

Although Spellman's support for South Vietnam remained as firm as ever in the latter half of the 1950s, Diem's seeming success in consolidating his power removed the urgency of the issue for the cardinal. Spellman confronted other matters as well and had a huge archdiocese to run, so he directed the bulk of his attention elsewhere. He was on hand, however, to play a cameo role during Diem's triumphant visit to the United States in May 1957. In addition to giving speeches to the National Press Club and a joint session of Congress and meeting with Eisenhower and his officials, the "miracle man" of Asia (as the president dubbed him) traveled to New York for a series of meetings and receptions hosted by the Council on Foreign Relations and such luminaries as John D. Rockefeller and Henry Luce of Time-Life. Spellman said a private mass for Diem and gave the invocation at a banquet hosted by Luce.[30] This attention was enough to provide grist for the mills of those who saw Diem as a creation of the cardinal, but what is more telling is the *limited* contact Diem had with the American churchman. His handlers from the AFV clearly preferred not to overdo their association, and there is little evidence of significant contact between them over the next few years. Moreover, there is no substantial evidence that Spellman sought to influence the Eisenhower administration's policies on Vietnam. Presumably, he was quite content with the American effort of nation building.

Of course, Spellman had not relented in any way in terms of his fierce opposition to communism. In 1959, he felt obliged to warn Eisenhower to remain firm on the Berlin issue in his coming discussions with Nikita Khrushchev, and in August 1960, he preached a sermon at the World Eucharistic Congress in Munich in which he bitterly denounced the communist powers and suggested the world was living through "the most dangerous summer since 1939." He listed the troublespots where communist-promoted crises threatened the interests of the free world—Cuba and Latin America, East Germany, China, and the Congo.[31] Notably, he left Vietnam off this list, and it was a few years into the new decade before events in Southeast Asia would reclaim the aging cleric's sustained attention.

During the early 1960s, Cardinal Spellman found some of the firm foundations of his church seemingly moving on him. His sponsor and friend Pius XII had died in 1958 and been replaced by Angelo Roncalli, better known as Pope John XXIII. The new pope convened the Second Vatican Council, designed, in effect, to bring the church up to date and to open it to the world. Spellman clearly preferred a more institutional and hierarchical church than the one fashioned at the council, which emphasized collegiality and the notion of the church as the people of God called on to serve the whole human family and to engage others in fruitful dialogue. Those of a younger generation who greeted the spirit and reforms of the council more ardently began to see the cardinal as being out of sync with the times, a throwback to an era now passed. Spellman's reaction to America's increasing military commitment in Vietnam only confirmed them in this view, for he responded to this developing conflict in the same way he had reacted to the American efforts in World War II and Korea.

The election of John F. Kennedy, the nation's first Catholic president, did not increase Spellman's influence in Washington because the new president saw political difficulties in being too closely identified with a prelate of his church. But Spellman supported the Kennedy foreign policy. He backed the increased American commitment to Diem, including a sharp increase in military advisers in 1961 and 1962 authorized by JFK to assist South Vietnam in resisting a Vietcong (VC) insurgency that had been launched in 1959. In what would become a familiar refrain, however, the American assistance proved insufficient to put down the communist insurrection, and in 1963 American attention turned to the limitations of the Diem regime in rallying the South Vietnamese population to fight the Vietcong. Diem's authoritarian style and the repressive measures he utilized against certain Buddhist groups eventually led American officials to demand that he dismiss his brother and key adviser, Ngo Dinh Nhu, who was held primarily responsible for the repression.

In the fall of 1963, as American officials led by Ambassador Henry Cabot Lodge applied unyielding pressure on Diem, Spellman found himself somewhat drawn into the controversy. Diem's older brother, Ngo Dinh Thuc, now archbishop of Hue, arrived in New York, planning to confer with the cardinal. His visit "touched off speculation that the Archbishop would appeal to the Roman Catholic hierarchy in the United States to intercede with Washington to help ease relations with the South Vietnamese Government."[32] Spellman clearly had not been expecting his South Vietnamese visitor, and just a day before his arrival the seventy-five-year-old cardinal had been in Miami Beach to receive the American Legion's Distinguished Service Medal. Thuc had gone to New York directly from Rome, where he had caused a stir by suggesting that "President Kennedy's Administration had spent $20 million trying to oust his family's regime." His imminent arrival in the United States had prompted Kennedy's national security adviser, McGeorge Bundy, to exclaim anxiously that "this was the first time the world had been faced with collective madness in a ruling family since the days of the czars."[33] But Thuc's visit apparently came to naught. John XXIII's successor, Pope Paul VI, wanted to play down the religious dimension of the clash between the Catholic Diem and the Buddhists and insisted that the conflict was political. He apparently had the Vatican Secretariat of State order Thuc to desist from public statements, and the archbishop, it seems, was kept under wraps in New York. What transpired privately between Spellman and Thuc is not known. What is clear, however, is that Thuc's visit did not prompt the prelate to make representations to the Kennedy administration on Diem's behalf.

Less than two months after Thuc's visit, South Vietnamese generals, with the authorization and complicity of American officials, launched a coup against Diem during which the onetime "miracle man" and his brother Nhu were brutally murdered. Spellman's private reaction is not known, but there is no official record that he protested the American endorsement of Diem's ousting. Presumably, he bought the administration line that the generals would bring new vigor to the anti-insurgency effort. But the South Vietnamese military proved inadequate to the task and developed an ever greater dependency on the United States, such that, a little over a year after the Diem coup, Kennedy's successor, Lyndon Johnson, would move to Americanize the war and introduce U.S. combat forces.

Spellman played no meaningful role in the Johnson administration's tortured decision making in 1964 and 1965 that culminated in the commitment of combat forces. The elderly cardinal was immediately on hand, however, to endorse the introduction of American troops once the decision was made. For him the conflict appeared as just another battle in the long fight that pitted America and Catholicism against communism. There was little nuance in his views: The war was just, for it aimed to defend South Vietnam against blatant aggression from the North, the success of which would mean the subjugation and repression of a people struggling to maintain themselves in freedom. The cardinal raised no questions of prudential judgment about the war. It had never been his modus operandi to weigh in on matters of military strategy or to provide evaluations of the determination and capability of the foe and the likelihood of success in a military endeavor. He had few doubts, if any, about either the righteousness of America's cause or its capacity to achieve it.

With America's fighting men in Vietnam in significant numbers by the end of 1965, it was natural that the vicar for the armed forces should plan to spend Christmas with them. On a five-day visit, during which he called at military bases and hospitals to say mass for and encourage American personnel, Spellman made clear his attitude to the war. After arriving in Saigon on December 23, the cardinal was asked by news reporters, "What do you think about what the United States is doing in Vietnam?" He replied without much deliberation, "I fully support everything it does." Then, he added, in words that paraphrased those of the nineteenth-century naval hero Stephen Decatur, "My country, may it always be right. Right or wrong, my country."[34] The cardinal's later critics have made much of his comment, suggesting that, given the choice, the old churchman would "follow his national leaders, even when they were morally wrong. Given a choice between Lyndon Johnson and Jesus Christ, he would unhesitatingly turn his back on Jesus Christ."[35]

Of course, Spellman hardly saw it that way. Given his patriotic fervor, it is quite likely the cardinal felt that his nation would inevitably be on the side of right. He certainly believed this in the case of Vietnam. In his formal Christmas message of 1965, he explained that "when the freedom and dignity of people anywhere are challenged, the freedom and dignity of people everywhere stand in peril. When tyranny is allowed to take one bold step in some distant land, it has begun its terrifying march across the world."[36] It was, he felt, America's historical burden and moral responsibility to oppose this march of tyranny in South Vietnam. The cardinal left the American soldiers in no doubt as to the morality and significance of their struggle.

The fervent and unqualified nature of Spellman's endorsement of the American war effort undoubtedly gave cheer to the White House, but Spellman was not a confidant of Lyndon Johnson in planning the war in 1965 and beyond. His name is notable only by its absence in the numerous deliberations and conversations in which America's course in Vietnam was fashioned by LBJ and such advisers as Robert McNamara and McGeorge Bundy. The president appreciated the cardinal's blessing of the American effort and his support for the U.S. troops in Vietnam, but he never turned to Spellman for serious counsel on the war.[37] The prelate had nothing of the privileged access to Johnson that he had enjoyed with FDR, and, in fact, Johnson demonstrated greater concern about Spellman's position on the issue of federal aid to education than he did over the cardinal's views on Vietnam.[38] Certainly, then, Spellman should not be asked to share primary responsibility for the American commitment in the war with LBJ and his "best and brightest" advisers.

Although the cardinal's stance on the war pleased the American president, it reportedly caused the Holy See some difficulty. Following the lead set by his predecessor in his encyclical *Pacem in Terris* (Peace on Earth) and reflecting the Second Vatican Council's more critical attitude to all warfare, Pope Paul VI favored negotiations and the avoidance of war. In a memorable declaration at the United Nations in October 1965, he had declared, "No more war, war never again."[39] But the hawkish New York cardinal seemed to be operating from a different set of principles. The Vatican's disfavor with Spellman was never openly stated, but American Catholic critics of his support for the war were not similarly restrained.

The cardinal first came in for significant criticism because of his alleged role in the "banishment" of the Jesuit priest, poet, and antiwar activist Daniel Berrigan, who had joined with Rabbi Abraham Heschel and Lutheran minister Richard Neuhaus to form Clergy and Laity Concerned about Vietnam (CALCAV). In late 1965, Berrigan was dispatched by his religious superiors to Latin America, presumably to silence him on the antiwar issue in the United States. Catholic liberals saw Spellman's powerful hand behind this action and reacted accordingly. On December 5, 1965, an advertisement protesting Berrigan's exile and demanding his recall appeared in the *New York Times,* signed by almost one thousand supporters.[40] Fordham students demonstrated outside the cardinal's residence, and the episode served to portray Spellman as intolerant of dissent on the war. Though the cardinal undoubtedly had no regard for the views expressed by Berrigan, it appears clear that this was an instance in which Spellman exercised his talent, as Wilfrid Sheed put it, "to be vilified beyond [his] merits." He apparently had no contact with Berrigan's Jesuit superiors and no direct role in their decision to order the priest out of the United States.[41]

Spellman's general support for the war in Vietnam attracted growing criticism during 1966. Catholic peace activists and concerned liberals increasingly asked how the official leaders of the church could refrain from making a critical moral assessment of the American actions in the war. As Timothy A. Byrnes noted, they "also attacked Spellman and others like him for their patriotic boosterism, and they condemned the 'scandal' of the hierarchy's 'near total silence' on the morality of the war." Such attacks had an ironic and somewhat confusing quality. Catholic leaders such as Spellman, as Byrnes noted, long "had been challenged by a hostile culture to demonstrate that it was possible to be a good patriotic American and remain a faithful Catholic." Now, they "were challenged by members of their own church to consider whether one could be a faithful Catholic and still remain a blindly patriotic, uncritical American."[42]

Spellman apparently did not take this challenge too personally or seriously. He must have wondered, if he wondered at all, at the critics' constant calls to consider the morality of the American role in the war. After all, he had done so long before and had found the effort just. His view was, for the most part, endorsed, although in more temperate language, in the pastoral letter of the American bishops, *Peace and Vietnam,* which was issued in November 1966. "In light of the facts as they are known to us," the bishops declared, "it is reasonable to argue that our presence in Vietnam is justified," as long as possibilities for a just peace settlement also were pursued.[43] Such a measured moral assessment, however, did not satisfy the antiwar critics, and its careful tone did not express well the cardinal's unqualified support for the war. As the year ended, Spellman returned to Vietnam to spend Christmas with the troops, and there, he gave his most fervent statement on the war.

In his familiar role visiting soldiers at the front, the seventy-seven-year-old Spellman told the troops that Vietnam was "a war for civilization." He expressed his hope and prayer "that through the valor and dedication of our men and women in our armed forces, we will soon have a victory for which all of us are praying." Then, in words that stirred up a hornet's nest of protest in liberal circles in the United States, he exclaimed that "less than victory is inconceivable."[44] The *New York Times* piously editorialized against Spellman on December 29, declaring it "a pity that he felt the need to speak at all in terms which momentarily forgot that of the three abiding Pauline virtues, the greatest is Charity." *The Nation* denounced him for his inflexibility. The liberal Catholic periodical *Commonweal* criticized the cardinal and argued that "the profusion of 'high Vatican sources' dissociating the Pope from Cardinal Spellman's Vietnam statements clearly adds up to a rebuke."[45] The cardinal's remarks also attracted criticism from the communist side of the Iron Curtain. *Izvestia* contrasted him unfavorably with Paul VI, and North Vietnam reportedly denounced him as a "reactionary under a priest's cloak."[46]

Spellman was not put off by the criticism at home or abroad. When he lunched at the White House on January 18 with Lyndon Johnson and Protestant evangelist Billy Graham, who also had visited Vietnam recently, the Catholic leader spoke positively about the war and emphasized the high morale of the U.S. forces. Graham remembers the cardinal as being "quite hawkish," and there is little reason to dispute his recollection.[47] Perhaps Spellman drew some sustenance from surveys showing that a majority of American Catholics still supported the Vietnam effort, but opposition was growing, and he became a target for it. The unalloyed militance of the cardinal's comments helped transform him into a symbol of unqualified support for the war and made him a special object for antiwar activists. On Sunday, January 22, 1967, demonstrators disrupted the high mass at Saint Patrick's Cathedral, where Spellman was presiding. Protestors also interrupted his public appearances with cries of "Draft Spellman!" and "Warmonger!" and columnist Drew Pearson reported with satisfaction that the Vietnam War had become known as "Spellman's War."[48] The cardinal proved unrepentant, and unlike many of his brother bishops, who were increasingly alarmed by the protests against their stand on the war (or lack of stand against it), he made no revisions to his positions. The night before his death from a massive stroke on December 2, 1967, Spellman attended a banquet at which he raised the possibility of going to Vietnam again at Christmas.

On the cardinal's death, Lyndon Johnson released a public tribute in which he made special note of Spellman's service as vicar of the armed forces. In Vietnam, Gen. William C. Westmoreland attended a memorial service for the man who had given his command such unflagging support. Thousands of mourners passed by Spellman's body, which lay in state in the cathedral for three days prior to his funeral on December 7—days that ironically coincided with Stop-the-Draft Week and a series of antiwar demonstrations in Manhattan. Concern about antiwar protests led police to take stringent security precautions to allow Johnson to attend the funeral. Presumably, it was for the president's benefit that a group of protestors gathered across the street from Saint Patrick's near the Rockefeller Center Promenade, holding aloft signs that read: "'Napalm: Johnson's Baby Powder,' 'Vietnamese Should Die So Good,' and the familiar 'LBJ, LBJ, How Many Kids Did You Kill Today?'"[49] Cardinal Spellman had gone to meet his maker and could be targeted no more.

Spellman's death in late 1967 spared him the turmoil that the nation and the administration experienced in response to the Tet Offensive of early 1968. No doubt, he would have tried to fight a rearguard action as the Catholic community in the United States, mirroring the American populace as a whole, became increasingly restive about the war. Four years after Spellman's death, as the war continued to drag on, the Catholic bishops described the "speedy ending of this war" as "a moral imperative of the highest priority."[50] Enthusiastic support for the war, such as Spellman had provided, was repudiated.

The cardinal's unqualified patriotism and his Manichaean assessment of the contest between communism and the Western democracies led by the United States prevented him from ever raising serious questions about the war's purpose. He took administration statements on the war at face value and was unaware of, and thus untroubled by, administration deception about Vietnam. Suggestions that the war was a crime or a sin struck him as bizarre and wrongheaded. He felt no need to examine the proportionality of means and ends. The old cardinal never appears to have been troubled that the cost of the war in lives and treasure seemed indeterminable by 1967, nor did he ever protest any aspect of America's conduct of the war. Even the massive air campaign against North Vietnam was insufficient to elicit from him any cautionary comments regarding the immorality of indiscriminate bombing. Such failures on his part leave him susceptible to severe criticism, especially given his responsibility as a Christian religious and moral leader.

It is unlikely, however, that Cardinal Spellman would have accepted such criticism graciously. Had he lived another decade or so, he assuredly would have directed his critics' attention to the political executions, the religious repression, the reeducation camps, and the Stalinism that drove well over a million refugees from Vietnam following the triumph of the North. He might have reminded them that that was exactly what he had warned against and tried to prevent, and he might have invited them to reconsider their own moral calculus in light of such developments. He might even have gone as far as Aleksandr I. Solzhenitsyn in his stinging 1978 commencement address at Harvard University and alleged that "members of the U.S. antiwar movement became accomplices in the betrayal of Far Eastern nations, in the genocide and the suffering today imposed on thirty million people there."[51] Above all, it is unlikely that he would have expressed any regrets for the role he played in supporting his nation's effort to sustain an independent, noncommunist South Vietnam.

Notes

1. James Carroll, *An American Requiem: God, My Father, and the War That Came between Us* (Boston: Houghton Mifflin, 1996), 164.

2. Robert Scheer and Warren Hinckle, "The 'Vietnam Lobby,'" *Ramparts* 4 (July 1965): 16–24.

3. The historian James T. Fisher is excellent on this subject. See his "With Friends Like These . . . ," *Reviews in American History* 25 (December 1997): 709, and his "The Second Catholic President: Ngo Dinh Diem, John F. Kennedy, and the Vietnam Lobby, 1954–1963," *U.S. Catholic Historian* 15 (Summer 1997): 119–21.

4. Spellman quoted in Dorothy Dohen, *Nationalism and American Catholicism* (New York: Sheed and Ward, 1967), 150.

5. Ibid., 58, 121.

6. Robert I. Gannon, S.J., *The Cardinal Spellman Story* (Garden City, N.Y.: Doubleday, 1962), 337.

7. For Spellman's efforts, see Donald F. Crosby, S.J., *God, Church, and Flag: Senator Joseph R. McCarthy and the Catholic Church, 1950–1957* (Chapel Hill: University of North Carolina Press, 1978), 10–12.

8. Wilfrid Sheed, *Clare Boothe Luce* (New York: E. P. Dutton, 1982), 114.

9. Crosby, *God, Church, and Flag,* 13.

10. Sheed, *Clare Boothe Luce,* 115.

11. McGuire's role is recorded in John Cooney, *The American Pope: The Life and Times of Francis Cardinal Spellman* (New York: Times Books, 1984), 240–41.

12. Joseph G. Morgan, *The Vietnam Lobby: The American Friends of Vietnam, 1955–1975* (Chapel Hill: University of North Carolina Press, 1997), 5. As Morgan noted, access to Spellman's personal papers is restricted, so further investigation there is limited.

13. On Douglas's role, see ibid., 10.

14. Gregory Allen Olson, *Mansfield and Vietnam: A Study in Rhetorical Adaption* (East Lansing: Michigan State University Press, 1995), 30.

15. Ibid. Olson well summarized this argument, although he did not agree with it. See also Morgan, *Vietnam Lobby,* 10–11.

16. Denis Warner, *The Last Confucian* (New York: Macmillan, 1963), 72, 81.

17. On the Diem-Lansdale connection, see David L. Anderson, *Trapped by Success: The Eisenhower Administration and Vietnam, 1953–1961* (New York: Columbia University Press, 1991).

18. Francis J. Spellman, "Dien Bien Phu: A Reveille," *Vital Speeches* 20 (July 1, 1954): 568.

19. "Text of Cardinal's Speech" [given before the American Legion convention, Washington, D.C., August 30, 1954], *New York Times,* August 31, 1954.

20. "Archdiocese Sending Aid: Cardinal Spellman in Letter Cites Refugee's Needs," *New York Times,* August 6, 1954.

21. Joseph J. Harnett to Edward E. Swanstrom, October 26, 1954, Box 2, Joseph Harnett Papers, University of Notre Dame Archives, Notre Dame, Indiana.

22. Charles R. Morris, *American Catholic: The Saints and Sinners Who Built America's Most Powerful Church* (New York: Times Books, 1997), 221.

23. Harnett to Swanstrom, January 16, 1955, Harnett Papers.

24. J. Lawton Collins, *Lightening Joe: An Autobiography* (Baton Rouge: Louisiana State University Press, 1979), 389.

25. Fisher, "The Second Catholic President," 121, 124–25.

26. Buttinger's claims are discussed ibid., 120–21.

27. Ibid., 121.

28. On the limited impact of the AFV, see Morgan, *Vietnam Lobby,* 44.

29. Quoted in Fisher, "The Second Catholic President," 129.

30. Anderson, *Trapped by Success,* 160–65, and Morgan, *Vietnam Lobby,* 50–52.

31. "Text of Sermon by Cardinal Spellman" [delivered at World Eucharistic Congress, Munich, Germany, August 6, 1960], *New York Times,* August 7, 1960.

32. Details of Thuc's visit are provided in Henry Raymont, "Vietnam Prelate Here from Rome," *New York Times,* September 12, 1963.

33. Bundy quoted in memorandum of discussion, September 11, 1963, in *Foreign Relations of the United States, 1961–1963,* vol. 4, *Vietnam, August–December 1963* (Washington, D.C.: Government Printing Office, 1991), 175.

34. "Spellman Arrives for Five-Day Visit with Vietnam's G.I.'s," *New York Times,* December 24, 1965.

35. Paul Hanly Furfey, "The Civilian COs," in *War or Peace? The Search*

for New Answers, ed. Thomas A. Shannon (Maryknoll, N.Y.: Orbis Books, 1980), 194.

36. Quoted in David J. O'Brien, "American Catholic Opposition to the Vietnam War: A Preliminary Assessment," ibid., 125.

37. For an example of Johnson's appreciation, see Walt Rostow to Spellman, August 12, 1966, Box 476, White House Central Files, Lyndon Baines Johnson Library, Austin, Texas. Rostow explained: "As you know, the burden of seeing through a crisis as severe and protracted as that in South Vietnam is heavy and lonely. Your public support and understanding have meant a great deal to the President."

38. Joseph A. Califano Jr., *The Triumph and Tragedy of Lyndon Johnson: The White House Years* (New York: Simon and Schuster, 1991), 71.

39. "Text of Pope Paul's Speech at U.N. Appealing for an End to War and Offensive Arms," *New York Times,* October 6, 1965.

40. "Open Letter to the Authorities of the Archdiocese of New York and the Jesuit Community in New York" [advertisement], *New York Times,* December 5, 1965.

41. See James Hennesey, S.J., *American Catholics: A History of the Roman Catholic Community in the United States* (Oxford: Oxford University Press, 1981), 319.

42. Timothy A. Byrnes, *Catholic Bishops in American Politics* (Princeton: Princeton University Press, 1991), 94.

43. National Conference of Catholic Bishops, "Peace and Vietnam" [November 18, 1966], in *Quest for Justice: A Compilation of Statements of the United States Catholic Bishops on the Political and Social Order, 1966–1980,* ed. Brian Benestad and Francis J. Butler (Washington, D.C.: U.S. Conference of Catholic Bishops, 1981), 51–54.

44. Quoted in O'Brien, "American Catholic Opposition to the Vietnam War," 126.

45. "The Words of a Cardinal" [editorial], *New York Times,* December 29, 1966; "The Cardinal's Mistake" [editorial], *The Nation* 204 (January 16, 1967): 69; "Cardinal, Pope and War" [editorial], *Commonweal* 85 (January 13, 1967): 391–92.

46. "Cardinal under Fire: Spellman's Views Irk Reds," *U.S. News and World Report* 62 (January 9, 1967): 14.

47. For a brief report on the lunch, see President's Daily Diary, January 18, 1967, Box 9, Diaries and Appointment Logs of Lyndon B. Johnson, Lyndon Baines Johnson Library, Austin, Texas. On Billy Graham's recollection, see his oral history interview with Monroe Billington, October 12, 1983, Johnson Library.

48. The material in this paragraph relies on the not always reliable Cooney, *American Pope,* 307–8.

49. Homer Bogart, "Helicopter Flies President to Central Park Meadow," *New York Times,* December 8, 1967.

50. Benestad and Butler, *Quest for Justice,* 78.

51. Aleksandr I. Solzhenitsyn, "A World Split Apart," in *Solzhenitsyn at Harvard,* ed. Ronald Berman (Washington, D.C.: Ethics and Public Policy Center, 1979), 14.

Suggested Readings

In addition to the sources cited in the notes, relevant works are Francis J. Spellman, *The Road to Victory* (New York: Scribner's, 1942), and James T. Fisher, *Dr. America: The Lives of Thomas A. Dooley, 1927–1961* (Amherst: University of Massachusetts Press, 1997).

2

Ambassador William Cattell Trimble and Cambodia, 1959–1962

Kenton Clymer

Prior to the 1950s the United States had exhibited only limited interest in Southeast Asia. Not only was it geographically and culturally distant from America, it also was a part of France's colonial empire for a century. Because France was a major European ally of the United States, American leaders deferred to French officials on policy matters for the region up to World War II. During and after that war, however, U.S. policymakers became increasingly critical of French efforts to maintain colonial mastery over the area. In the 1950s, Vietnam, Laos, and Cambodia achieved varying forms of independence from France, and U.S. representatives began to deal directly with the people of the region for the first time.

As U.S. ambassador to Cambodia from 1959 to 1962, William C. Trimble worked closely with Prince Norodom Sihanouk, Cambodia's proud and volatile ruler. The prince intensely disliked the imperious U.S. envoys who preceded Trimble, and Sihanouk believed, with some justification, that American intelligence agents were connected with rival Cambodian political factions. Through his personal diplomacy, Trimble was able to win Sihanouk's friendship and to improve significantly U.S.-Cambodian relations.

As analyzed by Kenton Clymer, the Trimble-Sihanouk relationship in many ways personified the U.S. policy challenges in Southeast Asia posed by the clash of global strategy with regional realities. The Cambodians deeply distrusted and expressed contempt toward their more powerful neighbors, the Vietnamese and the Thai. Because the United States was allied with South Vietnam and Thailand, this local tension made the U.S.-Cambodian relationship complex, interesting, and difficult, as did Sihanouk's insistence on neutrality at a time when the United States condemned that approach. Nevertheless, Washington tried through Trimble to maintain good relations and even provided ostensibly neutral Cambodia with military assistance. Ambassador Trimble's individual efforts, especially in cultivating Sihanouk, revealed both the importance and the danger of Indochina for Americans.

Kenton J. Clymer is a professor of history at the University of Texas, El Paso. He has also taught at universities in the Philippines, Malaysia, India, Indonesia, and Germany. He holds a Ph.D. from the University of Michigan and is the author of numerous books and articles on U.S.

From the William C. Trimble Papers, Public Policy Papers, Princeton University Library. *Courtesy of Princeton University Library*

relations with South and Southeast Asia, including *Protestant Mission-aries in the Philippines, 1898-1916: An Inquiry into the American Colo-nial Mentality* (1986), and *Quest for Freedom: The United States and India's Independence* (1995). He is currently working on a book on U.S. relations with Cambodia. Clymer gratefully acknowledges the assis-tance of William C. Trimble Jr. in obtaining information for this chapter.

When William Cattell Trimble arrived in Phnom Penh, Cambo-dia, in April 1959, he was only the third American ambassador assigned to that country, which had achieved independence from France in 1953–1954. (Cambodia dates its independence from Nov-ember 9, 1953, but France still had some authority until after the Geneva Conference the following year.) He arrived with at least two strikes against him. For one thing, Cambodia's leader, Prince Noro-dom Sihanouk, had disliked the previous American ambassadors. This was especially true of Robert McClintock, the first ambassador, who, as an Australian historian has recently written, "displayed an uncanny ability to offend Sihanouk."[1] Frank R. Valeo, an assistant to Sen. Mike Mansfield who accompanied the senator on many of his Asian trips, called McClintock a "martinet [who] carried a riding crop and walked with two poodles wherever he went. . . . I'm sur-prised that Sihanouk never asked for his removal, but he should have." McClintock was the epitome of the "ugly American," and Valeo thought his behavior was the source of future problems between the two countries: "[They] could be traced to that first ridiculous, stupid encounter."[2] McClintock "behaved toward Sihanouk as might an executive of the United Fruit Company toward the president of a banana republic," historian Michael Leifer wrote, adding that the ambassador's "failure to appreciate the sensitive nature of the Cam-bodian leader left a substantial legacy of insult."[3]

Another obstacle for Trimble was that Martin Herz, an Amer-ican diplomat stationed in Phnom Penh with McClintock, had re-cently published a good book about Cambodia that included observations about Cambodian politics that Sihanouk disliked. Inor-dinately sensitive to negative comments, the prince assumed that the book reflected official views and often thereafter criticized Herz by name and in public. The book, Trimble recalled, "constituted one of my problems upon arriving in Phnom Penh."[4] Yet, Trimble even-tually was the most successful of the early U.S. ambassadors to serve in Cambodia, becoming one of only two Americans whom Sihanouk ever really trusted.[5]

By the time Trimble arrived in his new posting, the United States had been interested in Cambodia for only a little more than a decade. Before World War II, Washington considered Cambodia (when it considered it at all) as a sleepy, backwater area in a minor part of the world: Southeast Asia. It had not always been so insignificant. At one time the Khmer empire stretched across mainland Southeast Asia, its powerful kings controlling much of what is now Vietnam and Thailand, as well as Cambodia. Centered in Angkor, near what is now the city of Siem Reap, it reached the peak of its power in the thirteenth century. At that time perhaps one million people lived in Angkor. The magnificent Angkor Wat, included on most anyone's list of the wonders of the world, is only one of hundreds of Hindu and Buddhist temples built in the area from the ninth to the thirteenth centuries.

For complex reasons, however, the kingdom declined in importance. The Siamese (Thai), Cham, and Vietnamese attacked the Khmer. The kingdom shrank, the temples of Angkor were all but abandoned, and the jungle reclaimed them. By the middle of the nineteenth century, it looked as if Cambodia might disappear altogether, the victim of the competing ambitions of its neighbors. It is possible that the arrival of the French in the region in 1863 inadvertently prevented the complete dissolution of the country.

By the end of the nineteenth century the French had gained control over most of the territory that today encompasses Vietnam, Cambodia, and Laos. The area became known as French Indochina, a name derived from the Indian cultural legacy in Cambodia and Laos and the Chinese cultural traditions in Vietnam. In all three countries the monarchy remained, but the French called the shots. The United States had no objection to French rule.

To the extent that Washington took an interest in Indochina before World War II, it was mostly concerned with Vietnam. Since the late nineteenth century, in fact, the United States had maintained consular offices in both Hanoi and Saigon. There was no American representation of any kind in Phnom Penh. Occasionally American representatives from Vietnam or Thailand visited the area, but official reports about developments in Cambodia prior to World War II were few and far between.

During World War II the Japanese occupied Cambodia and the rest of Indochina. Although they allowed the French to remain (because they were Vichy French, who had made their peace with Japan's European ally, Germany), the Japanese ruled behind the scenes. In 1941, shortly before the Japanese takeover, the French placed the young Norodom Sihanouk on the Cambodian throne. He quickly pledged eternal allegiance to France. When the Japanese overthrew the French colonial regime in March 1945, Sihanouk pledged his faith to the Japanese Greater East Asia Co-Prosperity Sphere, even as he, at Tokyo's request, declared the country independent.

Toward the end of the war, Washington concluded that the Cambodians would welcome a French return after the conflict because they feared the Siamese and the Vietnamese. The Americans were only partly correct. Even Sihanouk, whom they thought was very much a Francophile, informed the French that Cambodia had already achieved its independence. The French returned nonetheless, meeting little overt resistance.

After World War II the United States took more interest in Cambodia. American anticolonial sentiments inclined important U.S. officials to view the French-dominated regime as "a puppet government" and to urge American support for more autonomy or independence.[6] As the communists moved toward victory in China and the Vietminh made gains against the French in Vietnam, however, stopping the spread of communism became the predominant American concern. Pressuring the French to leave now seemed almost dangerous. Thus, in 1950, after France made a few concessions to the Indochinese peoples and granted them "independence," the United States recognized the quasi-independent governments of Cambodia, Laos, and Vietnam. It sent a low-ranking diplomat to Phnom Penh—but not an ambassador. Soon, America was supplying military and economic aid to Cambodia, as well as to Vietnam.

As Sihanouk took increasingly anti-French, nationalist positions, Washington pressured both sides to settle their differences peacefully, though it was worried about Sihanouk's neutralist rhetoric, which, as the Americans viewed it, played into the hands of the communists. Nevertheless, once Cambodia was genuinely independent, the United States recognized its government and strongly supported the Cambodians at the 1954 Geneva Conference negotiations. In particular, Washington successfully opposed any partition of Cambodia and vigorously resisted efforts to include representatives of Cambodian dissident movements at the conference. It also appointed its first ambassador to Phnom Penh and even negotiated a military assistance arrangement with Sihanouk. Cambodia was the only professedly neutral country in the world where the United States had a military assistance advisory group (MAAG). In theory, France was to train Cambodia's military forces, and the United States was to supply them. Gradually, however, America took on a training role, as well.

Cambodia's neutral posture posed a serious dilemma for Washington. The Americans viewed almost all developments through a Cold War lens. The struggle against "international communism" pushed other considerations to the side, and U.S. leaders found it difficult to understand why others did not share their sense of urgency. Sihanouk, however, was much more concerned with regional realities. Although he often suppressed domestic communists and other leftists at home, he believed (as did most Cambodians) that the main threats to the country's security were Thailand and Vietnam. Although he did fear a communist victory in Vietnam, he was quite willing to court the Soviet Union and the People's Republic of China if he thought they would be useful in his quest to guarantee his country's independence, territorial integrity, and national security.

The prince's visit to Beijing in 1956, as well as to several other communist countries, exacerbated American fears, as did Chinese premier Zhou Enlai's visit to Phnom Penh later that year. Furthermore, the visits resulted in some economic aid, which began arriving in 1957. The United States was furious when Sihanouk recognized the PRC in 1958. Such developments were very troubling, for if Cambodia succumbed to communism, it would be difficult to hold the rest of the region for the "free world" because, as one military official put it, Cambodia was "the hub of the wheel in Southeast Asia."[7]

Sihanouk's neutrality and his opening to China also further antagonized his neighbors. Both Thailand and South Vietnam increased their support of those who wished to destabilize his government and perhaps overthrow him. The United States was unquestionably aware of such plotting and almost certainly provided some support for the plotters. The Dwight D. Eisenhower administration had, after all, embraced covert action as a way to achieve its political objectives and had recently sponsored successful operations to overthrow governments in Iran and Guatemala and to suppress the Hukbalahap rebellion in the Philippines. Covert operations were also under way in Vietnam (these became the subject of Graham Greene's novel *The Quiet American*), and in 1958 the CIA secretly supported regional rebellions in Indonesia.

The major plot against Sihanouk involved Sam Sary, a Cambodian diplomat known for his pro-Western views who, until January 1959, had represented Cambodia in London. Accused of beating an embassy official who was his former mistress and who had borne his child, Sary was recalled in disgrace and immediately fled to Thailand, where he joined with other longtime Cambodian dissidents— the Khmer Serei (Free Khmer), as they were called—to oppose Sihanouk. The Cambodians immediately accused the United States of complicity.

About the same time, Dap Chhuon, another Cambodian who was then governor of Siem Reap Province and military commander of the northwest region, conspired to overthrow Sihanouk with the help of the South Vietnamese. Chhuon was strongly anticommunist, had a long association with the Thai, and disliked Sihanouk's policy of neutrality. This time, Americans appear to have been directly involved. Victor Matsui, a CIA agent serving as an attaché at the American embassy, had been in touch with Chhuon's brother, Slat Peou. Slat Peou had visited the United States in 1956 as a guest of the government, and the CIA probably contacted him at that time. In February 1959 an American pilot flew the small plane that brought radio transmitters to Dap Chuuon, and Matsui provided an additional transmitter a little later. None of these plots succeeded. Before the month was out, Chhuon had been captured and killed, and his brother had been taken prisoner. Although evidence of American involvement was not yet fully known to the Cambodians, they suspected it, and relations between the two countries were so tense that 1959 became, as officials in Phnom Penh put it in a retrospective analysis, "a Year of Troubles."[8] Thus, when William Trimble arrived in Cambodia in April of that year, he not only had to overcome Sihanouk's irritation with the behavior of his predecessors but also had to deal with Cambodian suspicions (amounting to virtual certainty) that the CIA was supporting efforts to overthrow the prince. More generally, American efforts to pressure Sihanouk to end his neutral stance put him on his guard. The new ambassador faced a difficult situation.

Trimble's background did not seem promising for a successful ambassadorship in Cambodia. Born in Maryland and educated at Princeton and Johns Hopkins, he appeared to be the embodiment of the eastern establishment that then filled the top ranks of the American foreign service. Though highly professional, the diplomatic corps of that age was clubbish, exclusive, and largely European oriented. Trimble had early assignments in Argentina and Mexico, and from 1954 to 1956, he served in Brazil, but after 1944, most of his career involved Europe. From 1944 to 1946, he was assistant chief of the Northern European Affairs Division of the State Department, and subsequently, he served in Iceland, London, and The Hague. Immediately prior to arriving in Cambodia, he was minister-counselor in Bonn. He had had no previous experience anywhere in Asia, knew no Asian language (although his fluency in French was useful in Cambodia), and, in fact, had never even traveled in the region. Despite helpful briefings in Washington, he acknowledged that he went to Cambodia "still a neophyte as regards the Far East."[9]

Just why the State Department selected him to go to Cambodia is not clear. Trimble had been in the foreign service since 1931 and had recently attained the rank of career minister, the second highest rank in the service, so he was eligible for an ambassadorship. Yet, at that very time, the government was under attack for sending representatives abroad who did not know the native language, were inexperienced in the region, and lacked cultural sensitivity. William Lederer and Eugene Burdick's sensational novel, *The Ugly American*—which made precisely these charges about the quality of American diplomatic representation in Southeast Asia—had taken the

United States by storm when it was published in 1957: In historian Robert D. Schulzinger's words, it "had an impact similar to Harriet Beecher Stowe's *Uncle Tom's Cabin* in the years before the Civil War."[10] Furthermore, recommendations were already percolating through the bureaucracy to address the shortcomings that Lederer and Burdick highlighted.

One problem was that Asian experts were in short supply. Only a few years earlier, Sen. Joseph McCarthy's destructive attacks on the State Department for harboring alleged communists and fellow travelers had resulted in an unconscionable purge of many Asian hands within the department, an action that had disgusted Trimble. Perhaps the Eisenhower administration also expected that Trimble would not be as feisty as his immediate predecessor, Carl Strom, who had wanted the United States to protest strongly against Thai and South Vietnamese efforts to destabilize Cambodia. This was, after all, Trimble's first posting as an ambassador. Yet, in the end and despite his lack of Asian experience or expertise, he put forward forceful recommendations, earned Sihanouk's trust, and helped improve Cambodian-American relations greatly. Neither before nor after his time in Cambodia would the relationship between the two countries be more positive than it was during his tenure from 1959 to 1962.

Part of the reason for Trimble's success was his deep devotion to public service. This ethic was inculcated into him by his family and by his teachers at the prestigious Gilman School in Baltimore, where he received his secondary education. As a history major at Princeton, Trimble found himself fascinated by international affairs. His professors, who had considerable influence on him, strongly encouraged him to pursue a career in public service. Indeed, he turned down a potentially lucrative offer in the business world to enter the foreign service, and he was extremely proud that his graduating class at Princeton produced more foreign service officers than any previous class, a record that lasted for decades. When World War II broke out, Trimble's devotion to the nation led him to try to enter the military. As a Reserve Officers' Training Corps (ROTC) cadet, he had been instructed in field artillery. But Secretary of State Cordell Hull talked him out of enlisting, saying that his expertise was needed in the State Department.

Trimble was raised by his mother, Margaret Jones Trimble, a lady of very strong character, and by his five older siblings. His father, the prominent surgeon Isaac Ridgeway Trimble, had died when William was only one year old, and this unfortunate loss resulted in a very close-knit family that valued honor, dedication, and hard work—traits that came to characterize his diplomatic career. Trimble enjoyed his job and worked very hard at it; he seldom returned from the office before 7:00 P.M. and worked half a day on Saturdays, as well. He had few diversions or leisure activities and, after his school days, did not engage in sports.

Like most successful diplomats, Trimble was also good at cultivating friendships with people from all backgrounds and nationalities, and he had a very wide circle of friends. Though reserved, he had an almost puckish sense of humor. He counted among his many personal friends the prime ministers of Holland, Germany, and Iceland. Later, he would add Prince Sihanouk to that list.

Devotion to service, hard work, and the ability to make friends easily helped Trimble navigate the treacherous shoals of the U.S.-Cambodian relationship. And if he arrived in Phnom Penh with several problems to overcome, he was also fortunate in two respects. First, shortly before the ambassador's arrival, President Eisenhower had responded to Sihanouk's almost desperate plea to intervene with Thailand and South Vietnam and stop the plotting. Eisenhower assured Sihanouk that the United States had consulted with both governments and had achieved positive results. In his first meeting with the prince, Trimble reiterated the president's assurances and added that J. Graham Parsons, the deputy assistant secretary of state for Far Eastern affairs, would soon visit the region and attempt to develop "greater confidence and trust in the relations among the three nations."[11] Although Eisenhower's response disappointed Sihanouk (in his reply, he noted pointedly that the rebels claimed American support), he also agreed that, as a result of American intervention, there had been a "marked improvement" in his relationship with the Thai.[12] Relations with the Vietnamese had not improved, and Sihanouk's suspicions of earlier American involvement with the plotters were not really assuaged. Eisenhower's letter, however, went far toward convincing him that, at least for the time being, the United States was no longer supporting efforts to topple his government.

The other fortuitous circumstance for Trimble was that the important Khmer-American Friendship Highway was being completed just as he arrived. The road connected Phnom Penh with the new, French-built seaport at Kompong Som on the Gulf of Siam. Conceived in 1954, funded in 1955, begun in 1956, and (happily for Trimble) finished on April 13, 1959, the highway cost $33 million and was the shining example of constructive American economic assistance to Cambodia. Even today, Cambodians remember the highway as a symbol of American helpfulness. The new road allowed Cambodia to import goods directly, without having to bring them up the Mekong River through Vietnam. The Cambodians very much wanted this, and the Americans funded the road for both economic and political reasons.

In July, Secretary of the Interior Fred A. Seaton went to Phnom Penh to dedicate the highway. By all accounts the visit was a huge success. Sihanouk entertained the American in royal fashion, even hosting a performance of the magnificent Royal Ballet. "We were touched—why not admit it—by [the] extremely eulogistic words Mr. Seaton used regarding our pride," editorialized an important Cambodian newspaper.[13] Trimble, too, reported on Seaton's excellent reception, a report that was passed along to the president.

These momentarily favorable circumstances and his own diplomatic talents enabled Trimble to initiate a dramatic improvement in Cambodian-American relations. As Nong Kimny, the Cambodian ambassador in Washington, told State Department officials, "Combined with Mr. Parsons' visit last April and Ambassador Trimble's fine conduct of US affairs in Cambodia . . . the Secretary's [Seaton's] visit had done much to improve and consolidate Cambodian-American relations."[14] To preserve this improvement, however, required bettering the relationship between Cambodia and its neighbors, and this task was not easy, especially in regard to the Vietnamese and the Cambodians. In Vietnam the Americans singled out Ngo Dinh Nhu as the most important obstacle to peace. The brother of President Ngo Dinh Diem and the Vietnamese official in charge of plots, Nhu had little patience with those who counseled restraint. "Persistent US efforts" would be required to get Vietnam to cease supporting the dissidents.[15]

Over the summer the Americans enjoyed some modest success in defusing the tensions between Cambodia and Vietnam. Trimble helped arrange for Sihanouk to visit Saigon for talks. The discussions were reportedly cordial and resulted in a rapprochement of sorts, at least for the moment. Furthermore, in response to improving relations with the United States, Sihanouk moved Cambodia's internal politics to the right. In July the United States was pleased that only two of eight proposed cabinet officials in a new government could be described as leftists. The next month, Sihanouk vigorously attacked the local communist press for criticizing the new cabinet. This was, thought an American diplomat, a "welcome turn of events."[16]

On August 31, just as relations were improving, however, a bomb exploded at the Royal Palace, killing Prince Norodom Vakravan (the palace's protocol director) and a servant and narrowly missing Sihanouk and his mother, the queen, who were in the next room. Eisenhower immediately expressed his shock to the royal family. The South Vietnamese, Sam Sary, friends of the late Dap Chhuon, and the Americans were all suspected of involvement. Trimble thought that the Vietminh or the Chinese communists were probably responsible, on the theory that they hoped the bomb would unravel the improving Cambodian-American relationship. Suspecting possible South Vietnamese involvement, the United States applied considerable pressure on Diem. Apparently convinced that, in the final analysis, America had too much at stake in Vietnam to abandon the government, Nhu continued to support anti-Cambodian plots. It is now generally agreed that the South Vietnamese—and in particular, Ngo Dinh Nhu—sent the bomb.

Although the French ambassador informed Trimble that Sihanouk did not blame the United States for the bombing, Cambodian suspicions of American intentions simmered just below the surface. Then, at the end of the month, another development reinvigorated Cambodian suspicions about American covert activities. On September 30, Slat Peou, the brother of rebel leader Dap Chhuon, was tried and sentenced to death for his involvement in the plot. In his testimony, he asserted that he was the intermediary between Dap Chhuon and intelligence officials from South Vietnam and the United States. In particular, he named Victor Matsui. The Americans, in other words, were implicated in the rebellions, something they had steadfastly and repeatedly denied. Whether true or not, this revelation had profoundly negative consequences. As a State Department official put it a few months later, "The importance of this development in shaking Cambodian confidence in US motives cannot be overemphasized."[17]

Trimble urged the State Department to issue a strongly worded denial, but Washington decided that quiet diplomacy would be more useful. The Western press had not picked up the story, and the department feared that a public statement would only bring unwanted publicity and inflame the situation. It did, however, prepare a statement. If it became necessary to comment, the department intended to deny Slat Peou's allegations, including his claim that Matsui was "a counter-espionage agent" who had given a radio to the plotters.[18]

With relations threatening to deteriorate, the State Department accepted Trimble's advice to put more pressure on South Vietnam. The United States wanted the Vietnamese to shut down a clandestine radio station beamed into Cambodia (Trimble later revealed that the transmitter was probably mounted on a truck and moved from place to place), close a training camp for Cambodian rebels, and arrest or deport those dissident Cambodian leaders who were in Vietnam. Still, Ngo Dinh Nhu remained almost immune to American pressure and continued to be a serious obstacle to better relations with Cambodia.

Although U.S. intervention with Diem had little impact, Sihanouk continued to take a strongly anticommunist line. "The only serious challenger to the Monarchy is Communism," he stated at one point.[19] Thus, by the end of the "Year of Troubles," the State Department concluded that "the situation was in most respects better than was to have been expected in the light of earlier experience."[20] Problems between Thailand and Cambodia were fewer, but serious difficulties still characterized Cambodian relations with Vietnam. Sihanouk's August visit to Saigon had cleared the air somewhat, but Nhu's continued plotting kept relations tense.

What had changed was the American approach to interregional problems. Initially preferring not to become involved, even while largely blaming Sihanouk for the problems, the United States now moved quickly whenever tensions developed. Although the Americans were not willing to allow Sihanouk to call for them on a whim, they *were* willing to protest to the Vietnamese or the Thai when justified. As Under Secretary of State C. Douglas Dillon put it, "We have no choice but [to] remain alert to and promptly protest any support by Thailand and Viet-Nam to anti-Sihanouk dissidents."[21]

By the end of 1959, then, the United States had moved far toward accepting Sihanouk, despite his sometimes irritating behavior. This trend continued, something for which Trimble was substantially responsible. On January 7, 1960, the ambassador dispatched to Washington a highly influential analysis of Cambodian politics, in which he stated that Sihanouk had the strong support of most of the people—notably, the peasants (some 80 percent of the population) and the "urban proletariat." Furthermore, the prince's policy of neutrality had "almost universal support." There were no opposition leaders of stature within the country, and the dissidents outside the borders had "no broad backing," Trimble reported. He continued: "Sam Sary is completely discredited. Son Ngoc Thanh [an important Cambodian patriot who had defected several years before] has lost most popular appeal he possessed during [the] independence movement." The army was loyal to Sihanouk, and the possibilities of organizing a successful revolt were remote. In sum, the implication was that Sihanouk's position was unassailable at present, and American interests were best served by supporting him.[22] The State Department commended Trimble for his "excellent assessment [of] Sihanouk's political position" and his "penetrating and concise analysis."[23]

Then, just as relations were beginning to improve, another incident threatened to unravel the tentative rapprochement—a common pattern. As Trimble recalled, "We would work hard and from time to time we'd go up, and then, BANG, something else would happen."[24] At the end of January, *Blitz,* a newspaper published in Bombay, India, printed a letter dated the previous September allegedly from Cambodian dissident Sam Sary to Edmund H. Kellogg, counselor and deputy chief of mission of the American embassy in Phnom

Penh. The letter not only suggested that the two men were on close terms but also implied that the United States was aiding Sam Sary. Washington went to unusual lengths to discredit the letter. Trimble immediately flew to Siem Reap to tell Sihanouk personally that it was a forgery—a Russian plant, he insisted. Handwriting experts from the United States Postal Service supported this view. But French experts thought otherwise, and most Cambodians accepted the letter's authenticity, gamely holding their ground against strong American pressure. "We were really in the doghouse on that one," Trimble recalled.[25]

American credibility temporarily increased as the result of yet another plot—the so-called Svay Rieng affair. On February 10 a young Cambodian, Reath Vath (or perhaps his name was Reath Suong) entered the American embassy and requested assistance in his plan to assassinate Sihanouk, whose foreign policy he said he disliked, during the prince's forthcoming visit to Svay Rieng. Trimble turned him over to the Cambodian police. Whether the man was a communist agent, someone sent by Sihanouk to test the Americans or even to distract attention from the *Blitz* affair, or simply a deranged individual was the subject of much debate. In a thorough review of the case, John C. Monjo, the third secretary of the embassy, concluded that most likely Sihanouk sent Vath to test the Americans, although Trimble subsequently maintained that the communists were to blame. Sihanouk later wrote that the man was a CIA agent (which is perhaps the least likely explanation). Whatever the truth, the Cambodian government at the time blamed the communists and praised the Americans for acting responsibly. "So having been down, we were suddenly up again," Trimble wrote. "We were fair-haired boys for about six weeks. But it was something."[26]

This bizarre incident helped improve relations, and for the rest of the year, Washington tried hard to remain in Sihanouk's good graces. As relations improved, the United States put much effort into attempts to persuade the prince that he could count on American protection and assistance. When Eisenhower went to New York to address the United Nations (UN), for example, he arranged a special personal meeting with Sihanouk. The prince also paid a successful visit to Kent State University. (Ironically, four students were shot at Kent State in 1970 while protesting an American invasion of Cambodia.) Toward the end of the Eisenhower presidency, the United States decided to offer jet aircraft training for six Cambodian military pilots, a proposal reluctantly made on the eve of Sihanouk's travels to communist countries.

Thus, by the time Eisenhower left office, the United States, although it continued to see events within a bipolar worldview, had come to accept Sihanouk and his neutralism. As long as he did not lean too far toward the communist countries, Washington intended to support him. The Cambodians suspected that the CIA was still working with Son Ngoc Thanh, at least, and, although covert actions to undermine Sihanouk's government would seem to have been counterproductive, it is not impossible that they continued.

Eisenhower's acceptance of Cambodia's neutral course was partial and grudging, but the incoming president, John F. Kennedy, felt less threatened by nations that pursued an independent course. Thus, for example, JFK worked closely with Sihanouk in devising a solution to the war in Laos, and he moved beyond the Eisenhower administration's position when he decided to provide jet aircraft for Cambodia. No American saw any military justification for the jets, and supplying them would undoubtedly complicate relations with Thailand and South Vietnam, but Sihanouk wanted them and probably could have gotten them from Soviet bloc countries. For purely political reasons, Trimble strongly supported providing the jets; in fact, he objected to the constant stalling and obvious reluctance with which the United States greeted many Cambodian requests for military supplies. Any aid given, he argued, should be provided quickly and without a sign of reluctance. Kennedy finally agreed to provide the jets but only after Sihanouk threatened to accept a Czech offer of twenty MIGs. The ambassador would have preferred a more forthcoming approach to Sihanouk's requests.

In June, Trimble strongly urged that the prince be invited to Washington for an official state visit as a reward for his good behavior in several areas. Although an invitation was not extended, Trimble was instrumental in seeing that the prince was very well treated when he attended the United Nations General Assembly meeting in New York in September. (Sihanouk had complained about inadequate and undignified arrangements during his visit the previous year.) On his way to the United States, the prince visited Italy, and the State Department went to extraordinary lengths to see him off at the Rome airport. Most important, however, was his visit with President Kennedy at the Hotel Carlyle in New York, a meeting for which Trimble was largely responsible, having argued vigorously that it ought to be arranged.

The meeting lasted nearly an hour, longer than Kennedy's meeting with any other head of state during the UN session. According to Trimble, who was present, Kennedy was masterly. Well versed on Cambodian and regional affairs, he engaged the prince in a serious discussion of current issues affecting Southeast Asia, all without a hint of condescension. At the end of the meeting, Kennedy invited Sihanouk to return on a state visit the following year.

Sihanouk "was in seventh heaven," Trimble later recalled, because Kennedy had taken him seriously.[27] Unfortunately the prince encountered considerable criticism at other points during his stay in the United States, which soured the good impression he had acquired in New York, and within a month, there was a dramatic change in the relationship. Once again, Sihanouk accused the United States of supporting dissidents and even referred to America as his enemy. A break in diplomatic relations seemed possible, and plans were drafted to evacuate U.S. citizens from Cambodia. The crisis passed when Kennedy reassured the prince of American intentions.

Another crisis soon loomed when journalist Robert Trumbull asserted in a *New York Times* article that there were Vietcong bases in Cambodia. Such allegations were not new, and some American officials—especially those stationed in Vietnam—believed them to be true. Still the charges infuriated Sihanouk. Trimble personally inspected by air the border regions, looking for Vietcong bases, and he supported Sihanouk's position, as did Gen. Edward Scherrer, the MAAG chief: "We believe there are none," Scherrer wrote to the commander of the American Pacific fleet.[28] Trimble even traveled to Saigon to examine photographic evidence of the alleged bases but found the pictures unconvincing. One photo was of a decaying, abandoned French fort. Other pictures purporting to show antiaircraft emplacements were nothing more than common rain pits.

In the end this issue that had threatened to destroy the fragile rapprochement helped better relations. At the ambassador's invitation, Trumbull went to Cambodia and, after a thorough investigation, concluded that there were no Vietcong bases there, as he had first thought. His article to that effect appeared in the *New York Times* on November 22. Thereafter, Sihanouk praised Trumbull and the *Times* and was in much better spirits. Indeed, Trimble found him positively euphoric at a party thrown for the departing Australian ambassador. The prince played the saxophone and the clarinet, danced with the guests, and sang, and the party ended so late, in fact, that it made the drive back to Phnom Penh difficult.

Some Americans, including the notorious and almost mythical Edward Lansdale, who was thought to be responsible for many of the covert actions undertaken in Indochina during these years, believed Trimble and Scherrer were, at best, naive. "I wonder if these folks who go looking really know what a Communist guerrilla really looks like?" he wrote. Scherrer's unwillingness to admit the existence of Vietcong sanctuaries particularly annoyed him. "It might be okay for American civilians to be lulled into a real lotus-land picture," Lansdale stated, "but our military need to look at the scene with hard realism."[29] Trimble, however, continued to maintain that there were no Vietcong bases at that time; this, perhaps more than anything else, endeared him to Sihanouk. In any event the crisis seemed nearly resolved. On January 19, 1962, Trimble could report that a "phased return to normality" was taking place.[30]

In 1961, he had asked to be transferred to the State Department. He had served a normal tour of duty, and his wife was not happy in Cambodia. The change in administration in 1961 may also have been a factor. Trimble admired Kennedy's diplomatic skills with Sihanouk, but he was clearly less comfortable with the administration's foreign service appointments. A strong believer in the career service, he objected that Chester Bowles, a close Kennedy aide who had considerable influence over foreign policy appointments, was inclined to recommend too many unqualified outsiders (often "deserving Democrats") for ambassadorial positions. He was also unhappy with reforms that had democratized the foreign service, bringing in many officers whom he considered unqualified.

Despite his request to return, Trimble remained in his post for an additional year. This delay may well have been because Sihanouk trusted him and wanted him to stay. In the summer of 1962, he returned to head the State Department's African Affairs office, an appointment for which he frankly admitted he was unsuited— though, as he accurately put it, few American officials knew anything about Africa.

It was a good time for Trimble to leave Cambodia. He had arrived at a tense moment, when evidence of American involvement with Sihanouk's enemies was surfacing. He successfully negotiated the diplomatic shoals and returned Cambodian-American relations to a state of relative cordiality. At a time when hard-line anticommunists in the United States were condemning neutralism, Trimble understood that Cambodia had no choice *but* neutrality, and he insisted that the United States accept this reality and work as closely as possible with Sihanouk. This course was difficult, given the closer relations that the United States had with Cambodia's enemies on both sides: the Thai and the South Vietnamese. Trimble handled the difficulties, however, about as well as anyone could have.

After his retirement from the foreign service, he continued to take an active interest in diplomacy. He consulted from time to time with the State Department on particular issues, wrote an occasional article for the *Foreign Service Journal,* and enjoyed attending meetings and symposia of the Foreign Service Association, in which he maintained a membership. When not involved in diplomatic affairs, he puttered around his wife's family's large, eighteenth-century country home in Maryland, and he annually attended the Williamsburg Forum, a gathering at which those interested in antiques could learn from leading museum experts.

After Trimble's departure from Phnom Penh, relations between the United States and Cambodia deteriorated. In part, this was a result of personal differences, for Sihanouk did not get along as well with Trimble's successor, Philip Sprouse, "a fastidious bachelor who was hardly Sihanouk's type."[31] More to the point was the increasing violence in Vietnam, a war that Sihanouk increasingly believed the communists would win and one that he greatly feared would one day engulf Cambodia. As the conflict intensified and the American commitment in Vietnam grew, there were more and more tensions with Cambodia. South Vietnamese troops and planes, sometimes accompanied by American advisers, crossed the border into Cambodia and killed civilians. The Khmer dissidents began to operate more freely on Vietnamese and Thai soil.

In November 1963, shortly before Kennedy's assassination, Sihanouk ended all American military and economic assistance programs. Later, in justifying his decision, he recalled his many problems with Washington in the 1950s and early 1960s: American support for the Khmer Serei; the U.S. failure to prevent South Vietnamese raids into Cambodia; Washington's refusal to allow him to use American equipment to repulse the Vietnamese and the Thai; the huge amounts of aid given to his neighbors (including even little Laos) as compared to what was extended to Cambodia; the interminable time it took to get four incompletely equipped jet planes (they lacked bomb racks, among other things); and, in general, the humiliating way he felt Cambodia had been treated. In the event of aggression, he stated, he would now turn to the Soviet Union or China.[32]

The Cambodian-American relationship lay in tatters. In May 1965, after another cross-border raid, Sihanouk broke diplomatic relations with the United States. They were not restored for four years. Washington had shown considerable flexibility at times, but in the final analysis, it had not found a way to reconcile its commitment to containing communism with regional concerns and neutrality.

Great tragedy lay ahead for Cambodia. In 1970, Lon Nol and Sisowath Sirik Matak overthrew Sihanouk in a coup that perhaps had American support. Finally, Cambodia was aligned with the United States—but at the cost of being swept fully into the Vietnam War. America unleashed its bombers over Cambodia (secret bombing had actually begun the previous year), and Sihanouk, now in exile, urged his compatriots to join the opposition Khmer Rouge. Five years later the Khmer Rouge prevailed and turned Cambodia into a great killing field. Although no one can say with certainty what might have happened if things had been done differently, it is possible that greater efforts on both sides to solve American differences with the Cambodians in the mid-1960s might have prevented the Cambodian holocaust.

Notes

1. Milton Osborne, *Sihanouk: Prince of Light, Prince of Darkness* (Honolulu: University of Hawaii Press, 1994), 94.

2. Francis R. Valeo Oral History Interview, July 3, 1985–March 11, 1986, p. 109, John F. Kennedy Library, Boston, Massachusetts.

3. Michael Leifer, *Cambodia: The Search for Security* (New York: Frederick A. Praeger, 1967), 103. William J. Duiker, however, considered McClintock's astute assessment of South Vietnamese leader Ngo Dinh Diem "prophetic"; see his *U.S. Containment Policy and the Conflict in Indochina* (Stanford: Stanford University Press, 1994), 106.

4. Martin F. Herz, *A Short History of Cambodia* (New York: Frederick A. Praeger, 1958); William C. Trimble Oral History Interview, August 12, 1969, p. 3, John F. Kennedy Library, Boston, Massachusetts.

5. David P. Chandler, *The Tragedy of Cambodian History: Politics, War, and Revolution since 1945* (New Haven: Yale University Press, 1991), 131. The other man was the chief of the American Military Assistance Advisory Group, Brig. Gen. Edward "Pony" Scherrer, who served under Trimble.

6. Edwin F. Stanton to secretary of state (hereafter cited as SS), January 13, 1947, despatch 244, 851G.00/1-1347, Confidential U.S. State Department Central Files, Indochina: Internal Affairs, 1945–1949 (microfilm), National Archives II, College Park, Maryland. (Citation to despatches in these files will hereafter be cited only by the despatch number.) Stanton was the American ambassador in Bangkok, Thailand.

7. Memorandum of Conversation, Walter Robertson et al., August 5, 1958, *Foreign Relations of the United States, 1958–1960*, vol. 16, *East Asia–Pacific Region: Cambodia, Laos* (Washington, D.C.: Government Printing Office, 1992), 244–46 (hereafter cited as FRUS 1958–60).

8. Cited in Richard E. Usher to John M. Steeves, March 11, 1960, ibid., 355.

9. Trimble Oral History, 3.

10. Robert D. Schulzinger, *A Time for War: The United States and Vietnam, 1941–1975* (New York: Oxford University Press, 1997), 98.

11. "Statement from the President to Prince Sihanouk to be delivered orally by Ambassador Trimble," March 28, 1959, Box: Cambodia 1959–61, Chronological File, September–December 1959, William C. Trimble Papers, Seeley G. Mudd Library, Princeton University, Princeton, New Jersey.

12. Norodom Sihanouk to Dwight D. Eisenhower, April 13, 1959, White House Office, Office of the Staff Secretary, 1952–61, International Series, Box 2, Folder: Cambodia (1), Dwight D. Eisenhower Papers, Dwight D. Eisenhower Library, Abilene, Kansas.

13. *Réalités Cambodgiennes*, July 25, 1959, quoted in William C. Trimble to SS, July 27, 1959, Telegram 116, Speeches Series, Box 33, Fred A. Seaton Papers, Dwight D. Eisenhower Library, Abilene, Kansas.

14. Memorandum of Conversation, Nong Kimny and State Department officials, August 12, 1959, ibid.

15. U.S. Embassy, Saigon, to State Department, May 20, 1959, FRUS 1958–60, 16:325 n.

16. Daniel J. Arzac Jr. to State Department, August 18, 1959, Despatch 46, 751H.00/8-1859.

17. Usher to Steeves, March 11, 1960, 355–56.

18. Christian Herter to U.S. Embassy, Phnom Penh, October 10, 1959, Despatch 318, 751H.00/10-859.

19. John C. Monjo to State Department, November 3, 1959, Despatch 132, 751H.00/11-359.

20. Usher to Steeves, March 11, 1960, 355–56. This memorandum discussed the American embassy's year-end assessment of U.S.-Cambodian relations for 1959.

21. C. Douglas Dillon to State Department, December 17, 1959, ibid., 348.

22. Trimble to State Department, January 7, 1960, Telegram 847, ibid., 349–52.

23. Livingston T. Merchant to U.S. Embassy, Phnom Penh, January 13, 1960, Telegram G-11, 751H.11/1-1660, Central Decimal File, 1960-63, Box 1751, National Archives II, College Park, Maryland (hereafter cited as CDF, 1960–63, with box number).

24. Trimble Oral History, 9.

25. Ibid., 60.

26. Ibid.

27. Ibid., 39.

28. Edward Scherrer to Harry D. Felt, November 15, 1961, FRUS 1961–63, 23:175–78.

29. Edward G. Lansdale to J. Lawton Collins, November 29, 1961, Airgram A-131, 751H.11/11-2861, CDF, 1960–63, Box 1752.

30. Trimble to SS, January 19, 1962, Telegram 490, 751H.00/1-1962, CDF, 1960–63, Box 1750.

31. Chandler, *The Tragedy of Cambodian History,* 132.

32. *Le Rejet de l'aide Américain: Trois Exposés de S. A. R. Le Prince Norodom Sihanouk* (Phnom Penh: Ministère de l'Information, n.d. [1963]), copy in Fonds "Affaire Etrangère" (No. 2), Boite 58, Cambodian National Archives, Phnom Penh, Cambodia.

Suggested Readings

Published historical accounts of American involvement in Cambodia are largely limited to the period after the United States began the secret bombing of the country in 1969. For the earlier period, see Kenton J. Clymer, "Decolonization, Nationalism, and Anti-Communism: United States Relations with Cambodia, 1945–1955, *Journal of American–East Asian Relations* 6 (Spring–Fall 1997). American policy is addressed in the Chandler, Liefer, and Osborne works cited in the notes and in Ben Kiernan, *How Pol Pot Came to Power: A History of Communism in Kampuchea, 1930–1975* (London: Verso, 1985). Useful sources for the general development of American policy in Southeast Asia include the Duiker and Schulzinger books cited in the notes and George C. Herring, *America's Longest War: The United States in Vietnam, 1950–1975*, 3d ed. (New York: McGraw-Hill, 1996).

3

Walt Rostow
Cheerful Hawk

Robert D. Schulzinger

When the youthful John Kennedy replaced the elderly Dwight Eisenhower as president in 1961, a transformation seemed to occur in the personality and temperament of America's leaders. Kennedy sought out and filled his administration with brilliant, forceful, and self-confident men (equal opportunity for women had not yet arrived). Labeled "the best and the brightest" by journalist David Halberstam, they came from major universities and corporations and from throughout the ranks of government. There was a palpable excitement in the air with the expectation that all of this talent could harness the great potential of the United States and transform the nation and the world. Among this gifted group of action intellectuals was Prof. Walt W. Rostow of the Massachusetts Institute of Technology (MIT). Kennedy appointed him to the White House's national security staff. An economist by training, Rostow had developed historical models of economic development and believed that the principal area of U.S.-Soviet competition would be in the underdeveloped world. In April 1966 Kennedy's successor, Lyndon Johnson, chose the hawkish Rostow to be his national security adviser.

Johnson liked Rostow's clearly stated and unqualified recommendations, according to Robert D. Schulzinger, and eventually, Rostow supplanted Secretary of Defense Robert McNamara as the president's principal adviser on Vietnam War policy. Rostow consistently urged the use of air power against North Vietnam and resisted negotiations with Hanoi. Through 1967, Johnson followed his advice. In 1968, however, with the heavy fighting of the Tet Offensive and growing U.S. public dissatisfaction with the war, LBJ decided that he had no choice but to de-escalate the conflict. Rostow's influence was slipping, but he never abandoned his belief in the appropriateness and ultimate effectiveness of using strong military force in Vietnam. Even after the war, he continued to insist that the United States had acted properly in pursuing military victory in Southeast Asia.

Robert D. Schulzinger is a professor of history and the director of the Program in International Affairs at the University of Colorado, Boulder, where he has taught since 1977. He holds a Ph.D. from Yale University and has written eight books on aspects of recent U.S. diplomatic and political history, the newest of which is *A Time for War: The*

Courtesy of Yoichi R. Okamoto / LBJ Library Collection

United States and Vietnam, 1941–1975 (1997). He is currently working on a companion volume, *A Time for Peace,* that will explore the legacy of the Vietnam War.

No one worked harder to commit U.S. forces to fight in Vietnam than did Walt Rostow, a loquacious former professor of economics and history at the Massachusetts Institute of Technology who served as a principal foreign policy adviser to Presidents John F. Kennedy and Lyndon B. Johnson. Rostow advocated American participation in the Vietnam War to show people in postcolonial societies that the Marxist model of economic and political organization would not meet their needs. He maintained his views for over thirty years.

Rostow was born in 1916 in New York City. His Russian Jewish immigrant parents had fallen in love with America. They showed their devotion to their new land by naming their three sons after heroes of the American radical tradition—Walt Whitman Rostow, Eugene Victor (Debs) Rostow, and Ralph Waldo (Emerson) Rostow. Walt raced through the New York public schools and entered Yale at fifteen. As a brilliant undergraduate, he decided to work professionally on the relationship between economic, social, and political forces. His academic achievement, wit, verbal skills, and ebullient, friendly personality won him a coveted Rhodes Scholarship to Oxford University. He continued to explore the intersection of politics, economics, and society at Oxford and then back at Yale, where he received a Ph.D. in economics in 1940.

Rostow taught economics for a year at Columbia before World War II broke out and spent the war years as a major in the Office of Strategic Services. In the five years after the war, he alternatively worked for the State Department and the Marshall Plan and taught at Oxford and Cambridge. In 1950, Rostow took a position at MIT, where he taught for the next decade. His work included scholarly analyses of the processes of economic growth in various countries since the sixteenth century and policy prescriptions for the United States to move more energetically in providing economic and military assistance to underdeveloped nations, especially those facing communist-led insurgencies.

In the nuclear age, Washington had ruled out initiating war against the Soviet Union or China. But, as Rostow wrote in 1955, "the alternative to war is not peace."[1] Consequently, he explored ways in which the United States could prevail in unconventional or guerrilla warfare. By the late 1950s, he concluded that the principal arena of the Cold War competition between America and the Soviet Union had shifted from Europe to the underdeveloped world. He subtitled his classic 1960 study, *The Stages of Economic Growth,* "a non-communist manifesto."[2]

Like many other so-called action intellectuals in Cambridge, Massachusetts, Rostow spent a lot of time in Washington in the 1950s advising both the Eisenhower administration and congressional Democrats. Officeholders could always count on him for prodigious work and a clever turn of phrase. He provided Eisenhower with the term "Open Skies," for instance, and came up with the slogans "the New Frontier" and "Let's Get America Moving Again" for Massachusetts Democratic senator John F. Kennedy. Rostow's cheerful good nature and his willingness to come up with a fresh memorandum, not just a recycled speech or article, deeply impressed Kennedy. Others noticed how eager he was to please prominent intellectual and political figures. He and his wife, Elspeth, entertained often—in Cambridge, New York, and Washington—and their guests remarked on how open, warm, and talkative both Rostows were. They held fast to strong opinions, but they were friendly with those who disagreed with them. Some people attributed Rostow's congeniality to an innately sunny disposition; others believed he was so committed to his beliefs that he did not really care what other people thought. It was also clear that Rostow desperately wanted acceptance in the world of the great and powerful. He very much remained a first-generation American—an outsider never completely at ease with members of the American establishment. He occupied an uncomfortable social space, working every day with the best and the brightest but ever aware of his own humble origins.[3]

Like most of his Cambridge friends, he ardently backed Senator Kennedy's 1960 presidential bid. During the campaign, JFK stressed some of Rostow's central conclusions about the Cold War: that recent trends ran against U.S. interests; that the success of Fidel Castro's revolution in Cuba represented a major setback for the United States; that the Eisenhower administration had complacently let U.S. nonnuclear military forces slip; that the major conflicts of the Cold War would take place in the underdeveloped world; and that the Cold War was a global conflict, so events anywhere in the world could affect American interests elsewhere. When Kennedy became president on January 20, 1961, he named Rostow deputy national security adviser, reporting to McGeorge Bundy, an old friend of Rostow's from Cambridge. Rostow immediately threw himself into crafting an assertive U.S. policy toward the communist insurgency in Laos and neighboring Vietnam.

Vietnam, he reflected in 1964, was the one problem that kept him awake at night. "My nightmare was that we wouldn't deal with it early enough. Things would go very bad. Then we would have to deal with it convulsively, in a war."[4] On February 2, 1961, he asked the president to read a somber report on the situation in Southeast Asia that had been prepared by Air Force general Edward Lansdale, one of South Vietnam president Ngo Dinh Diem's friends and supporters. Lansdale foresaw the possibility of a major crisis in Vietnam in 1961 if Diem did not reorganize his government and wage an aggressive war against the newly formed National Liberation Front (NLF). Vietnam could be saved, he asserted, only if the United States became more fully involved in encouraging Diem to reorganize his government. When Kennedy finished reading this discouraging account, he looked up and said to Rostow, "This is the worst one we've got, isn't it? You know Eisenhower never mentioned it. He talked at length about Laos, but never uttered the word Vietnam."[5]

Rostow went on to draw connections between the insurgencies in Laos and Vietnam. In the spring and summer of 1961, he participated in a joint White House, State Department, and Defense Department task force on Southeast Asia. The participants concluded that the region should be protected from what they characterized as communist subversion; furthermore, the United States had to be prepared to use military forces if the situation deteriorated to the point at which communists appeared to be victorious in Laos or Vietnam. The task force also recommended that Washington adopt a coordinated approach for all countries in the area, and it identified the Democratic Republic of Vietnam (North Vietnam) as the focal point of the problem. Working closely with Gen. Maxwell Taylor, President Kennedy's military adviser, Rostow concluded that the infiltration of troops from North Vietnam across the Laotian border put the Pathet Lao (the leftist insurgents in Laos) on the verge of taking power in Laos. The infiltration also threatened the authority of South Vietnam's president, Ngo Dinh Diem. In August, Rostow alerted Kennedy to the danger that the Vietminh (as the communist insurgents in Vietnam were then called) and the Chinese People's Liberation Army might enter northern Laos in large numbers. He recommended that "the best deterrent against such a Vietminh or ChiCom movement would be a positioning of more forces . . . which would signal to Hanoi . . . that the battle—if it is enlarged—will take place not in Laos but in North Vietnam."[6]

Rostow also spoke publicly about the dangers guerrilla wars in the underdeveloped world posed to the United States. In June 1961, he told the graduating class of the army's Special Warfare School at Fort Bragg, North Carolina, that the new Kennedy administration faced four crises in the underdeveloped world when it came into office: Cuba, the Congo, Laos, and Vietnam. Each, he said, had arisen from "the efforts of the international Communist movement to exploit the inherent instabilities of the underdeveloped areas of the non-communist world." But Rostow expressed confidence that, having identified the essence of guerrilla warfare ("an unsubtle operation, by the book, based more on murder than on political and psychological appeal"), the United States could help the South Vietnamese defeat the NLF insurgents.[7]

In October, Rostow visited South Vietnam with Maxwell Taylor. The two men found a crisis of confidence there. Across the political spectrum, people doubted whether the United States was committed to saving Southeast Asia from communist insurgents, and they faulted President Diem for employing bad military tactics and relying on a narrow cadre of advisers. On their return to Washington, Taylor and Rostow recommended to Kennedy that Washington increase its commitment to provide military assistance to the South. The war had to be won by the Vietnamese themselves, they stated, but the United States could help. The Taylor mission recommended that Kennedy increase the size of the U.S. Military Assistance Advisory Group and introduce an American military task force in Vietnam to "provide a U.S. military presence capable of raising national morale and of showing to Southeast Asia the seriousness of U.S. intent to resist a Communist take-over."[8] On November 22, 1961, Kennedy adopted some but not all of Taylor's recommendations when he signed National Security Action Memorandum 111 (NSAM-111). He resisted a substantial increase in U.S. forces in South Vietnam for the time being, but he did promise Saigon a sharply increased joint effort to resist the NLF. The Kennedy administration would increase economic aid and training for the Army of the Republic of Vietnam (ARVN) and would ship helicopters, light aircraft, and transports, all manned by U.S. personnel. In return, the South Vietnamese would agree to go on a wartime footing.

Kennedy's adoption of NSAM-111 represented a significant turning point in the American commitment to support the Republic of Vietnam in its war against the NLF. The president acknowledged that the stakes in Southeast Asia were very high and that the focus of the Cold War had shifted to the underdeveloped world. He agreed with Rostow that the insurgency in Southeast Asia was part of a global attempt by the communists "to impose a serious disease on those societies attempting the transition to modernization."[9] He was more cautious than his deputy national security adviser, however, about deploying U.S. troops in the war. Like Eisenhower before him and Johnson after, Kennedy hoped to defer decisions to turn the war in Vietnam into an American operation for as long as possible.

Rostow's role in developing U.S. policy toward Southeast Asia diminished in December 1961 when he moved from the White House to the State Department, where he served as director of the Policy Planning Staff and counselor of the department until the spring of 1966. Although he no longer had primary responsibility for setting U.S. policy toward Vietnam, he followed the deteriorating situation there from his post at the State Department and continued to see linkages between the insurgencies in Laos and Vietnam. As negotiations to reach a settlement of the Loatian war proceeded in Geneva, Rostow counseled greater boldness by the United States. In May, he recommended that Washington consider the "highly selective" bombing of North Vietnamese transport and power facilities and the mining of Haiphong Harbor to persuade the North Vietnamese to withdraw their forces from Laos.[10]

The Kennedy administration was more interested in ending the fighting in Laos than in bombing North Vietnam, and in July the Geneva Conference bore fruit with an agreement to neutralize Laos. The agreement disappointed Rostow, who soon worried that the North Vietnamese had sent more forces into Laos than permitted by the Geneva agreement: He called it "bad practice to connive at the violation of a solemn agreement by the Communists." He therefore urged that the United States bomb the North unless Hanoi removed its forces from Laos, and he recommended a speedy showdown, "before the Chinese Communists blow a nuclear device."[11] In November, he once more urged that the United States launch limited air strikes against North Vietnam if it did not stop infiltrating its forces through Laos into the South. He argued that Washington should "impose on North Vietnam limited, appropriate damage, by air and sea action, if infiltration does not cease."[12]

Rostow was largely on the sidelines during the climactic year of 1963. He watched in agony the burgeoning Buddhist crisis, as monks burned themselves to death to protest South Vietnamese government oppression and President Diem responded with violent attacks on Buddhist pagodas. Rostow had been one of Diem's strongest backers in Washington, but the grave situation in the summer and fall of 1963 convinced him, like most every other high official, that the South Vietnamese president had lost the ability to carry on the war. With more resignation that these things could happen than hope for the future, Rostow accepted the coup d'état led by Gen. Duong Van Minh. On the day of the coup, he advised Secretary of State Dean Rusk that the United States needed to "bring to a head the issue of infiltration from North Vietnam." He warned that "it is difficult, if not impossible, to win a guerrilla war with an open frontier."[13] In the months after the coup, Rostow worried that more and more South Vietnamese officials were becoming convinced that the United States had no clear strategy to defeat the communist insurgents and that these officials were toying with the idea of a neutral Vietnam. He believed the neutralization of Southeast Asia, as proposed by French president Charles de Gaulle, would be "the greatest setback to U.S. interests in the world scene in many years." As he had recommended for the past year, he reiterated that the only way to reverse this trend was for the new Johnson administration to force "a direct political-military showdown with Hanoi."[14]

In 1964, Rostow repeatedly urged President Johnson to publicly enumerate the high stakes involved in Vietnam. He saw crisis looming in Southeast Asia, with the United States facing dire consequences around the world. By March, he recommended exploring "the circumstances in which nuclear weapons would be used" by Washington in an Asian land war against North Vietnam and China.[15] He was also one of the first high government officials to advocate the adoption of a congressional resolution supporting the use of American military force against the North. Johnson demurred until the summer, fearful that a public debate over Vietnam might derail his ambitious agenda of domestic reform. Rostow recognized the way in which U.S. air strikes against North Vietnam and adoption of the Tonkin Gulf Resolution in early August altered the situation. In the following weeks, he advised the administration to make clear its desire to "impose on North Vietnam damage on a scale sufficient to put in question the advantages of pursuing the war in the South."[16]

Rostow was preoccupied with developing policies toward Latin America during 1965 when the Johnson administration took the final, fateful decisions to commit over one hundred thousand U.S. ground troops to fight in Vietnam. He did comment, though, and his analysis now included projections of the way in which the United States and South Vietnam might prevail over the insurgents. "There is no reason," he asserted, "we cannot win as clear a victory in South Vietnam as in Greece, Malaya and the Philippines."[17] He continually advocated a systematic attack of the North's oil storage and electrical power capabilities. He told President Johnson in late December that such bombing would be the best way to bring Hanoi to early negotiations on U.S. terms. Aware of the dangers of a protracted war, Rostow pointed out that "we have an enormous stake at home and abroad in forcing an early, rather than late, ending to the war in Vietnam."[18]

Johnson appointed Rostow to replace McGeorge Bundy as national security adviser on April 1, 1966. By the end of 1965, Bundy had borne the weight of service in that position for five years, and he had served President Johnson for more than two. When Bundy announced he was leaving to head the Ford Foundation, the president turned to Rostow. Johnson admired his enthusiasm, ebullience, and quick verbal skills. For his part, Rostow became the president's most loyal lieutenant. For the next two years, he was among the most ardent advocates of increasing U.S. military pressure on Hanoi. Until March 1968, Johnson relied heavily on his advice. Rostow's stature grew as Secretary of Defense Robert McNamara, once a vociferous hawk on Vietnam, changed his mind on the war and began to lose Johnson's confidence.

When Rostow surveyed the critical issues facing the United States in Vietnam in April 1966, he concluded that Hanoi hoped to wear down the American public. He observed: "They are playing us as they did the French in 1953. They know we are militarily stronger than the French. They are not yet convinced we have more stamina." Washington's task, therefore, was to show enough progress to keep domestic dissent to a minimum while encouraging the North to seek negotiations. "Hurting them badly around Hanoi-Haiphong" seemed to him the best way to force the issue with the North Vietnamese. As for domestic opinion in the United States, he encouraged the president to speak often about the stakes. "We are all being tested by this crisis," he said, and he urged the president to point out that "the Communists are counting on us to despair and give up."[19]

McNamara was less enthusiastic about bombing the oil storage facilities near Hanoi because he believed that such attacks would not directly affect the rate of infiltration into the South. He also thought that attacking near Hanoi would only harden North Vietnam's will to resist the Americans. Rostow disagreed. He contended that bombing the North had imposed serious costs on the enemy. Escalating those burdens, while making certain that the Soviet Union did not apply counterpressures on the United States, seemed to him the best way to lure Hanoi to the negotiating table. Johnson sided with Rostow, and U.S. planes began bombing the industrial installations around North Vietnam's capital in late June 1966.

In 1966 and 1967, Rostow looked for more ways to apply military force to the North. He wanted to increase pressure on Hanoi and mount a public relations offensive inside the United States to combat war weariness. A growing chorus of antiwar critics complained that the war had become stalemated. They argued that in a guerrilla war, the guerrillas won if they did not lose. Rostow responded that the war was being fought for people, not territory. In the two years after the American military buildup in Vietnam, he claimed that the percentage of the Vietnamese population living under the protection of the Saigon government had risen by one-half, while those under the control of the Vietcong had fallen by one-fourth.

Was this progress enough to bring the war to a successful end before 1967? In Rostow's estimation, it probably was not. In 1967, therefore, he advocated applying more pressure to force Hanoi to negotiate. He recommended invading the southern part of North Vietnam "in order to block infiltration routes, and to hold the area hostage against North Vietnamese withdrawal from Laos and Cambodia, as well as South Vietnam."[20] Johnson thought the risks of

Chinese intervention were too high, and he decided against invading North Vietnam. He also denied Rostow's appeal for a call-up of reserves. "Nothing we could do would more seriously impress Hanoi," Rostow observed.[21] But Johnson, alert to the political dangers, declined to mobilize reserves.

Rostow coordinated White House strategy toward the possibility of negotiations in 1967. He believed that the war would eventually end by diplomacy, but before that happened, he thought that Hanoi had to endure more hardship. But 1967 did present the best opportunity to negotiate a way out before Americans went to the polls to elect a president. Rostow detected a "possibility that Hanoi now estimates that the U.S. election of 1968 will not prove to be the pot of gold at the end of the rainbow"—either Johnson would be reelected, or North Vietnam would face even tougher conditions imposed by the Republicans. Consequently, he thought Johnson should encourage speculation that the Republicans might win. "We should make every effort to increase the pressure on the communists in the South and in the North," he advised.[22]

In 1967 the positions of the United States and North Vietnam seemed unbridgeable. Washington considered the conflict a case of international aggression: North Vietnam had attacked a sovereign state, South Vietnam. The United States labeled the Vietcong a terrorist organization, bent on gaining political power through intimidation. Washington believed negotiations should focus on ending what it characterized as aggression from the North and setting ground rules for the political future of an independent South Vietnam. Hanoi's opinion was nearly a mirror image of the Americans' position. For the Democratic Republic of Vietnam, the aggression consisted of the U.S. attacks on the North and the government of South Vietnam was only a creation of the United States. Thus, Hanoi's leaders contended that negotiations should address the ways in which the United States would leave the South.

Rostow believed that negotiations were possible as long as the field could be cleared of numerous meddlesome intermediaries. Confidentiality was key. He once likened a proposal to write a history of efforts to negotiate the end of the fighting to "publication by the *Chicago Tribune* of our breaking the Japanese code during World War II."[23]

In early 1967 Polish diplomats explored the possibility that Washington halt the bombing of North Vietnam in exchange for a promise from Hanoi to consider direct negotiations. The United States did not believe this proposal went far enough and stated that Hanoi would also have to agree to stop infiltration. Rostow and President Johnson felt that the Polish initiatives, code-named Marigold, were not serious, and the Poles never could get the North Vietnamese to promise to talk in exchange for a bombing halt. In February, Britain and the Soviet Union stepped forward, offering to arrange meetings between the United States and Vietnam. Their intervention irritated the White House. Rostow characterized it as "a pressure play which we should take seriously but not react to with excessive haste."[24] Johnson agreed, though he was more responsive to British and Soviet mediation efforts than he had been to those coming through the Polish channel. The Soviets asked the North Vietnamese to consider an end to infiltration, which Rostow thought "may have shaken and even frightened them." In the end, however, the Hanoi officials demurred. They replied that if the United States stopped bombing, they would consider negotiations. That was not enough for Washington. Rostow concluded that North Vietnam decided "to sweat us out to the 1968 election and, if they lose, withdraw silently rather than negotiate."[25]

By summer louder calls arose inside the United States for a negotiated end to the war. Prominent Senate critics of the war—including Robert Kennedy of New York, J. William Fulbright of Arkansas, and Majority Leader Mike Mansfield of Montana—called on the administration to go further and stop the bombing in exchange for Hanoi's promise to talk. The Johnson administration now sponsored its own informal exploration of the possibility of negotiations. Henry Kissinger, a professor of government at Harvard who had served as a part-time foreign policy adviser to both Kennedy and Johnson, shuttled between the United States and France from August through October.

In conversations with French intermediaries, code-named Pennsylvania, Kissinger thought he detected some movement in Hanoi's position. He characterized North Vietnam as "a small uncertain power, with a split government, facing an immense power whose intention it does not understand or trust." Rostow, however, thought that "with the best will in the world, none of us have been able to find anything other than a rather dignified negative" in Hanoi's response to the American conditions for a bombing halt.[26] Pennsylvania went forward for a few more weeks, but eventually, Johnson followed the advice of Rostow, the Joint Chiefs of Staff (JCS), and Supreme Court justice Abe Fortas, one of his most trusted counselors, and decided not to stop bombing. The consensus was that to do so would expose U.S. troops to danger without obtaining any real guarantee of negotiations. The other hawkish advisers also feared that it would be politically difficult to resume bombing once it stopped. Rostow thought that "it would be a good deal easier for the men in Hanoi (and their allies who carry the aid burden) to prolong the war and continue the strain on South Vietnam—and the U.S.— at lower cost to themselves" if the United States stopped bombing.[27]

The war did not end as he had hoped by the beginning of 1968. Still, he thought that the United States and South Vietnam were in a far more advantageous position than they had been when the American buildup began three years earlier. He was much more optimistic than the secretary of defense. McNamara had grown so disillusioned with the war that he wanted to stop the bombing and turn much of the fighting over to the South Vietnamese. By the fall of 1967, he was heartily sick of the war, and he wanted out of the government. Johnson, who had earlier called him the brightest star in his cabinet, now lost confidence in him. In late 1967, LBJ announced that McNamara would leave the following February to take up the presidency of the World Bank. He then named Clark Clifford, a longtime adviser to Democratic presidents, as McNamara's replacement.

On the surface, it seemed as if Rostow and Clifford might find more agreement on Vietnam than had the national security adviser and McNamara. During the July 1965 discussions surrounding the buildup of U.S. forces in Southeast Asia, Clifford had telephoned his reservations. Once Johnson announced that the United States was sending an additional hundred thousand soldiers to Vietnam, however, Clifford had kept his misgivings to himself, and in public, he had been one of the most vocal supporters of the war. With his appointment, it seemed as if Johnson's three senior foreign policy advisers—Rostow, Rusk, and Clifford—would be aligned in favor of a forceful American position in the war.

Everything changed on January 30, 1968. At two o'clock that afternoon, Johnson and Rostow were huddled in the White House, discussing a new Asian crisis—the North Korean seizure of an American naval reconnaissance ship, the U.S.S. *Pueblo*—when an aide burst in to announce that Vietcong sappers had stormed into the grounds of the U.S. embassy in Saigon. North Vietnam's Tet Offensive, the simultaneous assault on all the major population centers of South Vietnam, had begun. The bloodiest fighting of the war to date took place over the next six weeks, as U.S. and South Vietnamese forces fought to recapture the scores of provincial capitals and towns seized by the North Vietnamese and the Vietcong. In the process the American public's doubts about staying in Southeast Asia boiled over, forcing Johnson to reverse course on Vietnam. But Rostow did not change his mind. He continued to urge the president to do more militarily, and he remained skeptical of offering a bombing halt to the North without receiving ironclad guarantees from Hanoi that such an American de-escalation would result in prompt, productive negotiations. This time, though, he was overruled.

Rostow recognized immediately how seriously the Tet Offensive would affect public opinion. The day after Tet began, he set down his thoughts on how the administration should react to the new, more dangerous military situation. As usual, he saw connections between events over a large area. In this case, he perceived that just as Asia became more dangerous, America faced an economic crisis, for some European countries were demanding that their dollar holdings be redeemed in gold by the United States. Treasury officials feared a run on American currency as a result. The Tet Offensive, the seizure of the *Pueblo*, mounting North Korean pressure on South Korea, and the intensification of the war in Laos and Cambodia all threatened the will of the United States to continue the war. There was, he warned, "a widespread, desperate and dangerous Communist effort along the whole front in Asia to divert us from Vietnam, upset the progress made in Vietnam, and discourage and split the American people." He urged Johnson to tell his critics to "stop talking about a bombing cessation and keep clearly in our minds the bombings in Saigon, Danang and all over South Vietnam." As for the prospect of negotiations, Rostow stated that "when they are ready to talk about peace, they know where to get us."[28] He wanted Johnson to ask Congress for the authority to raise taxes and allocate funds to stabilize the dollar. To fight more effectively in Vietnam, he advised the president to extend tours of duty and call up individuals with special technical qualifications.

Rostow argued that only a successful counteroffensive in South Vietnam would turn the situation in favor of the United States. He told Johnson that Hanoi failed in its maximum objectives in the early days of Tet to foment a general rising among the South Vietnamese and a complete collapse of the ARVN. The offensive had badly shaken public opinion in the United States and around the world, however, and had undermined the government structure of the South. The offensive had also forced Gen. William Westmoreland, the U.S. commander in Vietnam, to divert his slim reserves away from mounting his own counteroffensive in the northernmost part of South Vietnam, known to the military as I Corps. Rostow thought that to reverse the defeatism in the United States, "there [was] one satisfactory answer: a clear defeat of the enemy in I Corps." He thought that action in I Corps, where the U.S. faced a large conventional force of North Vietnamese, was "our kind of battle. It has guerrilla elements, but is much more nearly conventional war."[29] Such a counteroffensive would work but only if Westmoreland received reinforcement and Johnson took the fateful step of calling up the reserves.

In late February and March 1968, Rostow tried to bolster the spirits of the Americans in Saigon and the South Vietnamese government. He advised U.S. Ambassador to Vietnam Ellsworth Bunker to *"go on the offensive,"* noting that "the enemy is badly shaken. . . .

Wherever forces can be taken from static defense to chase and harass the enemy, it ought to be done."[30] Washington believed that North Vietnam was trying to "force us into a negotiation on his [the enemy's] terms." To prevent that, South Vietnam had to convince the American public that Saigon was seizing the initiative. Tet was a "do or die offensive" for the North Vietnamese, who "may confront us soon with a diplomatic offensive." The South had to understand that "no one can do the job for the Vietnamese. . . . They must do it for themselves."[31]

General Westmoreland shared Rostow's views that Tet offered an opportunity to force the issue with the North Vietnamese. In February, he asked the president to send him an additional 206,000 troops over the next year and to call up U.S. reserves. The general's request set off one of the most important debates among high government officials over the future conduct of the war effort. The Joint Chiefs of Staff, Bunker, Rostow, and Rusk endorsed Westmoreland's request. On the other side were Clifford, congressional doves, Johnson's political advisers, and an informal group of foreign affairs experts called "the Wise Men," whom Johnson frequently consulted.

Rostow considered the case for the additional troops ironclad, for sending them would relieve pressure in Vietnam and elsewhere. As always, everything was connected in his mind. Without the extra forces, he reasoned, "pressure or aggression might be successful in the Middle East, elsewhere in Asia, and perhaps even in Europe." In Vietnam the communists believed that 1968 was the year of decision. Unlike the previous year, when they thought that the election would be a contest between President Johnson, committed to winning in Vietnam, and a Republican who was eager to escalate, Johnson now was under serious pressure to change course. Rostow thought he should accept the communist challenge and turn 1968 to the Americans' advantage. He believed that the U.S. public wanted to do more, not less, in the war. With frustration and even fear abroad in the land, he detected "a hawkish balance in the country" and "a desire to do something about the situation."[32]

Many of Johnson's other advisers were much more pessimistic. Clifford began a complete review of the military situation in Vietnam immediately on taking office. The prospects were not encouraging. Even with the addition of 206,000 troops, he could see no end to the war, and Westmoreland could not promise that he would not ask for even more soldiers in another year. For Clifford the events of 1968 bore an uncanny and unhappy resemblance to the events of 1965. This time, Clifford vowed not to keep his reservations so muted, and in intensive debates over the first three weeks of March, the civilian leadership of the Defense Department repeatedly warned against further troop commitments. Like McNamara, Clifford doubted the effectiveness of bombing as a tool to stop infiltration: Its only value was to bolster the morale of Saigon officials and American troops fighting in the South. Clifford thought it would be worth it to halt the bombing in order to start negotiations.

Rostow sensed the mood of the Defense Department officials as the discussions proceeded. The astonishingly good showing of Minnesota senator Eugene McCarthy in the New Hampshire Democratic primary demonstrated how far Johnson had slipped in public esteem. Then, a few days later, Sen. Robert Kennedy, the rival LBJ disliked and feared most, entered the presidential race. In this context, Rostow saw dark parallels between the current troubles at home and the American Civil War, though he held out hope. "About the only thing we've got," he concluded on March 25, "is [the hope] that the North Vietnamese *do* attack" and that the Americans "clobber them." Then Johnson would be "just like Lincoln in 1864," reviled in the press and seemingly unpopular but able to point to an improving military situation to win reelection in the fall.[33]

History did not repeat itself. The Wise Men held out far less hope for a sudden shift in the war news, and the president had to do something dramatic and immediate to halt the appalling collapse of public confidence. As former secretary of state Dean Acheson told Johnson, the United States could not "do the job we set out to do in the time we have left and we must take steps to disengage."[34] LBJ could barely believe what he was hearing from his senior foreign policy advisers, who previously had backed each move he made in Vietnam. "Everybody is recommending surrender," he complained.[35]

The president was as aware as anyone of the public's dark mood, however, and he knew they would not accept further troop commitments. On March 31, he announced that the United States was stopping the bombing over the population centers of North Vietnam and would end all bombing if Hanoi agreed to prompt, serious negotiations. He said that he was sending Ambassador-at-Large Averell Harriman and Deputy Secretary of Defense Cyrus Vance to Paris to try to arrange peace talks with the North Vietnamese. Then came Johnson's bombshell—he would not be a candidate for president in 1968.

Rostow was shocked and deeply disappointed. He did not think that any of the potential Democratic Party candidates—Senators McCarthy and Kennedy, both doves, or Vice President Hubert Humphrey—measured up to the president's stature. Nor could he, an advocate of Johnson's liberal domestic reform agenda, cheer at the prospect of a Republican in the White House. But he soldiered on for the rest of 1968. He consistently advocated that the United States should fight hard while it talked with the North Vietnamese, do more to bolster Saigon's morale, and not stop all bombing of the

North until Hanoi agreed to fruitful talks. Rostow, always eager to find historical parallels, saw similarities between the situation unfolding in South Vietnam, in which the United States would simultaneously talk and fight, and the last years of the Korean War. But this time, he felt things might go better. He reasoned: "In Korea we fought at a fixed line in which the enemy could impose casualties—and frustration within the United States—without losing anything of his bargaining position. Inside South Vietnam, we have the capacity to be steadily improving our position as talks proceed."[36]

The negotiations proceeded at a glacial pace until the fall. North Vietnam insisted that the United States halt all bombing before it would participate in any substantive talks, and the Americans were equally adamant that the North should not use a bombing halt to raise its troop levels in the South. Meanwhile, dramatic events in the United States and Europe—assassinations, student uprisings, the invasion of Czechoslovakia, and the tumultuous Democratic National Convention in Chicago—overshadowed these tedious negotiations for most Americans. Still, Rostow worked hard to persuade Harriman to avoid offering too much or receiving too little from Hanoi. Harriman had a different view. He shuddered at the prospect that Republican candidate Richard Nixon would be elected, and he believed that opening formal, substantive talks with North Vietnam would swing the election to Humphrey.

After leaving the Chicago convention badly trailing Nixon in the public opinion polls, Humphrey agreed that advancing the prospect for peace in Vietnam was his best hope for victory, and on September 30, he publicly called for a complete bombing halt. Then, in October, the logjam broke in Paris, where Hanoi for the first time indicated that it would not augment its force levels in the South if the bombing stopped. Harriman was eager to wrap up a deal before the election, and Humphrey began to eat into Nixon's lead.

In the early morning hours of October 29, President Johnson met his top foreign policy and military advisers to work out the final details of the bombing halt. Around midnight, just before going into the meeting, Rostow received a telephone call from his brother, Undersecretary of State Eugene Rostow, informing him that Anna Chennault, an official with the Nixon campaign, had been leaking information about the impending breakthrough to the government in Saigon. On hearing of this deal, South Vietnam's president, Nguyen Van Thieu, balked at agreeing to participate in talks before the election. News of his refusal arrived at the White House in the midst of the October 29 meeting. Eugene Rostow's information now took on new and sinister implications.

Johnson might have assured an election victory for Hubert Humphrey had he publicly assailed Nixon for meddling in the negotiations. He did not do so, however, wishing to remain above the political fray. Rostow concurred: "There is no hard evidence that Mr. Nixon himself is involved," he told Johnson at 8:50 A.M. on October 29. Moreover, "the materials are so explosive that they could gravely damage the country whether Mr. Nixon is elected or not."[37] Johnson agreed. As a result, announcement of the bombing halt was delayed for two crucial days, Humphrey's momentum in the polls stopped, and Nixon narrowly won the election.

Five years later, after Nixon had won a landslide reelection victory and the Watergate scandal began to unfold, Rostow privately expressed second thoughts. In a memorandum he originally intended to keep sealed for fifty years, he reflected on the Republicans' meddling in the October negotiations and found a direct connection to Watergate. As he saw it, the Republicans believed that "their enterprise with the South Vietnamese and Thieu's recalcitrance may have sufficiently blunted the impact on U.S. politics of the total bombing halt." It also set a precedent. "They got away with it," Rostow wrote, and they felt emboldened in 1972. "There was nothing in their previous experience with an operation of doubtful propriety (or, even, legality) to warn them off," he reflected further, "and there were memories of how close an election could get and the possible utility of pressing to the limit—or beyond."[38]

On January 21, 1969, Rostow left Washington for Texas with President Johnson, a man he venerated. Still a bundle of energy, he helped create the Lyndon B. Johnson School of Public Affairs and LBJ's presidential library. He also helped the former president prepare his memoirs, and he carried a full load as a professor of history and economics at the University of Texas, where his students admired him for his genuine interest in their lives and ideas. He never wavered in his support of the war in Vietnam and of President Johnson, nor did he become bitter. In a series of books and articles he authored, he justified the American enterprise in Vietnam as having successfully prevented a row of dominoes from falling throughout Southeast and South Asia. He argued that the survival of noncommunist Vietnam until 1975, when it would have become communist ten years earlier without U.S. intervention, allowed the other economies in the region to prosper.

In the end, two ironies stand out about Walt Rostow. The first is that he always saw regional connections among world events yet rarely reflected on the enormous costs and implications of continuing the Vietnam War, for either Southeast Asia or the United States. The second is that, though he expressed his opinions on the war in cold and bloodless prose, he was unfailingly the warmest, most positive, and most cheerful of all the advisers who committed America to fight in Vietnam.

Notes

1. Walt W. Rostow, *An American Policy in Asia* (New York: Wiley, 1955), VII.

2. Walt W. Rostow, *The Stages of Economic Growth: A Non-communist Manifesto* (New York: Cambridge University Press, 1960).

3. David Halberstam, *The Best and the Brightest* (New York: Random House, 1972), 156–59.

4. Walt W. Rostow, *The Diffusion of Power: An Essay in Recent History* (New York: Macmillan, 1972), 287.

5. Ibid., 265.

6. Rostow to president, August 4, 1961, *Foreign Relations of the United States, 1961–1963*, vol. 24, *Laos Crisis* (Washington, D.C.: Government Printing Office, 1994), 344.

7. Rostow to Army Special Warfare School, June 28, 1961, Box 6, Walt Rostow Files, Lyndon B. Johnson Library, Austin, Texas (hereafter cited as LBJL).

8. Taylor to president, November 3, 1961, *Foreign Relations of the United States, 1961–1963*, vol. 1, *Vietnam, 1961* (Washington, D.C.: Government Printing Office, 1988), 480–81.

9. Rostow to Army Special Warfare School, June 28, 1961, Box 6, Rostow Files, LBJL.

10. Rostow to Rusk, May 31, 1962, *Foreign Relations of the United States, 1961–1963,* vol. 2, *Vietnam, 1962* (Washington, D.C.: Government Printing Office, 1990), 433.

11. Rostow to Rusk, July 4, 1963, *Foreign Relations of the United States, 1961–1963*, vol. 3, *Vietnam, January–August 1963* (Washington, D.C.: Government Printing Office, 1991), 454–55.

12. Rostow to Rusk, November 28, 1962, Box 13, Rostow Files, LBJL.

13. Rostow to Rusk, November 1, 1963, ibid.

14. Rostow to Rusk, January 10, 1964, ibid.

15. Rostow to U. Alexis Johnson, March 9, 1964, ibid.

16. Rostow to Rusk, September 19, 1964, ibid.

17. Rostow to Rusk, May 20, 1965, *Foreign Relations of the United States, 1964–1968*, vol. 2, *Vietnam, January–June 1965* (Washington, D.C.: Government Printing Office, 1996), 681.

18. Rostow to president, December 23, 1965, *Foreign Relations of the United States, 1964–1968*, vol. 3, *Vietnam, June–December 1965* (Washington, D.C.: Government Printing Office, 1996), 696.

19. Rostow to president, April 21, 1966, Box 6, Rostow Files, LBJL.

20. Rostow, *The Diffusion of Power,* 513.

21. Rostow to Vance, May 22, 1967, Box 5, Rostow Files, LBJL.

22. Rostow to president, July 22, 1967, ibid.

23. Risotto memorandum for the record, January 11, 1968, Box 6, ibid.

24. Rostow to president, February 6, 1967, Box 5, ibid.

25. Rostow to president, February 15, 1967, Box 6, ibid.

26. Rostow memorandum of conversation, October 17, 1967, ibid.

27. Rostow to president, October 18, 1967, ibid.

28. Rostow to Rusk, January 31, 1968, ibid.

29. Rostow to president, February 12, 1968, ibid.

30. Rostow to Bunker, February 14, 1968, ibid.

31. Draft instructions for emissary to Saigon, n.d. [February 1968], ibid.

32. Rostow memorandum for the record, February 29, 1968, ibid.

33. Rostow note, March 25, 1968, ibid.

34. Clark Clifford, *Counsel to the President* (New York: Simon and Schuster, 1991), 517.

35. CIA and Defense Department Briefing, March 28, 1968, Box 1, Tom Johnson's Notes of Meetings, LBJL.

36. Rostow to president, April 3, 1968, Box 6, Rostow Files, LBJL.

37. Rostow to president, October 29, 1968, ibid.

38. Rostow, memorandum for the record, May 14, 1973, Anna Chennault, Reference File, LBJL.

Suggested Readings

In addition to the sources cited in the notes, see Robert D. Schulzinger, *A Time for War: The United States and Vietnam, 1941–1975* (New York: Oxford University Press, 1997), and David M. Barrett, *Uncertain Warriors: Lyndon Johnson and His Vietnam Advisers* (Lawrence: University Press of Kansas, 1993).

4

"The Expert"
Bernard Fall and His Critique of America's Involvement in Vietnam

Gary Hess and John McNay

Although American expertise on and experience with Southeast Asia was dangerously limited before the Vietnam War, the knowledge about the region that *was* available often went untapped by official Washington. Bernard Fall was the best known of a handful of American specialists on the history of Vietnam. A professor of international relations at Howard University, a journalist, and a prolific author, he was driven by a determination to understand the Vietnamese, their history, their culture, and their relationship with the rest of the world. Unlike the theorist Rostow or the diplomat Trimble, he had extensive firsthand experience in Vietnam, derived from many visits there beginning in the French Indochina War. His several books and numerous articles in prominent journals were widely read.

As the United States became more deeply involved in Vietnam, Gary Hess and John McNay note, Fall's writing increasingly focused on the limitations of American knowledge about the country. When Washington unleashed its massive firepower in Southeast Asia, Fall foresaw that, although the enemy might be annihilated, the North Vietnamese and National Liberation Front would only reluctantly, if ever, yield. The widespread devastation and the lingering bitterness that the war would cause left Fall, as he embarked on what turned out to be his final mission in Vietnam, fearing the worst for the United States. He stepped on a land mine while accompanying a marine patrol in Vietnam in February 1967 and was killed instantly. He was forty years old.

Had American leaders heeded Fall's cautionary advice, they would have taken another course in Vietnam. His writings remain timely, Hess and McNay maintain, for, in large part, they reflect much of what has become known as the "misguided containment" school of scholarship on the Vietnam War—that is, that the United States was not wrong to be concerned about Vietnam but that it pursued terribly wrongheaded policies.

Gary R. Hess is Distinguished Research Professor in the Department of History at Bowling Green State University, Bowling Green, Ohio. His Ph.D. is from the University of Virginia, and he is a past president of the Society for Historians of American Foreign Relations. His

Courtesy of Dorothy Fall

many publications on U.S. foreign relations include *The United States' Emergence as a Southeast Asian Power, 1940–1950* (1987) and *Vietnam and the United States: Origins and Legacy of a War* (1990). John McNay has a Ph.D. from Temple University, Philadelphia, where he wrote a dissertation entitled "Imperial Paradigm: Dean G. Acheson and American Foreign Policy, 1949–1952." He is a visiting assistant professor at Shippensberg University in Shippensberg, Pennsylvania. The authors acknowledge the research assistance of Jeff Grim.

When Bernard B. Fall was killed in Vietnam by stepping on a land mine in 1967, news of his death made the front pages of newspapers around the world. A professor of international relations at Howard University in Washington, D.C., he was widely respected in the 1960s as a principal authority on Vietnam, and he was lauded for his expertise in numerous obituaries. The *Times* (London) reported he was "one of the world's leading experts on the war in Vietnam." The *Washington Post* noted that Fall was considered "one of the Westerners best informed on Vietnam." The *San Francisco Chronicle* said that he was "widely regarded as knowing more about Vietnam than almost any other Westerner." *Newsweek* magazine described him as "the outstanding chronicler of the struggle for Indochina and perhaps the most influential academic critic of U.S. policy in Vietnam." Fall was "the best-known international commentator on Viet Nam," *Time* magazine observed. The *New York Times* reported that he "was a man of enormous enthusiasm as well as powerful intellect" and described him as "a well-built man . . . who cut a dashing figure." Fall, the *Times* continued, "spoke with contempt of those who wrote from the safety of the United States about Vietnam and the men who are fighting there."[1]

Bernard Fall's renown was the product of both circumstance and substance. As U.S. involvement in Vietnam escalated in the early 1960s, many educated Americans searched for authoritative accounts of recent Vietnamese history. They found a dearth of books and articles on the subject, but among the authors whom they did discover, the most prolific was Fall. Moreover, they were attracted by his concern with timely subjects, which he consistently placed within a broad historical and cultural context.

Fall's considerable skill in self-promotion and his outspokenness also helped to assure a wide audience for his ideas. Those traits, not surprisingly, also generated some controversy. Mainstream journalists, whose work he criticized for its shallowness, resented what they regarded as his pretense and arrogance. His detractors contended that he tailored his messages on Vietnam to his audiences. For instance an article he wrote for the establishment *New York Times* in 1966 was seen by some as notably less critical of U.S. policy in Vietnam than a sharply negative essay that he contributed about the same time to the antiwar journal *Ramparts*. (In defense of Fall, it should be noted that it is not unusual for writers, while preserving the essential integrity of their work, to "style" essays according to a given journal's political stance and audience.)

Nearly all readers of what was being written about Vietnam in newspapers, journals, and books during the early and mid-1960s would agree that Fall's work was in a class by itself. Although only a part-time journalist, he received the George Polk Memorial Award in 1966 for his reporting about Vietnam. He was also the recipient of a prestigious grant from the John Simon Guggenheim Foundation for a fifth (and final, as fate would have it) extended visit there. What gave Fall his unusual stature was the depth and forcefulness of his writing. He spoke with special authority on the French experience in Southeast Asia and on the nature of Vietnamese communism. He drew on his understanding of the country and his on-the-scene observations to offer an insightful critique of U.S. political-military policy in Vietnam. And unlike many other observers who tried to "explain" Vietnam (and the number of "authorities" increased substantially after the war was Americanized in 1965), he had no particular axe to grind. He was never an apologist for any particular party or cause in Vietnam.

Fall took pride in not being an armchair scholar, and, indeed, he lost his life while trying to learn more about the country that had absorbed his attention for fifteen years. He died on patrol with a company of U.S. Marines about thirteen miles northwest of Hue, just east of Highway 1—an area known as the "Street without Joy." Ironically, it was an area with which he was quite familiar: One of his best-known books was entitled *Street without Joy*, and in it, he detailed from firsthand experience the fruitless French attempt to oust the Vietminh from the area in 1953. In 1967, he was back in the same place, hoping to do a piece on the "Street without Joy Revisited."

A French citizen, Fall was actually born in Vienna of Jewish parents on November 19, 1926. He was raised in France and was living in Nice with his family as World War II broke out in Europe. The war years were among the most important and formative times of his life. At sixteen, he joined the Maquis, the underground movement that resisted German control of France. Soon thereafter, he would recall, things "got very bad—my mother was deported as a hostage and she never came back and my father was tortured to death in 1943—we found his body in a ditch with 12 other people two years later. I hadn't known my father was in the underground."[2] During his two and a half years in the Maquis, he was wounded twice in guerrilla fighting in the French Alps. Throughout his life, Fall took pride in the Resistance and the patriotism that it represented, and he insisted that the Maquis should be remembered as a real combat outfit. Twenty years after World War II, he reflected: "There was no such thing as living at home like a solid citizen and then go out and shoot up a few Germans and then go back home and stay camouflaged. . . . Oh, no, you actually fought all the way through. . . . For us there was nothing but the endless tunnel."[3] Fall's experience in the French Resistance gave him an insight into the world of guerrilla warfare that would serve him well when he later became a student of communist insurgency in Vietnam. It also helped to shape his strong identity with France, which contributed, in the judgment of some critics, to his tendency to view too sympathetically the French role in Southeast Asia.

After World War II, Fall returned to school, and in 1951, thanks to a Fulbright scholarship, he was able to pursue graduate study in political science at Syracuse University. He initially had no particular interest in Vietnam, but that changed when he had some free time in the summer of 1952 and enrolled in a course on Indochina at the School of Advanced International Studies at Johns Hopkins University. A professor there suggested that he make Vietnam his speciality, largely because of his French background. As Fall said in 1966, "This is how by pure accident, one sunny day in Washington, D.C., of all places, in 1952 I got interested in Viet-Nam and it's been a sort of bad love affair ever since."[4] To conduct research for his dissertation, which dealt with the political evolution of Vietnam after World War II, he paid his own way to Southeast Asia in 1953. He traveled throughout the war-torn country, aided by his French civil and military status, and was able to obtain cooperation from French and anticommunist Vietnamese administrative and military officials. Accompanying French troops as they waged war against the Vietminh, he gathered the material for *Street without Joy*.

Fall quickly turned into a prolific writer on Vietnam and a frequently caustic critic of American involvement in the country. During the next fourteen years, until his final return to the "Street without Joy," he produced a constant stream of history, analysis, and opinion about Vietnam, the American entanglement, and the French involvement. In fact, by the time he turned forty in 1967, he had written six books on Vietnam, ranging from studies of the organization of the Vietminh (*The Viet-Minh Regime, Le Viet Minh*), a journal of the French war (*Street without Joy*), a history of the interwar period (*The Two Viet-Nams*), an analysis of the American war (*Vietnam Witness: 1953–1966*), and a history of the battle of Dien Bien Phu (*Hell in a Very Small Place*). Fall also wrote many articles for journals, magazines, and newspapers. His works reflected his powerful memory, detached analytical skills, and a talent with languages that gave him fluency in English, French, and German, although he knew only a smattering of Vietnamese. He reached foreign policy elites throughout Europe and parts of Asia, as well as the United States, for his articles appeared in such influential journals as *Politique Etrangère, Foreign Affairs, Current History, Wehr-Wissenschaftliche Rundschau, International Journal, Revue Française de Science Politique, Pacific Affairs, China Quarterly, Naval War College Review, The Nation,* the *New York Times Magazine, India Quarterly,* and *New Republic.*

Because of the scope and subtlety of Fall's work and the changes taking place as he wrote, it is difficult to integrate and summarize the body of writings he left behind. Yet careful readers would have little difficulty discerning a series of clear messages about U.S. involvement in Vietnam. Fall's most basic criticism was that American policy reflected a dangerous ignorance and misunderstanding of the country. He had scorn for those Americans who arrived there in the early 1960s with the attitude that the only important segment of Vietnamese history started with the U.S. involvement and that anything that came before was inconsequential. Fall was incensed, for instance, by a 1962 United States Information Service booklet that described Vietnam's seven hundred thousand mountain tribal people as having "no social traditions, no tombs, no altars." Fall minced no words: "That incredible statement—a sheer anthropological idiocy if applied to *any* human society . . . explains why, after 10 years of being deeply committed in that country, Americans are still 'taken by surprise' by recent events in Viet-Nam."[5] Fall, by contrast, always tried to see Vietnam in its full historical context. One of his books began with the prehistory of the country and discussed the Vietnamese struggle against the Chinese that lasted a thousand years. Had Americans taken such a broad historical perspective, he implicitly suggested, they would have been aware of Vietnam's deep-seated mistrust of China and determination to avoid domination by its large neighbor.

Americans were ignorant not only of ancient Vietnamese history but also of more recent developments. Most important, they misinterpreted the Vietnamese communist movement, missing its essential nationalism. Elaborating on his general indictment of American assumptions about Vietnam, Fall criticized U.S. policy as it evolved during three distinct phases between World War II and 1967. During the first phase—the period beginning with World War II and continuing through France's defeat in its war against the Vietminh in 1954—the United States, he believed, engaged in an inconsistent policy that squandered opportunities to promote peaceful political change in Vietnam.

Fall argued that America's interest in influencing Vietnamese political development began during World War II. President Franklin Roosevelt's plan to detach Indochina from France after the war and to place it under an international trusteeship should have led to a more forthright anticolonial policy. The trusteeship scheme stemmed, in part, from Roosevelt's disgust over the French capitulation to Germany in 1940 and the subsequent collaboration of the Vichy regime. FDR's condemnation of the French annoyed Fall, who argued that the president failed to recognize the real situation in France, where hundreds of thousands of French citizens (including the youthful Fall) had been fighting the Germans. That indignation aside, he believed that Roosevelt's objective during the war should have led to a postwar attempt to force France to relinquish Vietnam. The lack of consistency in the policy, Fall believed, led to a missed opportunity.

The United States should have treated the French in Indochina just as it dealt with the Dutch in Indonesia, he contended. In that case, Washington bluntly insisted that the Netherlands abandon its warfare against Indonesian nationalists and grant independence to its Asian colony. Fall argued that the same pressure should have been used to force France to come to a peaceful arrangement with the Vietnamese nationalists. "France in 1947–48 was in no position to resist such pressure," he wrote.[6] Preoccupied with the Cold War in Europe and not wanting to antagonize the French, however, the United States ceased to be a diplomatic factor in Indochina until the outbreak of the Korean War in June 1950. As American troops were sent to resist North Korean aggression, Washington began to see the French as important players in slowing the onslaught of communism, and it provided extensive financial and material support to France for its war against the Vietminh. This heavy U.S. involvement, Fall said, changed the nature of the Indochina conflict from a purely French colonial struggle into an American one, as well. Thus, when the Vietminh won their military victory over the French at Dien Bien Phu, he argued, they also won a *political* victory over the United States.

With respect to the battle at Dien Bien Phu, Fall challenged the conventional American belief that President Dwight Eisenhower had wisely rejected France's request for a massive U.S. air strike on the North Vietnamese forces surrounding the French fortress. He denounced Eisenhower's inaction: "It put the United States in a position where, for the first time in her whole history, she would abandon an ally to his fate while the ally was fighting a war that the United States had encouraged him to fight far beyond his own political objectives and most certainly far beyond his own military means. . . . In that sense, there can be no doubt but that Dien Bien Phu, far from being a purely French defeat, became an *American* defeat as well."[7] Saving the French garrison, Fall concluded, would have stabilized Vietnam by leading to a North Vietnamese communist state that would have been "less conscious of its military superiority." Also, the South Vietnamese state would have been "less burdened by the shadow of crushing military defeat" than it was after the Geneva Conference "temporarily" divided Vietnam into two "zones." With a less decisive military outcome, the two Vietnamese governments would have been more successful in working out a peaceful arrangement. An accord between the two governments, he further contended, would have been facilitated by the continuing influence of France, which "would not have felt abandoned by two close allies in her direst hour of need, [and] might well have become a stabilizing factor in the Indochina area."[8] America's missed opportunities between 1945 and 1954 thus contributed to the political instability of Vietnam and the very problems that would command U.S. attention during the following decade.

Reflecting frequently on France's long war against the Vietminh, Fall believed that it offered lessons for the United States. He constantly and not always gently reminded his readers that the French had "passed this way before." But though he saw vital similarities between the French and American experiences, he also recognized significant differences. His concern with the French period led some critics to see him as an apologist for his native land. A careful reading of his work, however, suggests that it was Vietnam, not France, that he was trying to defend. U.S. policymakers and military commanders had a particular aversion to any comparison to the French, for such a comparison implied that America's efforts in Vietnam would end as had those of France—in failure. That was often Fall's implication. In particular, he saw the Americans, like the French before them, working from a weak political base in Vietnam.

This insight was a central point in Fall's writing about the second phase of U.S. involvement, the period beginning with America's movement to support an independent, noncommunist South Vietnam in 1954 and continuing to the large-scale, open-ended commit-

ment of U.S. forces in summer 1965. American policy during that
critical decade, he contended, was characterized by wishful thinking
and a lack of understanding about the political situation in Vietnam.
His critique began when he challenged the official view in the late
1950s that the government headed by Ngo Dinh Diem was building
a strong South Vietnamese nation. Even as American leaders were
trumpeting "the miracle of South Vietnam," Fall was emphasizing
the emergence of the Vietcong as a powerful military-political force.
On his return to Vietnam in 1957 amid assurances from the American and Saigon governments that all was well, he noticed the Saigon
newspapers carried numerous obituaries of village chiefs whose
deaths were attributed to "bandit attacks." He found a strange pattern to the attacks, plotted them on a map, and discovered they were
clustered in certain areas. Incredibly, he had discerned the begin-
nings of the Vietcong insurgency. A South Vietnamese government
official confided to him that the South already knew of the pattern
and had even plotted the existence of certain communist "cells" in
the rural areas, and Fall quickly recognized the significance of this
activity. He always took immense pride in the role that he had
played in calling attention to the rise of the Vietcong. For instance,
speaking a few years later to a seminar at the Foreign Service Institute in Washington, he said, "I have been one of the persons—I consider this with pride—to have been screaming about subversion in
South Vietnam since 1957."[9]

Having sounded the alarm, Fall received a grant in 1959 from
the Southeast Asia Treaty Organization to study communist infiltration in South Vietnam. His research concluded that the government in Saigon "was deliberately *encircled* and *cut off* from the
hinterland with a wall of dead village chiefs." By 1960 the killing
had accelerated to about eleven village officials a day. "This," he
wrote, "is control—not the military illusion of it."[10] His "screaming"
further underscored the essential point—one largely ignored by
Americans—that the struggle in Vietnam was fundamentally a *revolutionary* war, with its basis firmly entrenched in Vietnamese
nationalism. The war that began in the rural areas in the late 1950s
was really being fought on an ideological basis rather than a military one. He noted that recognition of the difference between revolutionary warfare and simple guerrilla actions had "enormous and
basic political implications of what we are facing in Vietnam."[11]

For at least three years, then, before President Kennedy committed large numbers of American advisers to Vietnam, Fall found
that the insurgency had been waging a successful war against the
Diem government. That is why he dated the beginning of the Second

Indochina War not with the buildup of American advisers in 1961 or the huge escalation in 1965 but when the killing of village officials first became clear in April 1957. Fall argued that to the leaders of the insurgency, the only worthwhile targets were the village leaders because, in an underdeveloped country, "it is the village head which is the essential link . . . between the population and the central government." Once the central government lost the village chiefs, there was nothing of what he called "feedback" from the villages. And once feedback was eliminated, he said, "the government begins, and there is a wonderful French expression for this, 'to legislate into the great void'" because it has lost control over the population.[12] The Vietcong exploited the peasantry's suspicion of the Saigon government as a tool of the West. The peasants increasingly saw the Diem regime as vulnerable, autocratic, and dependent on the United States.

In arguing that the war in Vietnam was essentially a nationalist struggle, his message was like a voice in the wilderness at the time. He recognized that the resistance was a response to the tyrannical rule of Diem, but he contended that more astute American and South Vietnamese tactics could have blunted the opposition. When the South Vietnamese government, with the active support of the Americans, opted not to have the scheduled reunification elections in 1956 and Diem escalated his crackdown on his opposition, those who were unhappy with his rule had no legal avenues to express their views. A better decision, Fall argued, would have been for Diem to provide legal channels for dissent, a step that would have isolated the communists and reduced their political effectiveness.

Instead, on December 20, 1960, Southern resistance leaders created the National Liberation Front. Such a united front against the "U.S.-Diem clique" had been advocated by some of the groups making up the NLF. "The guerrilla movement had matured," Fall stated, "into a full-fledged revolutionary apparatus."[13] The success of the campaign of political assassination and the capacity of the well-organized and opportunistic NLF to reach virtually all of rural South Vietnam meant, in his view, that the struggle for control of the villages, where 85 percent of the South Vietnamese lived, had been effectively won by the revolutionaries before the United States became involved militarily. The NLF sought and gained support from North Vietnam. Fall interpreted this support in the context of Vietnamese nationalism, rather than labeling it "aggression" from the North, as American officials claimed.

Like the NLF, he asserted, Ho Chi Minh was communist but mainly nationalist. In 1962, he was granted the rare opportunity to interview Ho in Hanoi; in fact, some of the most widely cited quotes from Ho come from that interview. When Fall tried to impress on him the tremendous military potential represented by the United States, Ho drew on lessons learned in the successful war against the French to conclude that the Vietnamese could outlast the Americans, as well. Ho said: "It took us eight years of bitter fighting to defeat you French in Indochina. . . . Now the South Vietnamese regime of Ngo Dinh Diem is well armed and helped by 10,000 Americans. The Americans are much stronger than the French, though they know us less well. It may perhaps take ten years to do it, but our heroic compatriots in the South will defeat them in the end."[14] After a pause, Ho continued, speaking slowly in flawless French and looking thoughtfully out of the high French window onto the manicured formal garden of his palace in Hanoi: "I think the Americans greatly underestimate the determination of the Vietnamese people. The Vietnamese people have always shown great determination when they were faced with a foreign invader."[15]

In 1963, using information gained in the interview and extensive research, Fall produced the first scholarly and authoritative biographical essay on the life of Ho Chi Minh. The lack of a full-length biography of Ho was itself indicative of the gap in Western knowledge about Vietnamese affairs. Although Fall emphasized that Ho's commitment to communism should not be doubted, he pointed out that his was a special kind of communism, adopted for special reasons. Ho, he wrote, "opted for Communism as a way out for Viet-Nam, on totally nationalistic grounds."[16] After reviewing Ho's career and his commitment to communism after World War I, Fall explained that the leader's whole drive was primarily toward Vietnamese nationalism: Communism was the best tool at hand to reach that goal, not an end in itself.

Fall's sympathetic portrayal of Ho contrasted sharply with his critical assessment of Diem. He observed the basic differences in the images the two leaders presented to the peoples of Vietnam. While Diem was seen either in full traditional mandarin's dress or in the snow-white suit of the French colonial tradition, for example, Ho was always attired in peasant dress and sandals. Diem's remoteness from his people was a metaphor for his government's distance from the villages where the Vietcong were in the ascendancy. To capture Diem's fundamental shortcoming, Fall relied on the observations of North Vietnamese premier Pham Van Dong and recounted a conversation he had had with the premier: "[Pham Van Dong said]: '[Diem] is unpopular and the more unpopular he is the more American aid he will require to stay in power. And the more American aid he receives, the more he will look like a puppet of the Americans and the less likely he is to win popular support for his side.' 'That sounds pretty much like a vicious circle,' I said. The Premier's eyes showed a humorous gleam as he said that it was more than vicious. 'It is really like a descending spiral.'"[17]

In 1962—a year before several American journalists and officials fully recognized Diem's weaknesses and began urging his replacement with a more democratic leader—Fall wrote that he saw parallels with France's failure to establish a strong political base to counter the Vietnamese communist movement. The French, he argued, had lost Vietnam to Ho's guerrilla armies "because they had no political program that could win the support of the peasantry. In South Vietnam today, Diem's regime remains a family autocracy in Saigon, with few reforms in sight, and there is no indication that it has attracted any real support from the majority of the people."[18]

The two decades of American ignorance, misunderstanding, inconsistency, and wishful thinking led to the final phase of U.S. involvement: the Americanization of the war in 1965. Fall lived long enough to observe just the first year and one half of the escalation of U.S. bombing of North Vietnam and U.S. ground warfare in the South and the resultant use of massive firepower. What he saw filled him with dread. The incredible might of the American forces brought not just a quantitative change in the war from the French period but also a *qualitative* change. He began to fear that the war could only end in the annihilation of Vietnam.

Witnessing American military power during a visit to Vietnam in 1965 led Fall to conclude that the war could not be lost militarily by the United States because the Americans seemed to be fighting without any concern for the impact on the Vietnamese and their country. He aptly labeled U.S. warfare "technological counterinsurgency," which was "depersonalized . . . dehumanized [and] brutal." The Americans might well win the military struggle with their techniques: "If you keep up the kill rate you will eventually run out of enemies," he wrote—"or at least armed enemies." Yet a military victory would not be a political one. Fall went on: "Of course, the whole country will hate you, but at least they won't resist you. What you will get is simply a cessation of resistance—an acquiescence in one's fate rather than a belief that your side and your ideas have really prevailed."[19]

As he reflected on the devastating war, he drew a unique and insightful historical parallel. He rejected the frequently expressed American view that the "lessons of the 1930s" necessitated U.S. resistance to communism in Vietnam. According to that view, the failure of the Western democracies to stand up to aggressive powers in the 1930s—notably, in the appeasement of Germany at the Munich Conference in 1938—had only encouraged aggressors to act more belligerently and had eventually led to World War II. So, in Vietnam, the theory went, America had to stand up to communism or ultimately fight a bigger war against the Soviets or Chinese somewhere else. Fall sharply disagreed with the Europe–Southeast Asia analogy. "[The] situation in Viet-Nam isn't Munich; it is Spain," he argued. Although there was a test of wills going on in Vietnam, he wrote, the real test was of "military technology and techniques and military ideas." The North Vietnamese and Vietcong believed they could win with a revolutionary war—a combination of guerrilla warfare and political ideology. Americans believed they could win through sheer military might. In that respect, Fall said, Americans might be able to prove, as did the Germans and Italians in their support of fascist forces during the Spanish civil war of 1936–1939, that superior firepower would mean victory. But for Americans, prevailing in Vietnam would have far-reaching implications in terms of the Third World. Vietnam was an example. He wrote: "What we're really doing in Viet-Nam is killing the cause of 'wars of liberation.'"[20] Accordingly, implicit in U.S. warfare was the assumption that the survival of an anticommunist South Vietnam would be worth almost any price, just as the victors in the Spanish civil war believed that the 1.5 million deaths during the three years of fighting had been a justifiable sacrifice to achieve postwar stability. Such thinking in regard to Vietnam profoundly troubled Fall. As he noted, "It is not straining the analogy to suggest that there are now Americans who would make the same judgment of the war in Viet-Nam: it may be a nasty claw-and-nail war, but what the hell, it's worth it if we come out on top."[21]

On the other side, Fall found that the communist leaders and their followers were oblivious to the magnitude of the war that America was prepared to wage. He recalled that Ho Chi Minh had told him that the North would outlast the Americans just as they had the French, and Fall found that analogy dangerous, for it risked underestimating the scale of American power and President Johnson's willingness to use it in Vietnam. During the entire fifty-six-day siege of Dien Bien Phu, he noted, the French expended less firepower than the Americans were unleashing in a single day.

Adding to his dread of a long and indecisive war was the attitude of the communist prisoners he interviewed. Inspired by the call for patriotic sacrifice from Hanoi, they were prepared to undergo enormous hardship and were convinced that they would ultimately prevail. Representative of America's enemy was one well-educated man, the holder of a degree in physics, with whom Fall spoke at length. A Communist Party member, he had come down from the North to fight with the NLF. Fall tried to impress on him the magnitude of America's military and Washington's willingness to fight the war. The prisoner was dismissive; he told Fall that "the Liberation Front forces will win in any case, because all the Vietnamese people help us. This war can only be settled by the Vietnamese themselves. The Americans and their allies must go. . . . Do the Americans think they can stay with this kind of war for 30, 40 years? Because that is what this is going to take."[22]

The absurdity of the warfare came home to Fall when the prisoner went on to claim that Americans were being killed in battles—he mentioned Chu Lai, Pleiku, and Tay Ninh—that the Vietcong considered major victories. Fall knew the American military either claimed these as victories (Chu Lai) or as firefights in which U.S. troops suffered only minor losses (Pleiku). Nothing he said could convince the prisoner of America's strength and staying power.

By 1967, given all his observations, Fall had a dark outlook about the final outcome of the war. An awesome military machine was being unleashed on Vietnam, and the Vietcong seemed oblivious to its destructive power. He had written that a massive air campaign against the North could crumble the resistance, but he had not foreseen President Johnson's restrictions on the bombing.

The protracted, inconclusive war that Fall envisioned did materialize. Although the United States unleashed its massive firepower on North and South Vietnam, causing an enormous number of casualties ("winning" the "body count"), it could never translate that military "success" into a strengthening of the political base of the South Vietnamese government. As he had foreseen, that political weakness plagued the Americans as it had the French. On the other side, Fall seemed to have underestimated North Vietnam's capacity to continue and, indeed, accelerate its movement of troops and supplies to the South, the American bombing campaign notwithstanding. He also seemed to have minimized the support that the Soviet Union and the People's Republic of China would provide to North Vietnam. And he appeared not to have anticipated the opposition to the war in the United States and the onset of war weariness among the American public. Still, Fall did foresee a long, bitter, and terribly destructive fight. More than any other observer of the American war in its early stages in 1965–1966, he warned of the immense tragedy of the conflict that dragged on for seven years after his death.

Reflecting on Fall's extensive writing on Vietnam, one is struck by some of the conclusions that he *failed* to draw. Despite his emphasis on the nationalist appeal of the communist movement in Vietnam, the strength of the NLF throughout the Southern countryside, and the chronic weakness of the South Vietnamese government, he did not see a unified, communist-led Vietnam as inevitable. In other words, he did not regard the U.S. effort as doomed to failure. He did, however, fault the United States for neglecting the political side of the struggle. Rather than emphasizing a military solution, Fall believed that a U.S. emphasis on the political aspect of the struggle could have salvaged an independent South Vietnam. Consequently, he urged American acceptance of the NLF as a legitimate political entity and its incorporation into the South Vietnamese political system. He was convinced that, through such a process, the NLF could be weaned away from its ties with North Vietnam. At the same time, the United States could have capitalized on Hanoi's determination to avoid dependence on the Soviet Union and China to foster its emergence as an independent communist state.

U.S. and South Vietnamese officials always dismissed any suggestion of NLF participation in the Saigon government, insisting that the group would subvert the political process. Inviting the NLF into a coalition government, they argued, would lead to communist domination. Such fears were well founded. The strength of the NLF throughout rural South Vietnam would have given it an enormous influence in any coalition government. Indeed, it seems that Fall's vision of a divided Vietnam, with a communist-led state in the North and communist involvement in a coalition government in the South, was wishful thinking on his part. Not only does the coalition concept appear inherently unworkable, it is also difficult to conceive of North Vietnam accepting the indefinite division of Vietnam. The leaders in Hanoi had been forced to accept a temporary division of Vietnam at the Geneva Conference in 1954, but their ultimate objective was always national unification.

Fall's refusal to abandon his hopes for an independent South derived from his identification with U.S. objectives in Vietnam. His extensive criticism of American political and military activities obscured the fact that he was fundamentally a "Cold Warrior." His view of the strategic importance of Vietnam paralleled the domino theory that was commonly used to justify U.S. policy. Like American officials, Fall believed that the outcome of the struggle in Vietnam would determine whether Southeast Asia came under communist domination. He wrote that the "Communists apparently have found Southeast Asia a propitious battleground where they can demonstrate the U.S. inability to stand up to the enormous stress of revolutionary war." Casting the struggle in Vietnam within the context of communist insurgency in Malaya and Laos and "Chinese terrorist guerrillas" along the Thailand-Malaya border, he contended that "all this spells a real challenge to the United States and one which the United States had decided to face up to in South Vietnam, regardless of cost." Failure to stand firm, he warned, would be disastrous. "With Southeast Asia no longer under American control," he contended, "India's position would become well-nigh impossible. What Indonesia's attitude then would be is anybody's guess. In other words, the negative stake of denying the adversary access to further Southeast Asian real estate is truly an important one."[23] In sum Fall's account of Vietnam's strategic importance could just as easily have been written by a U.S. official.

That he desperately wanted to see the preservation of an independent South Vietnam and an American-dominated Southeast Asia was not too surprising. In a sense, these hopes reflected his dual French and American heritage. Both France and the United States had invested heavily in achieving essentially the same objective in Vietnam, and, no matter how frustrating the situation might become there, it was difficult for any American or French citizen to acknowledge that that objective was not going to be realized. Fall had a curious way of referring to "you" Americans at certain times and, to "we" Americans at others. He used the former when he was lecturing Americans on their shortcomings and the latter when he was identifying with their cause. Like the preponderance of the intellectual elites in America and France, he was strongly anticommunist. Although he at times stressed the nationalist content of communist movements and the capacity of the United States to play off one communist government against another, he also was apprehensive of a general communist threat, emanating from China, to Asian stability.

Fall's writings remain an important contribution to the historiography of the Vietnam War. Today the opening of archives, the numerous memoirs by participants, and the perspective afforded by time provide an opportunity to study U.S. involvement in Vietnam in much greater depth and with far more understanding than was possible in the 1960s. By contrast, Fall's work is inevitably dated in some respects. Nonetheless today's scholars will find in his prolific writing illuminating firsthand accounts of a conflict as it unfolded. They will also discover the contemplations of a fellow scholar who, more than three decades earlier, was trying to understand the deeper forces at work in Vietnam—the kinds of issues that historians address. If journalists, as someone observed, provide the "rough-draft of history," then Bernard Fall fulfilled that role with unusual insight and prescience.

Notes

1. *Times* (London), February 22, 1967; *San Francisco Chronicle,* February 22, 1967; *Washington Post,* February 22, 1967; *Newsweek,* March 6, 1967; *Time,* March 3, 1967; *New York Times,* February 22, 1967.

2. Bernard Fall, *Last Reflections on a War,* ed. Dorothy Fall (New York: Doubleday, 1967), 16–18.

3. Ibid., 20–21.

4. Ibid., 22–23.

5. Bernard Fall, *Viet-Nam Witness, 1953–1966* (New York: Praeger, 1966), 190.

6. Fall, *Last Reflections,* 147.

7. Bernard Fall, *Hell in a Very Small Place* (Philadelphia: J. B. Lippincott, 1967), 461–62.

8. Ibid., 462.

9. Bernard Fall, *Military Developments in Vietnam* (Washington, D.C.: Foreign Service Institute, 1962), 25–26.

10. Fall, *Last Reflections,* 219.

11. Fall, *Military Developments,* 26–27.

12. Ibid., 28.

13. Fall, *Viet-Nam Witness,* 239.

14. Ibid., 105.

15. Ibid.

16. Fall, *Last Reflections,* 72–73.

17. Fall, *Viet-Nam Witness,* 112.

18. Ibid.

19. Fall, *Last Reflections,* 224–25.

20. Ibid.

21. Ibid.

22. Ibid., 254.

23. Fall, *Viet-Nam Witness,* 263.

Suggested Readings

In addition to the books cited in the notes, Fall's other works on Vietnam include *Street without Joy: Indochina at War, 1946–1954* (Harrisburg, Pa.: Stackpole, 1961), *The Two Viet-Nams: A Political and Military Analysis* (New York: Praeger, 1963); and *The Viet-Minh Regime: Government and Administration in the Democratic Republic of Vietnam* (Westport, Conn.: Greenwood Press, 1956). With Bernard Raskin, Fall edited *A Viet-Nam Reader: Articles and Documents on American Foreign Policy and the Viet-Nam Crisis* (New York: Random House, 1965). Other sources are Ho Chi Minh, *Ho Chi Minh on*

Revolution: Selected Writings, 1920–1966, ed. and intro. by Bernard B. Fall (New York: Praeger, 1967); Paul Mus, "Commitment," review of *Last Reflections on a War, New York Times Book Review,* December 10, 1967, pp. 1, 62–63; idem, "Victory and Defeat," review of *Hell in a Very Small Place, New York Times Book Review,* February 12, 1967, pp. 1, 31–34; and William W. Prochnau, *Once upon a Distant War* (New York: Times Books, 1995).

II

Americans Become Trapped in the Vietnam Quagmire

The old adage that young men fight old men's wars has rung true throughout history, but in the Vietnam era the disparity it suggests was aggravated by a generation gap that was more tension-filled than usual. Even before the war grew large and drew in hundreds of thousands of Americans, there was a youthful rebellion under way in the United States. In the 1950s the young movie stars Marlon Brando and James Dean symbolized the teenage rebel, whose persona and "attitude" were mimicked by many young people. The phenomenon of rock-and-roll music and the immense popularity of Elvis Presley, whose pelvic gyrations horrified older Americans, were other symptoms of a generational divide. By 1962, before most Americans knew much at all about Vietnam, the Students for a Democratic Society (SDS) issued their Port Huron Statement, which challenged the higher-education establishment to allow college students to participate in decisions made on their own campuses.

There are various explanations of why the so-called baby boomers, born in the years right after World War II, were so antagonistic toward their parents' generation. Some theories emphasize the depression-era experience of the parents in contrast to the postwar affluence in which these children matured. Another hypothesis notes that the dropping of the atomic bomb marked a divide between the older generation, which saw it as the end of a war, and the younger generation, which saw it as the beginning of an age of mass destruction. The sheer size of the baby boom population created a mass market for the music, clothes, and other elements of a youth culture. In addition university enrollments exploded and created some huge and increasingly impersonal campuses.

All of these changes were well under way when the escalation in Vietnam created a sudden need for large numbers of young men in the military services. In an effort to limit political controversy about the Vietnam deployments, Lyndon Johnson declined to mobilize the nation for war and refused to activate military reservists. Instead, his administration met the military manpower needs by expanding draft calls, which reached fifty thousand a month by 1968. Due to the rules in place for the draft and for combat enlistments, the overwhelming majority of the Vietnam-bound soldiers were nineteen years old, about seven years younger than the average age of U.S. soldiers in World War II. Not all male members of the huge baby boom generation were needed in the military even with the war, so various deferments were allowed, most notably to attend college or for specific medical conditions. Because working-class and poor families were less able to enroll their children in college or afford a well-documented medical history for them, they sent a disproportionate number of their sons to Vietnam.

As the war grew in size and duration, military service became increasingly controversial. There was tension between the leaders who made the decisions about the war (many of whose sons had deferments) and the young people who had to fight it. There were real questions of equity and fairness about which American youth were being exposed to the dangers of combat. And as the casualties mounted and the purpose of the war came under attack, the soldiers and potential soldiers began to feel trapped in the Vietnam quagmire rather than believing they were fulfilling a civic duty.

Although young men faced the prospect of combat in an ambiguous war, young women also found their lives dramatically altered by the conflict. The thousands of servicemen had sisters, girlfriends, and wives who became Vietnam veterans in their own right. In addition, a number of patriotic women, moved by the sacrifices being asked of men, volunteered to serve in various ways, especially as nurses.

This section presents the stories of four Americans who faced the reality of combat in Vietnam in different yet similar ways. Bill Weber was a draftee who could have avoided the war but instead went when called and was killed in action (Chapter 5). His death was only the beginning of years of trauma for his sister, Elizabeth, and the rest of his family. Seawillow Chambers was a young bride whose new husband went to Vietnam just weeks after their marriage (Chapter 6). He survived the war, but their life together was forever altered by that year of war-imposed separation. Nancy Randolph was an idealistic nurse whose tour in Vietnam transformed her (Chapter 7). Bill Henry Terry Jr. enlisted at nineteen to provide some financial security for his teenaged wife and baby (Chapter 8). Like many other African American men, he saw greater career opportunities in the service, even with the risk of death in Vietnam, than in civilian life.

These stories are only four of the thousands of individual dramas that made up the human experience of the Vietnam era. In many ways, they are the accounts of "ordinary" Americans, and in other ways, they are distinctive. Each is a single thread in the tapestry that was the American war in Vietnam.

5

In My Brother's Name
The Life and Death of Spec. 4 Bill Weber

Elizabeth Weber

Army Spec. 4 Bill Weber was killed by a Vietcong sniper on February 12, 1968, along the banks of the Diem Diem River, near the hamlet of My Lai, South Vietnam. He was the first man to die in his company, which had only recently arrived in Vietnam. One month later, on March 16, 1968, members of his company massacred every man, woman, and child in My Lai in the largest single atrocity committed by U.S. ground forces in the Vietnam War. Some of the men who participated in the rampage later claimed that revenge for Weber's death partly accounted for the killing.

Written by Weber's sister, this chapter not only chronicles the young soldier's life and death but also describes the family from which he came and the impact of his death on that family. He was a well-liked, all-American boy from Minnesota. In college, he spent so much time playing the guitar in a rock band that he flunked out and got drafted. His sister finds it bitterly ironic that after his death, the name of her guitar-picking, easygoing brother became linked with the tragedy at My Lai.

Elizabeth Weber recalls how news of her brother's death transformed every member of her family. Her parents damned Lyndon Johnson, Robert McNamara, and other national leaders. She herself went from being an honor student who attended church every Sunday to a counterculture dropout who shunned religion and stopped believing anything that politicians said. Years later, in 1996, she and her father went to Vietnam and to the spot where her brother had died. Some of their hosts were former Vietcong, one of whom may have fired the shot that killed young Weber. Surprisingly, she writes, she and her father found themselves apologizing to the Vietnamese for the American war in Vietnam and for her brother's part in it.

Elizabeth Weber is an associate professor of English at the University of Indianapolis in Indiana. She earned an M.F.A. from the University of Montana and a Ph.D. in English literature from the State University of New York, Binghamton. She teaches creative writing and has published a book of poetry, *Small Mercies* (1984), and numerous poems and essays in literary reviews and magazines. She is currently writing a memoir of her brother.

Courtesy of Elizabeth Weber

My older brother, Bill, was killed in Vietnam in February 1968, the winter of my senior year in high school. I remember the day clearly: a bone-cracking-cold Minnesota day with hardly any snow on the ground. In my bedroom over the front porch, I was studying for a calculus exam when I looked out the window to see our parish priest and a tall man in an army uniform walk up the steps to our house. Dashing for the stairs, I heard the doorbell ring. As I reached the living room, I heard my mother scream my brother's name. When she saw me, she pulled me to her and cried, "Oh my poor baby, your brother's dead, whatever will you do?" I looked up to see the foreign exchange student staying with us standing with her back pressed to the living room wall, her eyes wide. I felt sorry for her. My father came home about then. He saw the priest and the army sergeant and said, "What's going on?" He looked as if one of the cows he worked with as a veterinarian had kicked him hard in the head. As they told him the details, he kept saying, "Huh."

My parents kept me home from school the next day. When I went back to school two days later, I took my two best friends, one by one, into the nearest girls' rest room to tell them what happened. Every time I told someone, I'd break down in tears, unable to talk. The news spread, and a few other classmates came up to me and told me they were sorry. When they did, I'd break down crying and have to run away. I took the calculus test and flunked. I had a 94 percent average until then in the class, but when midterm grades came out two weeks later, I saw the teacher had given me a C+. All my grades fell that semester. I also started to talk back to teachers, something I'd never done before. I became belligerent and developed a "fuck you" attitude. I swore at a teacher when she wouldn't let me have an extra day to study for an exam I missed because of Bill's funeral. "I guess I goddamn flunk the fucking test," I told her. Later, I felt bad and apologized to her and told her the circumstances. New to the school and out of the gossip circle, she hadn't heard about my brother's death. She still didn't cut me any slack. I forged hall passes and release-from-school passes for myself and a friend using the name of the school librarian I worked for. During study hall one day, a friend and I found a copy of a James Bond book by Ian Fleming left by someone from the period before, and we tore it up into minute pieces. When the teacher, one of our favorites, caught us with the pile of torn pages and asked why we'd done that, we told him the book was sexist and promoted violence. He shook his head and said, "I'm surprised at you. You know better. You don't tear books up for any reason." He gave us each two days of detention. I also sassed back to another favorite teacher, the man who taught German, and mispronounced all the words in a dialogue we had to memorize. "What's gotten into you?" he asked angrily. "You know better than this." I was his star student, nearly fluent in the language from the time I'd lived in Germany when I was nine and ten. I didn't know what to say to him.

The things I did may sound mild compared to what other kids did then and now. But I went to a school that had mostly University of Minnesota professors' children in it. Many students went to Ivy League colleges. The majority took school very seriously. Before my brother's death, I had been a model student, a shy recluse who never talked back to teachers, never skipped school, never turned in work late, and never flunked exams. To me, a C was a bad grade. I was captain of the soccer team and an honor roll student in the top 10 percent of my class. I obeyed all rules.

After Bill died, I just didn't care. The world I knew seemed fake, and so did the people in it. All the rules and values I'd followed until then didn't seem to matter. Those rules and values had killed my brother, who always struck me as being one of the nicest, kindest guys in the world. I looked around me, and it didn't seem that many cared about what was happening over in Vietnam because it wasn't happening to them but to others. They didn't care as long as they could go about earning their money, promoting their careers, and going to parties and football games. They did not want their lives troubled. I hated them.

I should explain that my family was against the war. My parents told me it was unjust, that the United States was imposing its will on the people of Vietnam. The war was more about money and power than the freedom of a people, they said, and the government in South Vietnam was corrupt and oppressive. From what I read about the war in magazines and newspapers, the people of Vietnam, in both the North and the South, didn't want us over there. I felt that only a few people did—those who were benefiting financially. The corrupt wanted it. I could not understand why young Americans needed to go there and die. I did not buy the domino theory. After all, weren't some countries we supported as democracies just as oppressive and corrupt? Look at the Philippines or Korea.

The staff sergeant who told us of Bill's death also talked about what was happening in the war. We were being lied to about the number of casualties, he said, and much of the news about the war was buried on the back pages of our newspapers. After that, I always looked way in the back of the paper. He also told us that we were not winning. He himself was against the war. He had been a helicopter crewman there, and finally, when he couldn't stomach any more missions, they'd given him the job of telling families their boys had died. He hated what he saw happening.

All this shattered my beliefs. Then, Martin Luther King was gunned down in April. In June, Bobby Kennedy was shot and killed.

Later that summer the Democratic National Convention in Chicago brought rioting and violence. Also at that convention, I watched Hubert Humphrey, Minnesota's former senator, turn to the people behind him after he'd won the nomination and say, "Watch me wow them." He'd thought the mikes couldn't pick that up. I was disgusted.

I looked at the people with whom I had grown up, and for the first time, I saw them as shortsighted and filled with self-interest. They had killed my brother. They had sent him over to Vietnam to kill and to die. As long as it was not their sons who went and as long as their lives were not disrupted, they did not care.

I saw the leaders of this country as liars who just wanted power. They lied to the people about why we were in Vietnam, about the nature of the war over there, about who was winning, and about the number of casualties. They supported a regime that was corrupt, callous, and oppressive, and they did not care about the lives of the young men they sent to war.

I was also furious with my father and blamed him for my brother's death. Bill had been drafted into the army after flunking out of the University of Minnesota twice. For someone as smart as my brother, that must have taken some effort on his part or perhaps a sustained, concentrated lack of effort. He had gotten poor grades in high school also, mostly Cs and Ds. My brother's love in life had been music and playing the guitar. With two other guys, he first formed a folk band, then later a rock band, the Chasers, which was mildly successful locally until it dissolved when the members went off to the university in 1966.

He spent most of his high school years practicing the guitar. One of the enduring images I have of my brother is of him standing against the big picture window in our family room and playing his guitar while he looked out at the trees in the backyard. He would be totally absorbed in the music he was playing, and if I called to him then, he would not answer, or if he did, he would turn and look vacantly at me, his consciousness only coming partly back to listen. The first thing he did after he got a leave to come home right before being sent to Vietnam was to play music. I remember returning from school one afternoon in November 1967 to the sounds of the Byrds, backed by my brother's bass guitar, streaming out the front door. He had told no one he would be there, and I was the first home. I threw down my books and ran to the family room. There he stood, bass guitar in hand. "Hi, sis," he said. "So you bought the new Byrds album. Good choice."

All Bill wanted to do was play music. He spent all his time doing it, and that caused his downfall. Once during his first quarter at the University of Minnesota, I caught him playing with his band at a pep rally in our high school auditorium. He had not told us he was going to be there, and I knew he had a biology exam during that time. After the rally, I went up to him. "What are you doing?" I asked. "Didn't you have an exam at two?" He just smiled down at me and said, "Live for today, for tomorrow you die." I wanted to shake him and scream at him, "Are you nuts?" What was he doing? I was fifteen, but I knew what the consequence of flunking out of college was: Vietnam.

But back then, "Live for today, for tomorrow you die" was one of his favorite mottoes. In his last letter to me, he included a poem:

Life is like a drop of
salt water to the ocean.
From this thought arises
this question. Why waste life
on work? Why not just enjoy
what is so short.
To all who read this, search
for the answer,
I shan't.

In the same letter, he gave me this big-brotherly advice: "Always wonder, never take for granted." My brother, the philosopher. On the cover of a notebook for a college history course, he wrote, "Worry is a leak in the faucet of human potential." On a page inside, he recorded the grade for his first history theme—D+. Bill was not stupid, and he came from a home that had wall-to-wall books in the living room. When we didn't know a word or a fact, we looked it up in the dictionary or encyclopedia. Dinnertime discussions centered around politics, philosophy, or science.

My father hammered away at Bill about his grades. "Do you want to end up a ditchdigger?" he'd ask my brother, who merely stared back at him. Family opinion had it that the reason Bill did so badly in school was to get back at my father, who was a University of Minnesota professor with a Ph.D., a D.V.M., and thirteen years of college. Education was emphasized in my family. My mother had ten years of college and was only an exam away from a Ph.D. in genetics. My Grandmother Weber told us over and over that an education was the only thing no one could ever take away from you. To not do well in school was nearly a sin.

I look back on those last years of my brother's life and don't know exactly why he did poorly in school, but to say he was rebelling against my father is too simple an explanation. I know that he was embarrassed by his grades. One of his best high school friends was class valedictorian. Another graduated in the top 5 percent. One later told me that when they'd get tests back and ask Bill what he got, he would just shrug. Most of his friends said that he was not interested because he was not intellectual, but I don't agree. An intellectual even back then, I read extensively, devouring everything I could get my hands on, and from talking with my brother, reading the letters he wrote to me, and listening to the tapes he sent, I found him thoughtful and intellectual.

I also know that he could work hard. People who knew him on the few jobs he had remarked how hardworking and conscientious he was. At the Dayton's store in downtown Saint Paul where he worked in the men's department the summer before he was drafted, the manager told us that Bill had been one of his best salesclerks. In fact, I later was hired there because of his reputation. He was also a carryout boy at the local grocery store, and time and time again, I heard from women who shopped there how helpful he was. When I interviewed Bill's platoon leader and his company commander, both said that he was one of the guys they could always count on.

I watched Bill while he worked for my uncle one summer on his farm. He worked hard, getting up on time at five A.M. (unlike me), and my uncle wanted him to work for him full-time. I think Bill was a hard worker. He liked learning, reading, and thinking. But he did not like being told how to learn and what to learn and conforming to any set of rules. Also, he mostly liked playing music, pleasing people, and having people pleased with him. He worked hard at those things he liked.

My father's method of dealing with my brother's failing at school was to criticize him even more. He tried to shame him into doing well. That method worked with me because I got angry and had an "I'll show you" attitude, but it did not work with Bill. I think he began to believe he could not do well. All this may have straightened out with time, but during the late 1960s, young men did not have the luxury of gradually figuring out their lives because of the Vietnam War. So I worried about my brother and kept after him to stay in school, even if he didn't like it. But when I'd tell him that, he would just look at me as if *I* were clueless. Even after he flunked out and was just waiting to be drafted and I was after him to *do* something, for God's sake—go to Canada, sign up as a conscientious objector, *anything, please*—he would just stare down at me with this impervious, almost regal look. I was frantic with worry.

So when he died, I came down hard on my father. I let him know directly and regularly that I thought he had killed Bill by being too hard on him. Why hadn't he helped him more? Once when my father shouted at my younger brother, who also did not do well in school, I stood up and shouted back at my father that he had killed one of my brothers—was he now working on killing the other? Furiously, he told me to shut up or leave. I kept up my barrage at him until one day, I made him cry. I can't remember what I said to him, but he replied, "Ouch, that hurt." And I looked up to see tears in my father's eyes. I was horrified then and stopped my attacks.

As soon as I could, I left home to go to college and made sure I went to a school away from the Twin Cities, where we lived. At the time, I thought it was because I was so angry at my parents because they did nothing to help my brother. I was also angry because their way of living no longer worked for me. I wanted a different life—a life where brothers would not get sent away to wars, where wars and social injustice didn't exist. I saw everything my parents did as perpetuating those things. But now I know I also went away to be far from that house where one less person sat at the supper table and slept in a bedroom.

Unlike my brother, I did well in school and received mostly As and Bs and was on the dean's list my first two or three years of college. Majoring in biology, I thought about being premed, to carry on family tradition. With a love of learning and school, I was the type of student who read books for pleasure. I say this because of what subsequently happened. In college, I did not join any of the sororities because I saw them as perpetuating a system that no longer worked. How could anyone think about fraternities or sororities? They perpetuated the caste system, the materialism, the racism, the sexism, all that I felt was responsible for the way the world was. In the summer of 1968, before I went away, I addressed envelopes for Eugene McCarthy's campaign. I wrote letters to my congressmen, who, when they answered, never seemed to address the real issues but mouthed stale platitudes.

I took part in sit-ins and demonstrations. I remember two incidents most clearly. One was during a sleep-in we students held in front of the administration building in the fall of 1969 at the small college I attended. At that point, I was not what one would call a hippie, a member of the counterculture, and I remember one of the more hippie-looking students telling me to move, no one wanted me here, why didn't I go and be with my own kind? Sometimes, I found the people in the antiwar movement to be as callous as those who were prowar. In the other incident, I saw a group of students holding up placards that carried the names of those from Minnesota who had been killed in the war. On one of the signs dated 1968, I saw my brother's name. I was furious. My grief was personal and private. How dare they use his name like that? So I went over to argue with those holding the signs. Didn't they realize what they were doing? They were taking my brother and turning him into nothing but a cause, a statistic. I asked them to quit that or take his name off their sign. They tried to reason calmly with me. Didn't I want the war ended? Well, didn't I see that what they were doing was helping end the war by making people aware that actual people were dying there? I patiently explained to them how painful it was for me to see my brother's name up there. They patiently reasoned back. But our exchange ended with me screaming at them that they were as bad as the government that looked at my brother as nothing more than a tool to be used for its benefit. "Can't I have my grief? My memory of him?" I yelled in their faces. "Thank you for killing my brother twice," I raved as I snatched the sign and threw it to the ground. I walked away, aware of the murmuring at my back and the stares. I just didn't care.

During this time, I hated most people, even many of the people in the antiwar movement. Those not actively trying to stop the war I saw as murderers of my brother. And some of those in the antiwar movement I saw as sanctimonious or merely interested in the cause as a fad. Unlike most of them, I could not separate myself from the men who went to Vietnam. I did not hate the ordinary soldier who was drafted—I hated the American people; I hated those in power; I hated the generals and other commanding officers; I hated the South Vietnamese. I did not hate the Vietcong; I did not hate the North Vietnamese; and I did not hate those who went to Canada or those who didn't and fought. I did sometimes hate conscientious objectors, particularly if they took a holier-than-thou attitude. I figured they had just been graced by luck. I had utmost sympathy for the men sent to Vietnam. I saw them as my brothers.

After two years at the small private college, I transferred to the University of Minnesota. I did not like the complacent attitude most U. of M. students had. They seemed concerned with clothes, vacations in Saint Petersburg during spring break and Vail during Christmas break, their social calendars, and who was dating whom. They had queen contests in which the candidates had to be blond, blue-eyed, and Swedish. I was none of these.

The winter of my sophomore year, a story about a massacre in the village of My Lai started to appear in newspapers. Chu Lai, Charlie Company, Americal Division, Task Force Barker, Capt. Ernest Medina, and Lt. William Calley—those names stood out. When I called my parents, they confirmed my memories: The company accused of the massacre was the one my brother had been in. Medina was the captain who had written letters to us after Bill was killed. Calley was Bill's platoon leader. In fact, Bill had been his radio operator. Some of the guys from the company had been writing to my family: Tom Turner, Ron Grzesik, Bob Lee. I remember my parents wondering how they were involved. We all read the papers anxiously to see if those names appeared.

Soon after the reports became public, some of the guys from Bill's company went to visit my parents. I was away at school. My parents asked them what had happened that day in the village. They told my parents that they didn't know. They had stayed out of it, they said, on the outskirts of the village. They knew something bad was happening and decided to stay away. We sighed with relief. If they were guilty, so was Bill, and somehow by association so were we.

I know now after all the reading I've done since the war that those soldiers were lying. My parents probably knew that at the time, and I probably intuited it, though I was only nineteen and naive. In accounts of the massacre, I find most of the names of those men solidly in the center of the events. One of them told my father that they swore for every one of them that got killed they would kill one hundred Vietcong. One book I read reported that before they machine-gunned the villagers, some men from the company said, "And that's for Bill Weber."[1] My younger brother, who was nine at the time, told me later that one of the soldiers who visited my family looked like "someone whose vision of what the world was had been shattered, who did not recognize this world he had come back to and had found nothing yet to replace that world." He told me that the guy couldn't eat the steak my mother had served him and that even to smell it made him sick. The men and my family had gone to a hockey game at the University of Minnesota; my brother said that on the way, they had to cross a suspension bridge, and the guy smoked five cigarettes before he could cross.

Books and articles about the company and the massacre began to be published in 1970. They talked about Bill's death. I remember two accounts most vividly. The first was in an interview with Calley: "A rifle shot got my R.T.O.—radio-telephone operator—on his radio harness. The harness shattered and it tore his kidney out. He rolled off the levee saying to me, 'I've been shot.' . . . He was dead a good twenty minutes before the chopper could pick him up. It was horrible, but I was about to leave him there floating."[2]

Even though Calley got Bill's name wrong—he called him "Weaver"—I recognized my brother's death. In fact, many accounts got his name wrong; one called him "Ron Weber." The army had told us that Bill died instantly. The accounts I read did not seem to indicate that, and each told a different story. One described Bill as "moaning like an animal," crying, screaming, and saying, "I'm gonna die, I'm gonna die."[3] One of Bill's best friends and the medic, Doc Lee, came to aid him, but by the time the helicopter came, Bill was dead.

I wonder if most people reading such accounts think they are just like so many other stories of war and death, something read or seen in a movie. It is an impersonal death—something to cluck one's tongue about, but always something that happens to someone else. But as a twenty-year-old reading these accounts of my brother's death, I was sickened. I would slam the book shut, but every now and again, just as one picks at a scab, I would open it back up. I guess reading it and feeling the pain was one way of keeping Bill alive for me.

I also read all the accounts of the massacre I could find. I read them over and over again and tried to discover the truth about what happened. The details sickened me. I just could not imagine those guys—people who wrote to my parents, who had known Bill, and who had seemed so nice—doing such things. What had happened to them? I remembered that in his letters to us shortly before he died, Bill had mentioned that he and the others went on search-and-destroy missions. My parents were angry at that. I remember them saying, "What do you expect when you send guys out on missions like that? Particularly when it's hard to tell who's an enemy and who's a friend." They said that the generals, President Johnson, and Robert McNamara should be tried in court.

All these years later, I cannot block out the cries of those villagers. When I meet someone for the first time, I have a tendency to tell them that my brother was Lieutenant Calley's radio operator—you know, the one who was convicted of killing those villagers in My Lai. To most Americans, My Lai is an aberration, something done by guys who went berserk and were probably a little on the edge to begin with. But for me, it is not an aberration. It is the whole war for me, and the guys who did it are my brothers. And they break my heart. I cannot separate my brother from that massacre. He has become synonymous with it. When I think of him, I think of all those people crying and screaming before they were gunned down.

In the spring of 1971, I was preparing to take an exam in organic chemistry, a course in which I had a 94 percent grade average. Instead of studying for it, I found myself drifting over to the literature section of the library and reading all the books on the shelf about Edgar Allan Poe. I passed the course with a C. The next fall, I was in an honors seminar on eighteenth-century philosophers, and when I was supposed to be studying for a midterm exam on Spinoza, Leibnitz, and Descartes, I instead stayed up all night and listened to Beethoven's Ninth and read e.e. cummings's poetry. I got the third-lowest grade in a class of sixty students. I dropped biology as a major and changed to German, a language I knew almost as well as English. After I did that, my grades improved. I went back to getting As with a few Bs thrown in here and there. German was easy. Upset that I'd changed my major, my father asked, "Why did you stop taking bread-and-butter courses?"

I began spending more time doing activities that were considered countercultural. I joined a commune, food co-ops, hardware co-ops, and a woman's health co-op. I hung out at the women's liberation office on campus. I stopped cutting my hair and let it grow long and tangled. I stopped wearing a bra, stopped shaving my legs and my underarms, and stopped wearing shoes in the summer, even in the city. I vowed not to become "part of the establishment," not to "sell out to the system," and instead I looked for alternative ways to make money. I didn't want to be part of the power structure that oppressed, robbed, and killed people. I took menial jobs. I know this upset my parents. At one point my father, on seeing the place where I lived (a condemned house off Franklin Avenue in Minneapolis), asked me how far down I thought I might go before I decided I was low enough. I just shrugged.

I went through probably about a six-month period during which I shoplifted groceries, record albums, water colors, watercolor paper, and textbooks. I did it to get back at the capitalists who ran the country and made their money by oppressing people and who had helped kill my brother. I quit stealing for two reasons. First, the manager of the bookstore where I did a lot of my shoplifting was a very nice woman. Second, I realized that I would never touch those who made all the money. They would simply raise the prices and pass their loss on to the people who shopped at their stores. By stealing, I hurt only the poor. So I gave it up.

I finally gave up my down-and-out counterculture life, too, and finished college. I later earned a Ph.D. in English literature and started teaching at a university. I am not one who likes to suffer much, particularly when it seems pointless, so I stopped my overt social protests. I have never regained my faith in our government, however. I still see it as basically corrupt. Also, I have never regained faith in people. Most are out to make a buck and to get as much as they can. They do not want to jeopardize their comfortable lives, and they would sacrifice their neighbors to keep living their lives as they do. I'm sorry I feel this way. I wish I didn't. I have never forgiven the people in the United States for the Vietnam War. When I walked past the Vietnam Veterans Memorial in Washington, D.C., a few years ago and saw the line of people passing by and looking sad, I felt angry. What right did they have to mourn those men? What right did they have to look sad? Where were *they* back then? What did they do to stop the war? What did they give up to stop the killing? I found myself elbowing my way through the crowds and not caring if I hurt someone. I know it is wrong to feel this way. I know I am being unfair. But my heart hardens into a tight fist and won't let go, no matter what I say to it.

After McNamara's memoirs came out, a friend asked me what justice I thought he deserved. I decided I wanted him to feel what I felt, the pain my parents had felt. I answered that I wanted him to watch as his children were killed one by one. I know this is horrific and that such desires caused My Lai. They are evil. I have been taught that I should bless my enemies, pray for their souls. I guess I'm not there yet. I will keep trying.

I have reconciled with my father. I quit blaming him for my brother's death a long time ago. A few years ago, I wrote him a letter asking him to forgive me for ever blaming him for what happened to Bill. I have no idea why my brother seemed so bent on destruction, but he chose the way his life ended. He flunked out of school and did nothing about being drafted when he did have alternatives. He turned down officer candidate school in Germany, where, because of his fluency in German, he could have spent his time in the army, and then he put in for the most exposed position in a platoon, that of the radio operator. I told a friend right after Bill's death that I thought he had a death wish. I don't care so much anymore about reasons. I am just sad that all that potential is gone, and I'm sad that when I remember my brother, I also have to remember that miserable war.

Not long ago, my seventy-eight-year-old father, a writer friend named Bob Ross, and I traveled to Vietnam to visit the site of the My Lai massacre and to find the spot where my brother was killed. I knew my father needed to go to be at peace about Bill's death. My mother did not want us to go because she felt it uncovered things best left undisturbed. Upset at my persistence, she stopped talking to me about two months before we went and died suddenly about four weeks before our trip. Despite her angry silence, she had bought our tickets to Vietnam. I wish my mother could have made the trip. She never found peace about Bill's death. Since going, I find that I am less upset about his death. He used to come back to me in dreams. He no longer does.

My father and I met with members of the People's Committee in Quang Ngai, Duc Pho, and My Lai, all the places where Bill was during the war. One rainy day in December just before Christmas, they helped us find the place where Bill was probably killed on the Diem Diem River, near where it flows into the sea about two kilometers outside the village of My Lai. The levee where he was killed was gone, and the river had swollen far over its banks because of the never ceasing torrents of rain. The men—the same ones who, twenty-nine years earlier as Vietcong, had taken part in the battle that killed Bill—pointed to a spot about a hundred yards into the swirling river. "Over there," they said. They gestured to a far line of trees and told us that was where they were shooting from. "We knew we had killed or wounded some GI that day because we saw the helicopter land here where we stand now," they told us.

Earlier, over tea and cookies, my father and I apologized to them for my brother's part in the war. "He was a good boy. He was only doing what his country asked of him," my father said as he shook his head sadly. I told the People's Committee of My Lai that I was glad that my brother was dead because I would have hated for him to be part of that massacre. I would have hated what it would have done to his soul. Did I mean that? My friend Bob was angry at me for saying that. He told me that as he was sitting with all those former Vietcong, he had suddenly felt angry. Hadn't they killed also? What are we apologizing for? He told me my mother would be doubly angry at me now. How could I be glad my brother was dead?

These days, I keep thinking about the others in Bill's company who survived and what I have read about their lives. I also remember what my father said about Bill when he was killed: "He was probably watching the butterflies in the outfield, just as he did when he was a kid playing baseball. I'd look up and there would be old Bill daydreaming out in left field and missing all the balls hit to him."

Notes

1. Martin Gershen, *Destroy or Die: The True Story of My Lai* (New Rochelle, N.Y.: Arlington House, 1971), 37.

2. John Sack, "The Continuing Confessions of Lieutenant Calley," *Esquire,* February 1971, 55.

3. Gershen, *Destroy or Die*, 204.

Suggested Readings

For background and analysis on the My Lai massacre, see David L. Anderson, ed., *Facing My Lai: Moving beyond the Massacre* (Lawrence: University Press of Kansas, 1998), and Michael Bilton and Kevin Sim, *Four Hours in My Lai* (New York: Viking, 1992). Moving accounts of the impact of the war on individuals are found in Myra MacPherson, *Long Time Passing: Vietnam and the Haunted Generation* (New York: Doubleday, 1984), and in the memoirs, poems, and novels of Vietnam veteran writers. For an example of the latter, see Tim O'Brien, *The Things They Carried* (Boston: Houghton Mifflin, 1990).

6

Seawillow Chambers
Soldier's Wife

William J. Brinker

In a 1989 interview project with Putnam County, Tennessee, Vietnam veterans and their wives, Seawillow Chambers, a new bride at the time her husband was sent to Southeast Asia, remembered the crucial early days of her marriage with honesty and frankness. She had married hastily, having but a few weeks with her husband before he went to war. She reported that she felt cheated of what she believed a typical young bride experienced—a romantic first year exploring and learning to know one's mate. Although she "patriotically" accepted the appropriateness of her husband's decision to answer the nation's call to duty, her understanding of the war was minimal at best. Her concerns, by and large, lay elsewhere. During his time in Vietnam, she found some degree of security in her own family but had no young women friends in whom she could confide. Thus, she spent his Vietnam year psychologically alone. Remembering a visit with her husband in Hawaii on his rest and recuperation (R and R) leave, Seawillow told a moving story of their brief reunion, recalling how she felt as if she had encountered a stranger. She returned to Tennessee while he returned to Vietnam and safely finished his tour. They were finally reunited, but the lingering influences of his and her separate experiences affected their relationship until her death in an automobile accident in 1991. Although her husband served in Vietnam for "only" one year, Seawillow Chambers's entire adult life was affected by that war in distant Southeast Asia.

Her story is retold here by William J. Brinker, who conducted the oral history interview. He is a professor and chair of the Department of History at Tennessee Technological University, Cookeville, and serves as the editor of the *SHAFR* (Society for Historians of American Foreign Relations) *Newsletter*. He received a Ph.D. from Indiana University and specializes in U.S. diplomatic and East Asian history. He is also the editor of *A Time for Looking Back: Putnam County Veterans, Their Families, and the Vietnam War* (1992).

Late in World War II, James Henry Malone was stationed on Staten Island, New York City. Newly married, he and his wife, Geraldine ("Gerry"), soon had their first son. At war's end, he returned to civilian life and began a long, slow climb out of relative poverty. The family lived in Alcoa, Tennessee, on a dead-end street in an almost

Courtesy of William J. Brinker

entirely African American neighborhood. James drove a truck for the city of Alcoa before becoming a city fireman and later supervisor of the city's sanitation department. The Malones had a second son and then, late in July 1948, a daughter. James gave his new daughter an unusual name: She was to be Seawillow, named after an old family friend. While James was slowly making progress at his job with the city, Gerry was a homemaker, busy raising the three children. When Seawillow was eleven, the family income allowed a move across town into a more comfortable house in a white neighborhood.

Site of major facilities of the Aluminum Company of America, Alcoa was a small, prosperous, working-class community about ten miles south of Knoxville. During the immediate post–World War II years, growing up in Alcoa meant being inculcated with what would now be dubbed "family values." The Malone family was politically conservative, practicing the then-dominant civic virtues of stability, patriotism, and duty—patterns that were familiar and expected in the 1950s. Secure in this mode, the Malones stayed, and prayed, together. When the children were very young, James would take them and their mother to church, drop them off, and return home. He then began staying for services and gradually became a committed believer and eventually a deacon in the Alcoa Central Baptist Church. Hence, he and his children developed their formal religious conviction at the same time, perhaps intensifying the youngsters' ties to their church, and his two sons eventually became Baptist ministers. Seawillow remembered that her father "raised us all to be very independent, very strong." As the children moved through the school experience, they were involved in circles of friends, sports, and church. As was common in mid-twentieth-century American families, all three were given piano lessons; in her case, Seawillow said, they "didn't take."

James, now deceased, was described by his children as having been "strong," with a suggestion of being a strong-willed and stern man who was uncomfortable showing affection. According to one of Seawillow's brothers, only after their father physically disciplined his children would he reassure them of his love. This characteristic weighed heavily on his daughter, who, according to her siblings, inherited some of her father's traits. Although popular and attractive, Seawillow as she grew to maturity, doubted that her accomplishments really pleased her father. It was her mother, Gerry, who furnished the emotional support needed by the growing children.

In high school, Seawillow was an academically average student. She was chosen to be on the cheerleading squad and was team captain in both her junior and senior years. She was active in church youth activities, culminating with being crowned "queen" in Acteens, a Baptist girls' missions organization. In addition to school and church activities, she did a little modeling for a Knoxville department store. Predictably, she had a steady stream of male admirers. In the summers, she worked at a community swimming pool, where she first met a crosstown high school athlete who was a few years older. A fondly remembered family story has it that on their first meeting, this young man, Ron Chambers, told Seawillow that he would marry her. Three and a half years later, he did.

Seawillow and Ron dated while she finished high school and took a year of secretarial training at Knoxville Business College. During this time, he was a lackadaisical student in prepharmacy studies at East Tennessee State University and a more interested drummer in a rock band. These were the years of the large buildup of American involvement in Vietnam, and draft boards were processing young men into the armed services. Ron was well aware he might be called for military service at any time. A tragic auto accident involving a close friend caused him to reassess his life. According to Seawillow, a kind of guilt or shame over his lack of interest and effort in his university studies and his participation in the rock-and-roll scene led him to a significant and abrupt change. At the time of the accident the friend (who recovered) was going home to participate in a weekend religious revival, whereas Ron was going to Knoxville to help open a nightclub. Seawillow remembered that Ron made a spiritual decision at that time; he "just felt like the direction his life was going was not the way that the Lord had intended it." He told her that he was considering volunteering for the army.

In the spring of 1967, these two young people made a decision that would affect the rest of their lives. Youthful arrogance and ignorance had captured them both and, coupled with an inbred sense of morality, made his entering the military at the height of the Vietnam War seem natural and proper. Seawillow, then eighteen, "had no problem with it." She had been raised in what she called a "strong" background.

> I felt a very strong sense of him doing what he needed to do for his country. I supported him in that decision. It did not matter to me. . . . I didn't think too much about what was going on in the world. . . . And I guess I thought there might be a possibility [of Ron going to Vietnam], but I just always thought that that's part of a man's responsibility to his country, to serve in whatever capacity it was.

Once the decision was made, Ron reported for basic and then advanced training at Fort Benning, Georgia. While in Alcoa on a weekend leave, he and Seawillow became engaged. On his return to the training camp, their long-distance relationship continued, and they talked of marriage. If he received orders for Vietnam, Ron wanted them to wed before his departure. The possibility of being killed was in his thoughts, and he hoped that he might experience as much of life as possible while he could. Seawillow accepted his wishes, and they began to plan a wedding. Her family was actively supportive of the young couple and their plans. Soon after, toward the end of Ron's advanced individual training, he received orders for Vietnam and was granted three weeks of leave. He returned to Alcoa, where he and Seawillow had a traditional church wedding, with white gown, attendants, and flowers. Following the ceremony and reception, the couple went on a short honeymoon in Florida. Returning to Alcoa, they stayed briefly at his sister's home, which was vacant at the time. Seawillow later recalled:

> We did have some time to ourselves, . . . but that doesn't constitute a marriage. I'd been married for three weeks, and that was great, then all of a sudden, that stopped. It's like I built up nineteen years to that point, and then I've got to shut that door again. And so, for those months [following] I was living in limbo. I was neither married nor single. . . . I think it was a mistake that we got married before he left because that messes you up, or it did me. . . . It didn't affect Ron as much . . . things were different . . . he had the effects of the war, but as far as . . . well, women are emotional, so you talk. . . . Everybody talks about their first year of marriage, how special it was. Well, I feel robbed because I felt like we never had that first year. When he came back from Vietnam, it seemed like we'd been married for five years instead of one year.

Seawillow was but one of many women from whom war stole the anticipated romance and excitement of late adolescence and early adulthood. Many girls and young women of her generation were trained to believe that these years were the high point of life. Instead, war took away their beaus and husbands, the excitement of dating, and the exploration of their own and their spouses' emotional and physical needs and responses.

At the time of her marriage, the young bride was employed in the offices of a small manufacturing plant in Knoxville, and after Ron left, she continued working there and living in her parents' home. Looking back, she saw that this further complicated her thinking and her development. "Still living at home with Mom and Dad . . . I never did get to break from one role to another. Basically, I was still [their] little ol' girl."

Wives of absent servicemen often experience financial difficulties, but for Seawillow that was not the case. Living at home, working in a good job, driving Ron's fairly new car, and having additional money sent home by her husband meant that she had few material concerns.

First time in my life I'd ever had a car to drive of my own, so that was a lot of fun. And first time in my life I'd ever had any money to speak of. I'd always [had] little part-time jobs. . . . So I was buying what I wanted to and doing what I wanted to because I had no rent or any responsibilities. . . . It was great. It was glory for me. I thoroughly enjoyed it.

She learned firsthand, however, that having money and managing it wisely were not the same thing.

I did run out of money because I wasn't used to handling or budgeting money. I do remember my girlfriend and I running out of money, pooling our money to go and share a piece of pie at a drive-in with a glass of water because we didn't have enough money between us.

Seawillow's memories of the drive-in are revealing. Although somewhat past their heyday, drive-in restaurants were still a major focus of socializing among America's youth in the late 1960s. Cruising these eateries in a showy car, being seen, seeing others, and perhaps even ordering something to eat were high on a young person's list of things to do. Seawillow and her girlfriend had not grown beyond that phase. Remembering, she continued:

Doing that was just a ploy of not going home. See . . . that's part of how I adjusted during that year. We just didn't want to go home. So we'd do anything . . . to keep from going home to the loneliness and the emptiness of being by ourselves.

Some months later a longtime male friend returned to town, further complicating her situation. She readily agreed to meet the old school chum for dinner, and the young man confessed his love for her and his desire that they marry. Distraught, she returned home and tearfully described her confusion and turmoil to her mother. Mother and daughter talked of loneliness and vulnerability. Seawillow then reaffirmed to her mother that it was Ron whom she loved.

At that point in her life, she would have benefited from sharing her feelings with someone in a similar situation. She did have one good friend whose husband was in the army, but he was stationed in Panama, not a war zone. The two women "never discussed particulars of it." She had "no one to identify with . . . unless they had had a spouse that had been in World War II," and that was of little help. Years later, she realized that there must have been other wives with husbands in Vietnam living in her community, but she "wasn't exposed to them." She neither sought out such women nor felt encouraged to do so: "I was by myself, basically. So I didn't seek out anybody." At the time of her interview an older and wiser Seawillow said, with some regret, "I would do that now. I would have the insight to do that, to seek out somebody or call and say, 'How could I get in touch with another wife, so that we can have a common bond?'" At the time, however, it was in her heritage to tough things out on her own.

Seawillow's youth and immaturity partly account for her lack of knowledge about or even interest in the Vietnam War. Although her husband was in Southeast Asia, she remembered that

> when you're nineteen, the world is rose-colored, and you just don't think about the seriousness of it. . . . I was still more or less involved in what teenagers do, . . . going to movies or going shopping. Just staying busy.

But as a young wife whose husband was in Vietnam, she did react to the tumultuous events of 1967 and 1968. War protesters and draft evaders raised her ire, for she supported the U.S. effort.

> Now we know it didn't accomplish much, but we had to do what we had to do at the time, thinking that we were doing the right thing. . . . I had the feelings that if I were a man, I would have wanted to go and serve my country. I had that strong male input into my life. . . . I have more that side than the weaker, female side. . . . I feel very strongly about it, and anybody that did protest the war or go to Canada to avoid the draft, I don't have very much respect for. I feel if their family can afford for them to evade the draft . . . it just gives you sort of a sick feeling. Especially if you know that someone that you love, a family member, is putting their life on the line. I guess I think of them as a weaker person because they don't have that sense of responsibility for their country and fighting for freedom. It's just not fair in a lot of ways. You don't think that they would go to that extent to avoid . . . what I was raised to believe is a responsibility in life. That if we go to war, we fight. The men go to battle.

She did, of course, know something of what Ron was enduring in Vietnam. For instance, she was fairly certain that he spent about eight months as a squad leader at a firebase in the Central Highlands, near Pleiku. He wrote that "he fired a 4.2 mortar . . . and that they would be fired upon, but he was mostly in a firebase and he wasn't experiencing hand-to-hand combat." She knew, however, that the likelihood of combat remained because in another letter, he said that he and his squad had been scheduled to go into the field but that due to a last-minute change in plans, another squad actually went. In fact, he happened to be standing behind a radio operator at the base when a message came in that he had been hit. He wrote her about his reaction at the time: "No, no, I'm here, I'm here."

Seawillow recalled that learning of that incident "sort of scared us because if he hadn't been at the right point at the right time, the message might have gotten back to the United States that he was dead or missing in action. So we were real thankful for the way it happened and process it went through."

Even after hearing of her husband's chance avoidance of tragedy, the young wife resisted thinking seriously about the war. She realized, though, that her resistance was no longer attributable to youth or immaturity but was, in part, a psychological defense mechanism.

> I guess at that point, I didn't really care, or even realize what the United States was even involved in, in depth, . . . of what was going on. My main concern was him, and him getting back. I've talked with and shared with other wives of veterans, and we all shared that the first three months, you're scared to death, you're afraid they're going to get killed. And the last three months, you think they're going to get killed. Particularly the last month, the last week, because it happens all the time during their tour, that's usually the most times that it does. So in between times, you're more or less numb. And you're just trying to keep the letters rolling. To keep the support going. But as far as what the United States was doing . . . I don't remember being involved in that because I was just busy trying to keep busy.

Ron spent the last three months of his tour near Pleiku, working with the Montagnards—the primitive tribal people who inhabit the highland regions of Vietnam. Of this experience Seawillow recollected little, again perhaps reflecting a conscious and unconscious blocking of the war.

By chance, Ron escaped involvement in the Tet Offensive, but after the worst of it had run its course in March 1968, he secured R and R, and Seawillow arranged to meet her husband in Hawaii. For her the trip to Honolulu was filled with anxieties over the adventure of traveling by herself and of meeting a man she had not seen in eight months. Looking back, she told of the kindness of strangers who befriended her en route:

> I'd never flown on an airplane when I went. I boarded the Knoxville plane . . . and we flew to Chattanooga and Atlanta. I change[d] flights in Atlanta. I had never done that in my entire life. I was petrified. Here, this little green person was experiencing all of this, and I thought, "What will I do? Well the Lord takes care of us little dumb animals that wander around by ourselves. These [military] career wives saw me, and they must have seen green written all over my forehead. They asked me if I was an army wife and if I was going to Hawaii to meet my husband. I told them I was, and they said, "Come go with us." They got my ticket changed, got me on my

flight, and . . . took me under their wing. . . . I never would have made it. I probably would have missed the flight somewhere along the way. But when we got in Los Angeles, I wouldn't have known, but they knew that when we got to one part of the airport, we had to literally run to the other end of the airport to meet our flight. If I hadn't been with them, I would have missed it at that point. So we flew . . . to Honolulu. When we got there, I'd never ridden in a taxi. They hailed a taxi and two or three of us went together. I was hoping someone would be in the same hotel. . . . Nobody was, so they took me to my place, where I got out [at] this fifteen-, sixteen-story hotel. Never seen anything like that in my life. I went in and got my room, and I think, "What will I do until three o'clock in the morning?" I had to meet [Ron] at three. Luckily, I was across the street from the international marketplace, and I went over there and got me some supper. When, having an unusual southern accent, I asked for a hamburger, the guy asked me where I was from. I said, "Tennessee," and he said, "I thought so." I had to go and went back to my room and had them give me a call for the middle of the night so I could be up.

The hotel arranged for a taxi to take her to the R and R Center to meet her husband, and thereby, Seawillow found herself in another situation that aroused her anxieties:

Well, in the middle of the night, me . . . nineteen years old, never been to a strange place in my life, had to get a taxi. It was a black taxi driver! I was terrified. I didn't know whether he would take me where I would need to be or [whether] he would take me somewhere else and kill me or whatever. . . . I sat in that back seat, froze.

This episode is both surprising and significant on several levels. In her interview some twenty years after the event, she prefaced this part of her story by noting that "being raised in the fifties and sixties [meant being exposed to] a lot of prejudice. And [I] was not used to a lot of integration at that time. They integrated my high school my junior year." Just why she was so racially conscious and fearful is uncertain. Perhaps the mores of the community she lived in from the age of eleven onward fostered her fear, overcoming her early childhood experiences in a black neighborhood. Perhaps her prejudice was the product of being a young white person in a small Tennessee town in the early 1960s, when the civil rights movement and the tensions associated with it were sweeping the nation. Another possible explanation was offered by her husband. He had been told that when Seawillow was a child, her father fell into a violent rage when he saw her walking with a black neighbor boy— sending a powerful message that black boys and white girls were not to associate in any way.

The incident involving the Honolulu taxi driver raises yet another perplexing issue. What in Seawillow's background would cause her to enter a taxi driven by a man, any man, of whom she was terrified? Did she have no choice but to walk into what she perceived as a dangerous situation? Could she not say, "No thanks"? Was her encounter with the taxi driver part of a pattern, as in her hurried marriage, of doing things she really did not want to do?

In any event, to her enormous relief, the black driver delivered her at her destination. But once there, she did not know what she was supposed to do; she had no further information. She entered a large building where busloads of soldiers were arriving. She sat and watched. "I'd see one after another, and I never could see him. Then finally, . . . this strange person came over and grabbed me. . . . It was Ron." After debriefing, they were free to go, but another adjustment was imminent.

Seawillow remembered returning to the hotel she was staying at and walking down a hallway:

> I had the strangest feeling. I thought, "Here, I'm going to a hotel room with a man I barely know." We'd been apart for eight months, and I'm supposed to respond to this man and be his wife again. . . . Everything was so strange. My mind was just so messed up because I'd had so many shocks to my system. . . . To him, there was no adjustment period because I was "The World," I was home, and he was at home because I was familiar. [But] he was the unfamiliar, and everything around me was unfamiliar. So it took us until the next day to get where, you know. Meeting in the middle of the night, and your days and nights and everything mixed together. . . . I do remember the strangeness of the whole situation at that time.

They spent about three days in Honolulu. She was unsure how to count the days exactly, in part because he arrived in the very early morning and, some days later, left at night.

For Seawillow, the adventure of returning home lay ahead. She telephoned a woman named Renate with whom she had traveled to Hawaii. Luck would have it that Renate was booked on the same flight. Comforted by traveling with a friend, she got under way. Once in the air, however, Seawillow became sick—sick enough to be moved into the first-class compartment, where she rested and was nursed by Renate and a flight attendant for the entire flight. She attributed her illness to nerves and quickly recovered after reaching home and being on solid ground. All in all, the events and emotions of her Hawaiian trip loomed large in her mind even twenty years later, and, indeed, there was much there for her to work through at the time.

Three months later, in August 1968, Ron returned safe and sound from Vietnam. On his first day home in Alcoa, his parents held a "welcome home" celebration. Understandably, the reunited couple wanted to be alone on their first night together and arranged reservations at a local motel. Shortly after checking in to the motel, they were surprised by a knock on the door. On opening the door, they were greeted by the motel manager, who began telling them that the motel had a policy of not allowing a man and a woman with local addresses to stay at this respectable establishment. Forestalling any demand that they leave, Ron explained that he had just returned from Vietnam and that they were a married couple. More than a little embarrassed, the manager welcomed them and wished them a good night.

A little more than six months of Ron's two-year army obligation remained at the time of his return from Vietnam, and he was assigned again to Fort Benning. This time, Seawillow quit her job, and they prepared to move to the base. A married couple who had been among Ron's high school friends in Alcoa were living in a trailer park in Fort Mitchell, Alabama, close to Fort Benning, and they found a nearby trailer for Ron and Seawillow.

Physical and social isolation, mindless and automatic household chores, boredom, and loneliness set the tone of Seawillow's life over the next months. Living in a trailer in Fort Mitchell was a difficult adjustment:

> Fort Mitchell, Alabama, is a very desolate place. . . . It's the end of the world; there's nothing there. They got us a trailer so we just took the bare necessities in a little U-Haul. . . . So that was easy for us not to have to look for housing. . . . So we just drove to that [trailer park that] had a little bitty grocery store across the road, and that was it for miles and miles and miles. [The store] was not a very clean place; it was a very rough grocery store. So if I ran out of any food, I had to go there. That was the only part of civilization that there was out there.
>
> My biggest thrill of the day was going to the mailbox to see if there was any mail, washing every day and hanging out clothes, [doing] his uniforms, and mopping. I did a lot of mopping and waxing, kept a real clean trailer. There was nothing else to do.

Curiously, Seawillow was not able or willing to form a close friendship with the other Alcoa wife at the trailer park. Her recollections reflect her need for a relationship in which she would be looked after, not one between equals.

> I couldn't really spend much time with the other couple because right after we got there, about a month or so, she had a new baby.

So I didn't feel like I could spend much time with her because she was too busy to trouble with me.

So, without human distractions, Seawillow grasped at the little things that were available to pass the time.

The TV program I watched at that time was *Dark Shadows*, a soap opera–type thing, but it had to do with werewolves and vampires. I had no telephone, just had that little TV. I put together picture albums.

Her one salvation was Ron. They were, after all, finally together, even if he was absent all day. When he returned home from the base, she recalled,

I'd say, "Let's go to the mall." There was a mall in Columbus, Georgia, which wasn't far. . . . This was just when malls were beginning to come into being. [I'd say,] "We don't have to buy anything. Just get me in the car and let me ride somewhere."

[At other times, we] did go to the commissary, and we would get two buggies and fill them full. We'd buy groceries once a month, which now I cannot imagine. . . . Between times, we'd get milk and things like that in the little store across the road.

Ron must have recognized a kind of desperation in his wife, for shortly after arriving at Fort Benning, he bought a small motorcycle to ride to the base each day, leaving his car for her to use. Seawillow now had wheels, but that did not give her what she had hoped for and needed. "I still . . . had no money, no friend, no way. I never did really go anywhere."

Occasionally, she did some grocery shopping alone, and she remembered vividly one visit to the commissary and its consequences. She also recalled that the army had many forms and many regulations that, if not followed correctly, might cause problems.

Being the little green person that I was, you had to stamp your checks in a certain way before you went into the commissary. So I had [Ron's] check from the army. So this guy, it was a black man again, and he was very rude, said, "Well, you stamped this way and this way, front and back." Well, I did what I thought he told me to do when I first went in there. [However,] I wasn't supposed to stamp a government issue check on the front. . . . And that meant we were out of money. We had no money until they could reissue us another check. So pandemonium went. I can't remember now whether we had to wait a month or just a few weeks or something . . . but that was another biggie in the life of a young wife.

Once she had use of the car, she could have made her life more pleasant and less lonely by getting a job, but she chose not to take that road.

> There wasn't any purpose in me trying to do anything. No one would hire me for that. You know, at that time, there wasn't a lot of fast-food places. I probably could have done it and not told them, but as honest as I was, particularly in those days, if I would have told them I was only going to be here seven months, they wouldn't have hired me.

She didn't fully realize how much her inactive social life and the boredom of trailer living had affected her until her mother, father, and sister-in-law traveled to Alabama to see her. Their visit occasioned an outpouring of suppressed feelings.

> I wasn't raised in a real affectionate home where we did a lot of hugging and kissing. But as soon as I saw them pull up, I burst out the front door and ran and hugged them and grabbed them, and I knew then how lonely and what I had been experiencing at that time. . . . I didn't realize how empty . . . it was. It was a big shock to my system.

Visits from family and the realization that Ron's military commitment was running out led the couple to finish formulating plans for their future. Ron had long since abandoned thoughts of becoming a pharmacist, and Seawillow had never planned a professional career; she had secured her secretarial degree, and for her, "that was it." A typical young woman of the 1950s and early 1960s, she had never been encouraged to consider a career. Her business school training was intended to bridge the gap between high school graduation and marriage. Seawillow really wanted nothing other than to be married, have children, and be a homemaker.

While in Vietnam, Ron had decided that he wanted to work with young people—to try to influence them and help them form their lives. His obvious choice was to become a teacher and a coach. This goal required, however, that he finish his university education in a new academic major. For Seawillow, that meant that she would need to work.

On his release from the army, Ron enrolled at Tennessee Technological University. The newly civilian couple lived in the school's married student housing, and while Ron attended classes, Seawillow first worked at a finance company. Shortly, the busy couple became the parents of a son, making their lives a bit more hectic. Ron eventually got a job teaching and coaching at the local junior high school, and their family grew to include a daughter and, finally, twin boys.

For several years, Seawillow was able to be the wife, mother, and homemaker that had been her dream.

Through those years, Seawillow believed that she and Ron complemented one another.

> Ron is a very positive person, and he's able to look at life very positively. He finds the good things. . . . As far as the effects of the war, . . . nothing . . . altered his personality or changed his attitude toward me or his children that you hear about—veterans, where they had abused, were abusive or anything. He's never been that way. . . . He looks at life positively and through spiritual eyes.

By contrast, she described herself as a pessimist who came from a negative home environment.

> So we brought together two very strong forces. Him 150 percent positive; me 150 percent negative. So then you clash the two together. He's helped me, and I've pulled down his ego a little bit, you know. But that helped him.

Seawillow eventually went back to work in a satisfying job as an elementary school secretary. Although she also had four children to care for and a house to maintain, she found time to enjoy crafts and to play an active role in the family church. She supported her husband in his coaching duties, attending his games and taking charge of things at home when he was frequently at practice and on scouting trips. To make ends meet, Ron usually had an additional part-time job. Sadly, Ron and Seawillow's life together ended prematurely, for she was killed in a car accident in 1991 at the age of forty-three.

One recurring theme in her interview in 1989, some twenty years after her husband's return from Southeast Asia, was her enduring resentment that the Vietnam War had taken her husband so abruptly from her. As she put it:

> When Ron and I were talking about me coming [for the interview], we were talking about the effects [the war] had on us, our life, and the biggest thing I could think of [was] I had said many times that I think it was a mistake that we got married before he left because that messes you up, or it did me. . . . In the days that I grew up, you saved yourself for the man that you married. . . . So I had saved myself for marriage to give myself to this man. So then after three weeks time, I've got to lock all that back up and store it away for another year, and then re-open that door again to be a wife to him again. . . . It's had its effect for many, many years on me.

Author's Note

In 1989, Seawillow Chambers agreed to an interview concerning her recollections of the time her husband served in Vietnam. She spoke about her late teenage years from the perspective of a mature woman. Her candor was especially significant in terms of her willingness to discuss her immaturity at that time—her self-centeredness, her lack of curiosity about the world and Vietnam in particular—and how, in some ways, the war and the absence of her soldier-husband had surprisingly little impact on her. In other ways, his absence during their first year of marriage cast a kind of shadow over her subsequent life.

Recently, several family members, including her mother, a brother, and her husband, graciously complemented and corroborated her account. Seawillow's death in 1991 prevented her own clarification or elaboration of her interview. We are left, principally, with her story of a young woman whose experiences may well have paralleled those of numerous other young women of the Vietnam War era. I have strived, as much as possible, to let Seawillow tell her own story. The quotations are all from her oral interview.

Suggested Readings

Although there are few published accounts like that of Seawillow Chambers, she shared much with the women included in Brett Harvey's *The Fifties: A Women's Oral History* (New York: Harper-Collins, 1993). For reading on women during World War II, see D'Ann Campbell, *Women at War with America: Private Lives in a Patriotic Era* (Cambridge, Mass.: Harvard University Press, 1984), and Judy Barrett Litoff and David C. Smith, eds., *American Women in a World at War: Contemporary Accounts from World War II* (Wilmington, Del.: Scholarly Resources, 1996). Portions of the following works are also relevant: Peter Karsten, *Soldiers and Society: The Effects of Military Service and War on American Life* (Westport, Conn.: Greenwood Press, 1987); Aphrodite Matsakis, *Vietnam Wives: Women and Children Surviving Life with Veterans Suffering Post-Traumatic Stress Disorder* (Kensington, Md.: Woodbine House, 1988); and Patience H. C. Mason, *Recovering from the War: A Woman's Guide to Helping Your Vietnam Vet, Your Family, and Yourself* (New York: Penguin, 1990).

7

Nancy Randolph, Army Nurse
"Ten Thousand Patients in Nine Months [and] All Downhill since Then"

William J. Brinker

Nancy Randolph volunteered to serve as an army nurse and spent a year, from October 1968 through September 1969, in Vietnam. While there, she served three months in a Vietnamese ward and thereafter worked in intensive care and recovery room settings. As might be expected, her experiences in Vietnam could not be duplicated in a nurse's career in the United States. In this combat setting, nurses accepted responsibilities that would have been denied them except in a war zone. She greatly expanded her skills and daily faced the tragedy and pathos of the wounded and dying. Only twenty-two when she enlisted, the harsh realities of Vietnam fostered a degree of cynicism and fatalism in her that effectively and abruptly ended her youth. Her return to the United States was not a smooth transition. Suddenly faced with army procedures that she found offensive, she soon left the military. Yet returning to the role of a civilian nurse was equally difficult. Civilian doctors were unable to accept that nurses had had the responsibilities that were commonplace in Vietnam. As a woman and as a nurse, Randolph has, with difficulty, adjusted and compensated for that momentous year in Southeast Asia.

William J. Brinker, of Tennessee Technological University, Cookeville, prepared this account of Nancy Randolph's Vietnam experiences from the oral history interviews that he and others conducted in 1989 with Vietnam veterans and their families in Putnam County, Tennessee. He published some of those reminiscences in *A Time for Looking Back: Putnam County Veterans, Their Families, and the Vietnam War* (1992), but Randolph's story and that of Seawillow Chambers in the previous chapter were not included in that collection.

Nancy Randolph traveled halfway around the world from Ravenscroft, Tennessee, a former coal-mining village about five miles from Sparta, to spend a tour of duty in Vietnam attached to the 312th Evacuation Hospital in Chu Lai. Little in her background prepared her for the year she spent as an army nurse in Vietnam. That year introduced her to wartime nursing practices

Courtesy of William J. Brinker

and responsibilities, many of which were far removed from those encountered in stateside nursing. Her Vietnam experience changed her as a woman and as a nurse, with lifelong consequences.[1]

Sparta is a small county seat in the midstate region between Knoxville and Nashville, each nearly 100 miles distant. Growing up in a rural and essentially isolated section of Tennessee meant being inculcated in conservative religious, political, and social values. Looking back, Nancy remembers her mother as a warm and caring woman, but her father was emotionally distant. She had two brothers and two sisters and was the youngest child. Alternately teased and pampered, Nancy grew up in a secure environment that allowed her to be both naive and tough but not so much of either to cause her problems after leaving home. The family lived a simple existence; there was no money to waste. For the children, there were no allowances, just money they occasionally earned themselves. That modest upbringing came in handy in Vietnam, where common creature comforts were often lacking. Over the years, Randolph frequently felt the pull of family, and she returned home for physical and emotional shelter when needed.

Asked when or why she decided to become a nurse, Nancy can give no clear answer. She cannot recall any definite moment or even an approximate time when she chose nursing as a field of study. According to her mother, she often played the role of nurse to her dolls. In any case, on graduation from high school, she enrolled in the nursing program at Saint Thomas Hospital in Nashville. At the time, a nurse's training commonly consisted of three years of study in a hospital; no college degree was required. But studying at Saint Thomas Hospital entailed significant expenses for food, lodging, and travel, and after two years, Nancy found herself in debt and fearful that she would be unable to finish her training.

A solution to her problem presented itself when army recruiters visited the hospital. They told her the Army Nurse Corps would pay for her remaining year of study in exchange for her accepting an army commission, which meant she would finish the third year of training and serve two years on active duty. Nancy sought advice from her parents. Her mother supported her plan to enlist, but, to her surprise, her father, a World War II veteran, balked at the idea. He failed to make clear the exact nature of his apprehension. In frustration, Nancy pointed out that he could only delay her decision because she would accept the commission over his objections on becoming twenty-one, only a few months hence. He reluctantly agreed to her plans, with one caveat: She should not accept an assignment to Vietnam. Nancy readily agreed and signed on the dotted line.

It was not by deceit that she had agreed to her father's terms, for Vietnam was unreal to her and thus not somewhere she might be sent. In spite of the growing domestic opposition to America's involvement in the Vietnam War, Nancy, like many young Americans in the middle of the 1960s, was largely ignorant about the conflict in Southeast Asia. In retrospect, she confesses surprise that she had little inkling that by accepting a nurse's commission, she might be sent to a war zone. A youthful concern only for the immediate and the personal and a naive trust in her own immunity from harm took this Tennessee woman on a course that led her into America's war in Vietnam.

Having agreed to the army's terms, Nancy finished her training at Saint Thomas Hospital, passed the state board examinations, attended her commissioning, and headed for Fort Sam Houston, Texas. There, she completed six weeks of officer basic training. Many doctors and other medical personnel were trained on the base, and men outnumbered women. Nancy remembers those weeks as a period of serious training interspersed with an active social life.

From Fort Sam Houston, she was assigned to Fort Gordon, Georgia.

> I spent one year at Fort Gordon—all working on the orthopedic wards—much to my dismay at first. I had already decided I would not like it, so I spent the first three months trying to get transferred. No such luck. During this time, I also learned to love taking care of the orthopedic patient. Ninety to 95 percent of the patients I cared for while at Fort Gordon were Vietnam veterans with injuries and oftentimes amputations—both of the body and soul. While at Fort Gordon, I learned what it was like to give more than was necessary, so to speak. I loved those guys with all my heart. They reciprocated. They broke the rules, and I covered for them. They went home on pass and came back brokenhearted—I listened. They tried to kill themselves while I was on duty—I helped revive them. They became addicted to Demerol, and I tried to wean them. They were sent to the VA [Veterans Administration hospital], and I received letters. And they tried to talk me out of going to Vietnam. They had that in common with my daddy. I didn't listen to either of them. It was not a choice that I had to make; it was something I had to do.
>
> At the end of my year at Fort Gordon, one by one, my friends were receiving orders for Vietnam. It made you feel guilty every time another set of orders came down and your name wasn't on it. And you wondered *why* them and not you? I decided, if I was in the army and the true army nurse that I should be and was, I needed to go to the war just like everyone else. I put in a request for transfer. . . . I received orders for Vietnam within three weeks of my request.
>
> I must say that I believe there were more reasons than one for my decision to go to Vietnam. . . . I was curious. And when you are

twenty-two, glory presents itself in various ways. To be a combat nurse brought all sorts of visions to mind—few of what reality brought. And then, as I said, my friends were being sent. Peer pressure meant that I should go, too: peer pressure not from my friends but from within myself. And then what I had learned at basic—I was an army nurse, my job was to help conserve the fighting strength (the mission of the army nurses), the army and soldiers needed me.

With hindsight, she faults the army training for not preparing her for Vietnam. The wards where she worked gave her a "little insight as to the wounds [we would see] . . . except they were healed. You didn't see them when they first happened; the trauma you did not see. You just saw the result of it." In addition to the nursing experience, some preparation for service in Vietnam was provided by the army in 1968, but it was only halfhearted and poorly conceived. The personnel with orders for Vietnam were sent through what was called RVN (Republic of Vietnam) training. There everyone was put together. She remembers:

> There was no segregation as to my medical skills or anything. I was with the guys that were going to go out and fight. They had a village . . . set up . . . we had to go through, and they gassed us and fired weapons, and we saw where they [the enemy] were supposedly living. But no one ever talked to me about what I would have to do as a nurse.

Even the nurses at Fort Gordon who had returned from Southeast Asia were silent about their experiences. After Nancy received her orders to Vietnam, she asked several of these veterans to tell her what she would be doing and what things were like there. She remembers that "they had their answer down pat—'You'll see.'" Amazingly, "they offered no insight, nothing." Other parts of the military may have tried to prepare their personnel for service in Vietnam, but in Nancy's experience, "the medical branch didn't." Making matters worse, she discovered after receiving her orders for the 311th Field Hospital that "nobody [at Fort Gordon] even knew what that was. . . . Nobody'd ever heard of it, they didn't know where it was."

It is fair to say that the medical profession was, as late as 1968, still learning how to deal with battle casualties in Vietnam. Although significant medical advances had occurred in the Korean War, even more innovations were being utilized in Vietnam. In Korea, 22 percent of all the wounded died; in Vietnam that number fell to 13 percent. The mortality of hospitalized wounded in the Korean War was 4.5 percent; in Vietnam, it was 2.5 percent. Medical treatment was vastly different due to the ubiquitous use of helicopters in evacuating the wounded directly from the battlefield.

The speed with which they were delivered to hospitals and given effective treatment (often in less than one hour, sometimes within ten to fifteen minutes) meant that men who once would have died on the battlefield were given prompt medical treatment in modern facilities during the Vietnam War. Hospital staff members were treating men in hemorrhagic and traumatic shock. According to one account, "It was now frequent for patients to arrive at hospitals with no blood pressure, with a nearly halted circulation, with dramatic metabolic defects, but *who were still alive.*"[2] Incorporating new methods, equipment, and drugs was part of the learning process taking place in Vietnam.[3]

For physicians and nurses alike, practicing medicine in wartime requires reformulating assumptions based on what is practical, possible, and ultimately humane for patients who differ in significant ways from patients in a civilian and peaceful world. To begin with, the vast majority of the soldiers suffering from wounds are young men in the prime of life. They are physically fit and not suffering from the various infirmities of a random population. They are, to be sure, wounded, but the rest of their bodies may be functioning perfectly. There is some parallel with patients arriving in an emergency room, but even here, the differences with the uniformly young men wounded in battle are obvious.

About to advance her medical education, Nancy left Fort Gordon and went home for one last visit before heading to Vietnam. "Everything was fine until I had to tell my daddy good-bye, and then I just lost it completely. Cried all the way to Nashville. . . . I can't remember, to this day, being that hysterical [before]. It was like I'd let him down."

After flying from the United States, Nancy landed at Cam Ranh Bay and was taken to Long Binh, near Saigon, where the new arrivals assembled and "some guy wanted to know how many of the people in this group had orders to the 311th Field Hospital." Nancy, along with perhaps two others, put up her hand. He told her that the 311th was a prisoner of war (POW) facility and that women would not be sent there unless they were willing. It was time for a quick decision. Nancy decided, "Well, no, if I have a choice." Her orders were changed. Her trip to her new post was prolonged because the army was replacing its military currency. She spent five days at the coastal city of Da Nang and from there went to the 312th Evacuation Hospital in Chu Lai, which was to be her home for the next eight months.

Her welcome at the new unit was less than satisfactory. On arrival at the 312th, she was assigned a room in the male bachelor officers' quarters (BOQ) "because there were no rooms in the other one. I was the first girl put in the men's building, and they didn't necessarily think they were going to like that." After checking in at the hospital, there was no orientation: "It was just like . . . here's the new one. There was no meeting with the head . . . or chief nurse." Nancy was assigned to a ward having patients with "malaria, gastritis, skin diseases, and things like that, no wounds. And I worked there three weeks, which was very, very boring. And I don't mean [that] for the guys; they were very sick, but medically . . . there was not a lot to do. Kind of like a babysitter."

Coinciding with her arrival, the hospital staff began segregating the American soldiers and the Vietnamese patients. Nancy volunteered to work on the two Vietnamese wards, believing "anything will beat sitting . . . for twelve hours, you know, passing out pills." She got the new post and spent three months caring for the Vietnamese, a new nursing experience in more ways than one. The wards were designed for twenty-five patients each, but normally, they accommodated seventy-five to a hundred people "because all the family came with them!" In these wards the majority of the patients were civilians, but there were some South Vietnamese soldiers and some captured Vietcong soldiers and North Vietnamese Army (NVA) regulars. The VC and NVA had guards, but beyond that, they were not segregated. The patients, friend and foe alike, were in one large space; there were no screens, no curtains, and no rooms to separate anyone. Also, in the intensive care unit (ICU) and recovery rooms, there was no segregation at all, although, Nancy noted, "we did attempt to put the Vietnamese, especially the prisoners . . . in the back part of the ward, because we didn't feel that the American soldiers should have to wake up and look at the same face that put them there."

She recalls that the enemy wounded occasionally made the bad situation worse:

> It was very difficult to take care of them [the North Vietnamese prisoners]. Even though you're a nurse, and even though you're trained and you're supposedly compassionate and humane and all that stuff, he's also probably the guy that blew this GI's brains out that you've just got through wiping out of his ears. You know, you could not . . . stay removed from it. We had one, that I remember, that was supposedly a prize catch. He was hostile the whole time. He had an armed guard in ICU when he was on the respirator, and he was restrained in four-point leather restraints. He made threats against us and threats against the Vietnamese. We had a little Vietnamese girl that was like a nursing assistant that worked with us. While we were changing his dressing, she just started hysterically crying. He had said something to her, you know, in between being on and off the respirator or made some sort of threat that she understood. I remember a physician coming to her rescue and

taking the guy off the respirator and saying a few choice words whether in English or otherwise [that] I'm sure he understood. So there was some feeling against those people, even though they were patients. You couldn't help it. I would like to say that I have never seen or don't remember seeing any of the Vietnamese, whether they were civilians or prisoners, mistreated by the people that I worked with. We may not have been nice to them, and they may not have gotten a backrub every night.

Nancy felt differently, though, about the wounded Vietcong children in her ward.

Most of the Vietcong that I took care of were children. And I'm sure children can kill, too, but I just kind of looked down and thought, "God, do they know why or anything about it, or are they trying to get supper tonight?" You know . . . they were never offensive to us, they worked hard on the ward. They had jobs to do, so those I don't have any hard feelings against.

The 312th Evac was a four-hundred-bed hospital, some of whose physicians, nurses, corpsmen, and support personnel were army reservists called to national service. To Nancy's knowledge the arrangement was unusual in Vietnam. The reservists had arrived in Southeast Asia from Winston-Salem, North Carolina, in July 1968—about three weeks before her arrival. Most of the nurses, like Nancy, were regular army.

It was just really kind of funny because you had a group of people from Winston-Salem . . . totally removed from the military as I'd known it. But they were running it, so the army was played down, very much so. Military protocol went out the door . . . and stayed out the door because we were so busy medically. We didn't have time for it. [We] saw approximately ten thousand patients in nine months. . . . I ran across that information when I was up at the Pentagon. . . . Although that's not official, it's a good estimate.

The patient load required that the staff work twelve hours a day, six days a week. "And we did a good job, the patients had excellent care, and they [the entire staff] were a super group of people—perhaps the finest that I have ever known . . . anywhere. The intensive care unit had all the specialties, neural surgeons, chest surgeons, and all of that." Those civilians-turned-military medical personnel "were extremely professional in their jobs." Before being activated for Vietnam, some of the corpsmen and the people in personnel held a variety of nonmedical jobs and were "only medical when they were performing their reserve duties (and that's the same that we have now), . . . they weren't full-time medical."

After a short time, Nancy transferred to the intensive care and recovery wards. "I was twenty-two years old. I had had one year of nursing experience. In other words, I didn't know a whole hell of a lot. . . . I hadn't had any intensive care training." She remembers that the emotional stress was "the thing that stands out most." On the ICU ward "the wounds were [often] gross; these people were mutilated but yet they were awake. And there was not as rapid a turnover with patients as people probably thought there was." Some of the wounded spent lengthy periods in the ICU. "To me, one of the hardest things is they bring this kid to you, and you save his life, literally, in the hours when he first came in. Then you stabilize him, and if something goes wrong, you pull him out of that. Some ended up being with us three and four weeks." During that time "the emotional attachment between the nurse and the patient was just tremendous. You represented everything to them, you know. They were all in love with their nurses, so to speak, and you know, you ended up being their nurse, their mother, their sister, their girlfriend, their wife. You wrote their letters home, good or bad. . . . You saw them twelve hours a day . . . and you, literally, were probably one of the few good things that had happened to them in the war." And, of course, because of the nature of their wounds, sometimes "they would die on you" despite the best efforts of the medical team.

For Nancy, the role of nurse in the midst of war presented contradictions and confusions that defied resolution:

> The saddest thing I'd ever encountered after I'd been there a while [was] to see the human body and what war does to it. . . . We [the soldier and the medic] were so different, and this is one thing I don't know if people comprehend. When you send a medic to war, you're sending him to do something exactly opposite from what you train the soldier to do. The more people the soldier kills, the more medals he gets pinned on his chest. The medic can't kill. I mean not only can't, won't. It's not our job. It's not why we're there. So there we are. Our goal is to put them back together, and the goal of the war is to kill . . . and, and it gets your mind screwed up. How do you keep the thing separated?

The 312th did not have a lot of equipment. It had no computers and no "invasive monitoring techniques like in an ICU unit today. We only had one or two cardiac monitors in the unit, in ICU and in the OR [operating room], and they were used back and forth. The only invasive technique that we used was the central venous line," a very basic procedure by which a catheter is inserted into a major vein to measure body fluids.

On reflection, Nancy downplays the lack of sophisticated aids. "You don't want a lot of state-of-the-art equipment in a war, takes too much time to operate [it]. We had what we needed." She continued, "We didn't have a lot of capabilities of sterility, and we didn't practice sterility and sterile techniques as I was taught in school or as I know it today. For example, today, in America, you would never think of using a catheter on someone and then reusing it. We did it all the time. We soaked it in a red chemical, or we autoclaved it to sterilize. Today, you open one package and use it, and you throw what's left away. We did not do that in Nam. No."[4]

Fortunately, she recalls, the hospital was never short on narcotics. "[Patients] that were terminally ill because of wounds and/or infections were medicated around the clock, not on a PRN, that is, as you need it [basis]. They were medicated every four hours all the time once we knew they had no chance of surviving the wounds that they had received. We did not always have as many antibiotics as we needed because we used them so much." To her knowledge, however, the patients never endured "any pain that could be avoided."

Nancy found "the expectant category" one of the hardest things to handle. Patients in the expectant category were expected to die. She explained:

> You triage patients [sort patients by category or need] in mass trauma, whether it's stateside or war. And you triage them probably out in the field; the medic did. He knew which ones to try to get back and which ones to just give some morphine, and they, when they got to us, they were triaged again. We triaged them from the point of view of how much time it would take in the operating room versus . . . is it worth it? We didn't have the time to waste. Once the doctor triaged them, if they were put in the expectant category, . . . they were brought to the ward, and they were cared for—they were given a bed or a gurney or whatever. . . . They were medicated, and they were bathed if they were dirty. Their wounds were dressed, not in the manner that you would dress the living wound or the wound of someone that's going to live. They were cared for, but still, it was so sad just to put them behind a curtain and check them every so often so you could get the time of death right.

Patients in the expectant category usually lasted a few hours, but a few endured their injuries for longer periods. Nancy recalled one especially tragic soldier who had been a prisoner of the Vietnamese before being retaken by American forces.

> He came to us after a raid-type thing, with severe head trauma. His head had been beaten to a pulp. But he had these old wounds to his legs, fractured both legs, that had healed without being set, so they were just gross, grotesque. And the story is that the enemy had hit him when they heard the Americans were coming to keep him from making any noise. . . . They just beat him over the head and left

him. He was brought in unconscious . . . and certainly had no prognosis to live, but he wouldn't die either. We didn't know who he was, and that was just one thing that really touched my heart. To have a U.S. number on a patient that you're taking care of. He was with us about three weeks to a month.

The GIs always had the priority. . . . We never had to refuse any, and I think that speaks highly of our unit because we could have. I've seen . . . the beds full, in a twenty-bed ward, and litters lying under the beds to the point where you had to walk around them. So far as refusing them, we could have always, at some point in time, routed them to another hospital. . . . They may not have gotten real good care sometimes, simply because the load was so heavy. But if it came to giving one of the respirators to a patient, the GI would have always gotten it.

Concern for the fate of the patients never ceased, and nursing in the ICU wards meant frequently working in an atmosphere of crisis. She reflected: "Trauma nursing of that caliber is extremely exciting, even though it was a war. And it's, it's been all downhill since then."

In addition to the emotional highs and lows, nursing in these wards was hard physical work. Each intensive care unit contained twenty beds. On the night shift the ratio of patients to nurses could be ten to one. Two registered nurses and perhaps three corpsmen cared for anywhere from twenty to forty total-care patients. Even with the heavy work load, however, there was never any question regarding morale.

The morale of the whole hospital was tremendous. We had a big sign up in the ER [emergency room], something to the effect: "You are now entering the best hospital in the world." The morale among the staff . . . was probably passed on to the patient. You worked hard; you played hard. . . . You know they learned in a hurry that this was a team effort. . . . Hospital personnel went over and above to do that. I think for the patient's benefit as well as our own. We regressed quite a bit and went back to childhood games and, you know, squirting people with syringes and all this sort of things, to let off the tension.

Yet even things that might, in other circumstances, be helpful diversions from stressful work, things such as newspapers and television, sometimes had the opposite impact.

It was very depressing to see what we saw, day in and day out, and then pick up a newspaper, which we did get quite frequently— they were several days old when we got them—or see the news. The TV shows were several days behind, coming in. . . . It was very traumatic to see all of the anti-Vietnam things going on at home. . . . So, I tried to keep myself removed from that and have tried to maintain that throughout the years because I've never doubted what I did in Nam as being useful. I'm glad I did it. I know, from remembering the looks in the guys' eyes when I was taking care of them, that the service that I provided was invaluable.

When first arriving at Chu Lai, Nancy was rightly concerned about safety—the hospital's, the staff's, and her own. She wondered how to distinguish incoming and outgoing shells. She questioned experienced nurses, asking, "What does it sound like?" Their response was the familiar "you'll know." In time, she learned that they were correct. "You do know. You learn the sound, immediately, if it's coming at you or going away." For the medical personnel at Chu Lai, such sounds came very near. Located only a mile from an Eleventh Infantry Brigade base camp, the hospital itself occasionally came under enemy fire. "If I'm not mistaken, the hospital had three hits. . . . One time the rocket didn't go off, it was kind of a dud and [only] sputtered. It missed headquarters by five feet. . . . The second time, they demolished our sailboat. We were very upset about that. Some doc had brought a sailboat back from Japan, and there was nothing left of that." It was the third hit that confirmed that the hospital was in a war zone. "It was a Sunday morning, June 8th, between five-thirty and six. The rocket or mortar—I never knew the difference—made a big explosion." The incoming projectile hit the covered walkway between the two Vietnamese wards. "When I walked over, I'd never seen anything like that. There were live wires . . . smoke . . . and smells. . . . It was just a rubble. There were still people in the ward, and there were bodies. . . . Two or three Vietnamese were killed and several wounded." It took a long time to restore order and to treat the wounded. Some family members of the Vietnamese patients were injured, as well, "so we spent the majority of the day operating on those people." In the midst of the tragic results of the attack, two special incidents are vividly remembered.

Lt. Sharon Lane, a nurse and coworker, was killed, the only American female killed *by enemy action* during the war. Lane was working that night and resting on the edge of a bed during "a kind of lull time, [when] you've got the majority of your work done and you're waiting to finish it up. She never knew what hit her. Killed her instantly." Sharon's death intensely personalized the war for Nancy. Initially, in the chaos of the destruction, a kind of numbness set in, and Nancy remembers getting dressed and reporting to the ward for what became a twelve-hour shift. Slowly the reality of Sharon Lane's death permeated her thoughts. Nancy remembers experiencing the conflicting emotions of guilt and relief—guilt that it was not she lying dead and relief that she was alive. Other emotions, fear and anger, surfaced also, for Sharon's death meant that even nurses were not immune to attack and death.[5]

Years later Nancy composed a poem dedicated to all of the nurses who shared that day. Two stanzas of "We Went to Work" follow:

> We went to work—with a sadness of heart
> and a numbness of spirit
> because Sharon lay dead
> as we went to work.
> We went to work—with a profound sense of loss
> without time to mourn
> more wounded coming in
> no choice but to work.

Nancy also remembers that dreadful attack for another, not-so-tragic reason:

> We had this one little kid that we'd had to operate on, and when he woke up in recovery, which was where I was working, he was just wild from all of this trauma. He'd been in one explosion, why he was there at the hospital to start with, and now he was in another one. We tried to bring all these different people in to see who the kid belonged to, to try to pair them up because our interpreters were so busy with other things. The kid wasn't old enough to tell you, [he] was only about two. Well, he quit crying [when another] little boy came in. It calmed him down, so we assumed they belonged together. You know it was . . . probably the most emotional, traumatic day of my life. I know it was the most traumatic of Nam. And then we all went to work, just like nothing happened. What are you going to do? Can't go to the movies.

To be sure, movies or other distractions could not alleviate the anxieties and sorrows of the wards, but a special event might mitigate them or even prove that serving in a medical capacity in Vietnam was much appreciated. Nancy poignantly remembers Christmas of 1968.

> At Christmas time, Bob Hope came to Chu Lai. We had this huge amphitheater that sat right behind the hospital. And the troops had been coming in for five days before he was due. His guest that year was Ann-Margaret. And so they were coming, bringing their gunnysacks and their sleeping bags, all this stuff. They camped out down there for several days before he came. But we had reserved several of the first-row benches for some of the hospital patients, and we took the ones that couldn't walk down in ambulances. And, of course, the nurses were going down with them. I don't know how many thousands of people were in that theater, but it was a lot. And . . . we're moving some of the patients around. We had our backs to the stage, and we heard this just tremendous cheer, and they're

standing up and . . . we thought, "God, we're missing the show," you know, so we turned around, and there's nothing on the stage. It was the nurses, it was us, as we were bringing those patients in, that these guys were standing, cheering.

That brought tears to my eyes, and I still get cold chills when I think of that. And then, during that presentation before [Hope's] show was over, the entire group there stood and joined hands and sang "Silent Night." And, you know, that's one song that I just really have trouble with even today. Just to think, here we are . . . in the middle of a war, and it shouldn't be that way. It's quiet, there's no fighting, and . . . it's really hard to put into words those feelings of that.

The nurses of the 312th were special beings. They were American women in distant Vietnam, they were officers, and they were nurses. The army did its best to secure and protect them. In general the 312th was "a very closed unit, and we weren't allowed to travel that much because of all the hostilities." There were guards at the gates to the compound, and the nurses were supposed to be in by ten o'clock. Nancy noted, "Of course, that's absurd, especially when you're twenty-two. I mean, you know, who's going to do that?" So she and some of her friends traded some preventative medical supplies for an old ambulance, and after that,

> we came and went as we pleased. . . . And if you did it, you had to break the rules and run the chance of getting caught. And we did it all the time because what are they going to do to you? They already sent you to Vietnam. The only thing they could do was send you home, and we knew they weren't going to do that.

Nancy's travel horizons were expanded further through her boyfriend. He was a "dustoff" pilot, that is, a helicopter pilot who picked up wounded men during or immediately after a battle. "I never flew any missions with him," she recalled. "We would go up to Da Nang shopping because they had a better PX [post exchange] and make beer runs. You know, you could get hurt going to the PX on Coke and beer day—when those items were restocked." The 312th benefited from their Robin Hood and Maid Marian activities when they were able to "liberate" unused equipment from U.S. military installations. They would "steal air conditioners and things that we came across that we felt we needed more than the person who had left them there."

The nurses occasionally left the hospital compound on official business. Sometimes, Nancy did Medical Civic Action Programs (MEDCAPs), "which were little clinics for the Vietnamese village people, and I went to their schools to pass out some clothing and candy and things like that that my mother had sent. But I didn't actually see village life, and I certainly didn't see city life because Chu Lai was way out in the country." Like most military personnel, Nancy and her fellow nurses saw little of Vietnam. She never went to Saigon or the old resort of Vung Tau. "The pressure of work combined with the reality that this country was at war meant that you did your assignment and directly experienced little of the wider picture."

One exception to the parochial nature of serving in Vietnam were leaves and R and R breaks.

> They had it all set up where you could take five or six days' leave and then you had the seven-day R and R. . . . I had put in orders to take leave to go to Hong Kong [but] that was canceled because of casualties.

After about eight months in Vietnam, Nancy did spend a week in Hong Kong with another nurse. In addition to enjoying a break from the stress of nursing, of living in an uncompromising environment, and of doing without commonplace creature comforts, Nancy best remembers her week at the Hilton Hotel in Kowloon, across the bay from Hong Kong, as a brief, luxurious respite of warm showers, access to cosmetics, good food, and hotel service, in approximately that order.

After being with the 312th for about eight months, the Winston-Salem reservists returned stateside while the regular army nurses joined other units. Nancy served with the Ninety-first Evac, which was transferred to Chu Lai. However, she doesn't consider herself a member of the Ninety-first; she was "a member of the 312th because that's the unit I did most of my service with."

In 1969, Nancy finished her required two years of active duty. Because her terminal date came up in Vietnam, she was discharged directly from there. She flew from Cam Ranh Bay via Japan to the West Coast, where she "came through Seattle for the paperwork." Her return was anything but a heroine's welcome. She arrived at the airport near Seattle along with about five hundred GIs and one other nurse and was met by a first sergeant. He told the nurses that he did not know what they were supposed to do: He did not have beds for women, he had not been told that they were coming, and they could not get on the waiting bus. He told them to do whatever they thought necessary.

That the army, personified by the sergeant, cared so little about her situation left Nancy angry and disoriented. Being a lieutenant, she outranked him, but instead of ordering him to provide transportation and quarters, she simply watched him depart, leaving her in the middle of the airport "wearing . . . jungle fatigues." Left to their own devices the two women got a cab, found a motel room, and reported to Fort Lewis the next day.

At Fort Lewis, Nancy received a routine debriefing, a quick and extremely superficial physical examination, a recalculation of her pay records, and a discharge with an inactive reserve obligation. Officers at Fort Lewis were not sympathetic to the predicament she had faced the previous day on arrival at the airport. They suggested that she should have known what to do; a call to the nursing offices at Fort Lewis would have solved everything.

From Fort Lewis, Nancy went to visit her sister in Los Angeles before returning to Tennessee. Traveling in uniform, she felt she was "looked at quite sternly, in LA especially" but received no negative comments or signs. In fact, "[people] didn't talk to me at all!" Her sister, thinking to distract Nancy, took her to Disneyland. The distractions proved not to come from the Disney characters and fantasy but from watching all the people. "I was just kind of in a state of shock." When she had left the United States, the flower children "had begun to grow out in California"; now, she "came home to people with long hair and ragged clothes," and she was "just appalled."

On the flight from Los Angeles to Nashville, she encountered the only person who talked to her on her whole journey.

> The gentleman sitting next to me in the airplane asked what the patch on my arm meant. . . . When I told him, he just kind of looked at me real funny and said something to the effect, "Well, that must have been some experience." That's all he said, and he didn't elaborate.

Once she was back home, people seemed curious about her experiences, and she was willing to meet them halfway.

> I was still naive and thought they wanted to know, and I'd start to answer [their questions]. Before I got through, they'd just look at me kind of funny and say, "Really?" They weren't really interested, so then I just clammed up about it.

Nancy then lived in a separate apartment in her parents' home and worked as the director of nursing in the small county hospital in Sparta, which was a learning experience for her because she lacked any administrative background. Occasionally, she found herself becoming concerned with what she saw as less than a full commitment to patients. Her Vietnam experience had instilled a sense of attention to detail, and that, she felt, was sometimes lacking in the staff.

During the year, at home she made substantial progress in healing her ravaged emotions. It was a slow process, however, and she believed she needed something more, something different. She decided to go to southern California to visit her sister, whose husband was in the navy and often at sea. Retelling the story later, she realized that she was planning something more than a visit, for she had packed her car with most of her things, including her cat and her stereo.[6]

Nancy stayed with her sister for about three months. She then got a job working nights in intensive care and found her own housing. But a kind of restlessness began to surface, and she soon moved on to a new VA hospital in not-too-distant La Jolla, where she remained for about three years. She found comfort in the familiarity of intensive care nursing and for several years deliberately sought such jobs.

Nancy also found security in the anonymity of living and working in California. For over two years, she told no one that she had been in Vietnam: "It just seemed an easy solution." One day while at work, however, she noticed that a new nurse was being treated gingerly by the hospital staff. Inquiring about the new coworker, Nancy learned that she had just returned from Vietnam and, by implication, was something to be handled with caution. Overcoming her habit of keeping thoughts of Vietnam to herself, she asked the veteran where she had served. Curtly, the nurse said, "Chu Lai," in a dismissive tone that suggested that Nancy (or anyone else) could not possibly know what she was talking about. Nancy asked what unit she had been with; the answer came—the Ninety-first. When Nancy revealed that she, too, had served with that unit at Chu Lai, it was as if a wall had been breached; the two women formed a bond that has lasted to this day. Each had found another who understood, who had shared the joy and the pain of Vietnam. For both women, this chance meeting was enormously beneficial. The new friend credited Nancy for making her adjustment to stateside living possible.[7]

Nancy realizes that her own adjustment was furthered by their friendship as well, and although that process was essentially completed during those California years, it had not been easy.

> When I came home from Nam, it was difficult to play the boy-girl games, you know. It was difficult to come back into my age group and go to the discos and all that. After what I'd been through, it wasn't fun. It took me almost two years to see *M*A*S*H*. . . . Everybody was telling me about this movie, and I'm saying I don't think it's funny. Two years . . . and I went, and I laughed my head off. I certainly appreciated it. . . . It was a riot, and it was so true, just reminded me of so many things.

In 1973, when the American military finally withdrew from Vietnam, Nancy had mixed emotions. She was glad because all the nurses and all the GIs were coming home and because the war was over. Nonetheless, there was a tremendous amount of sadness, and what did we accomplish other than losing so many lives? We left Vietnam in worse shape than it was when we went over, I understand, or at least as bad. . . . And there were some of the Vietnamese people that truly wanted a different life, and I felt like we went over there and we promised them the world and then we say, "Hey, we can't stand this shit. We're leaving."

When her sister and brother-in-law were returning to Tennessee in 1975, Nancy, feeling that she, too, was ready to move on, returned with them. Once again, she lived with her parents and commuted to a nearby town to work.

Being back in the United States as a professional nurse has had its complications. The Vietnam nurses were good. You had to be good. You didn't have a lot of time. And nursing has been kind of a bore ever since. And that's another thing people don't understand. They don't understand my attitude. . . . I've always been good, and I've always been professional. I don't mean that to sound egotistical. I just am a good nurse. And I feel that the patients that I'm taking care of deserve that, but it hasn't been as much fun.

I came back to these rural counties, and I . . . have to ask permission to give an aspirin? Come on, give me a break, you know. Or I'd have to listen to some doc, egotistical asshole that he is, chew me out for whatever, after what I'd seen and done for a year, you know. I just didn't need it.

Within a year, she relocated. She was becoming a kind of professional nomad, frequently changing jobs when either boredom or dissatisfaction set in. Then the need for change began to abate. With a new job, a new apartment, and later a house of her own, Cookeville, Tennessee, became the closest thing to a permanent home for Nancy. Curiously, she had not distanced herself far from her roots; Sparta was only about fifteen miles away.

Ironically, in 1982, Nancy joined the Tennessee National Guard. At the time of her return from Vietnam and her discharge, she had not seriously considered remaining in the military as a career. But nearly fifteen years later, joining the guard seemed "the right thing to do." Being in the guard meant attending drills one day each month and fifteen days each summer. She enjoyed this reassociation with the military and saw this commitment as an easy way to earn additional money.

A decade and a half after the U.S. withdrawal from Vietnam, construction of the Vietnam Veterans Memorial got under way in Washington. Nancy was angry at first. She thought, "Why build it now? Fifteen years [later]?" Then, she read and thought more about it and realized that "America did not build it for the Vietnam veteran; the Vietnam veterans built it for the Vietnam veterans." In time, she went to Washington to see it.

> [I] was prepared to look at it and be able to tell people, "Yeah, I've seen it." But you can't do that. I couldn't do that . . . because all of a sudden, I was standing there with tears streaming down my face, not caring. I was there in 1985 in July, the Fourth celebration. There were thousands and thousands of people, and it was just like I was the only one there. The tremendous emotions. It took me back to Chu Lai. I'd see the guy's name that I had taken care of when he died. I'd see his face. I could tell you his last words. I could tell you the bed he was lying in and all that. And I just went down the wall, the panels, finding the ones that I could remember by name. And, you know, that in itself is sad because there's many patients I took care of I can't remember their names. I can remember their faces [but] can't recall their names. I can recall their nickname or their first name, but not their last. So the ones that I could find on the wall, it was just like, . . . it's so much more than a name, you know. . . . I can't tell you what it was like to go.

Meanwhile, her work at the Cookeville Hospital included an introduction to home care and to offering instruction in practical nursing. Although she found the teaching especially satisfying, she was still not entirely settled. Professionally, she realized that times had changed and that advancement would require having an undergraduate degree. Fortunately, Cookeville had a small university with a nursing school, enabling her to continue at her job and take classes when time allowed. To finance the schooling, she took a most interesting step. She assumed a six-year National Guard responsibility in exchange for getting her degree financed through a government program known by the acronym STRAP.[8]

The adage that timing is everything came into play for Nancy. No sooner had she committed herself to the six-year obligation than her entire 230-person guard unit was mobilized during the Gulf War. They were activated in December 1990 and told that their destination would be Europe. During two weeks at Fort Campbell, Kentucky, she learned that she would be assigned to a medical unit in Germany. The Tennessee guard unit was split, with some members going to Great Britain, some to Germany, and some elsewhere. Nancy went to Stuttgart for just over three months. Fortunately, the facilities there were not put to the test, for the success and speed of the U.S. war effort meant that there was little for the medical teams to do. Consequently, the staff gave care primarily to civilians and dependents of American military personnel stationed in Germany.

In March 1991, Nancy returned to Cookeville and held various jobs until finally finding that elusive position that would prove fulfilling. She presently works in a two-nurse outpatient program that offers diabetes education on either a one-on-one or a group basis. The clinic is assocated with a hospital about forty miles from her home in Cookeville and is owned by a large health care corporation. She likes the work and especially enjoys being largely her own boss. At least for the present, her life is good.

During the interview conducted in the late 1980s, Nancy responded to a question concerning what impact the Vietnam experience had on her:

> It made me a better person. It showed me, up front, at the ripe old age of twenty-two, what I could do without and still survive—what was important and what wasn't. I'm not a person of trivia.

In a more recent correspondence, she elaborated:

> I believe, for the most part, Vietnam made me a better person. It gave me an inner strength. But there have been times in the past thirty years and sometimes still when I feel such a sadness, such a loss. Sometimes I feel as if I don't belong—like a square that must fit into a round hole, and no matter what you do, you cannot make it fit. When I feel that way, I try to grasp that strength that is there and let it hurt without allowing it to overcome me.[9]

She later reflected further and listed the things that Vietnam had taught her. Among her thoughts were these words of hard-won wisdom:

> Don't take yourself so seriously. Ego is nothing but an enemy.
> Be self-reliant, no one owes you anything.
> A sense of humor goes a long way. Laugh—the load will be easier to
>   bear.
> The comforts we are accustomed to may be nice, but they are
>   nonessential.
> Live for and in today.
> Be true to yourself. People are going to believe what they want
>   regardless of what you say or do.

Most poignantly, she added:

> War is never the answer—the price to the innocent is always greater than to those who initiate it.[10]

Notes

1. In 1989, Nancy Randolph participated in a community history project that included interviews of veterans of the Vietnam War. Funded by the Tennessee Humanities Council, the project resulted in a museum display, a public television program, and an edited book—William J. Brinker, ed., *A Time for Looking Back: Putnam County Veterans, Their Families, and the Vietnam War* (Claremont, Calif.: Regina Books, 1992). Prior to her interview, Nancy had not talked publicly about the war for many years, and she gives credit to the project for helping her to deal with her experiences. For purposes of this chapter, she agreed to talk with the author in 1997 and augment the earlier interview. She also wrote a few pages of her thoughts in 1998. In this chapter, unless otherwise noted, the quotations are from the 1989 interview. Her 1997 conversations with the author and her written thoughts are cited in the notes that follow.

2. Robert M. Hardaway, *Care of the Wounded in Vietnam* (Manhattan, Kans.: Sunflower University Press, 1988), 30 (emphasis added).

3. Ibid., 12–13.

4. An autoclave is a steam-pressure device used to sterilize equipment.

5. This paragraph is based on conversations with the author from October to December 1997.

6. Ibid.

7. Ibid.

8. Ibid.

9. Written note given to the author in January 1998.

10. Written list given to the author in January 1998.

Suggested Readings

For more reading on women in Vietnam, especially military nurses, see Kathryn Marshall, *In the Combat Zone: An Oral History of American Women in Vietnam* (Boston: Little, Brown, 1987); Keith Walker, *Pieces of My Heart: The Stories of Twenty-six American Women Who Served in Vietnam* (Novato, Calif.: Presidio, 1985); and Lynda Van Devanter, *Home before Morning: The Story of an Army Nurse in Vietnam* (New York: Beaufort Books, 1983).

8

Bill Henry Terry Jr., Killed in Action

An African American's Journey from Alabama to Vietnam and Back

David L. Anderson

Bill Henry Terry Jr. was twenty years old when he was killed in action in Vietnam on July 3, 1969. Corporal Terry's name is one of the 58,219 names inscribed on the Vietnam Veterans Memorial in Washington, D.C., which honors those Americans who gave their lives in service to their country in the controversial war. When the U.S. Army returned Terry's body to his hometown of Birmingham, Alabama, in July 1969, however, the local reception was not that befitting a fallen soldier. He had volunteered for the army, and after he was ordered to go to Vietnam, he had told his sixteen-year-old wife and his mother that, if he was killed, he wanted to be buried in Elmwood Cemetery, the city's oldest and largest burial ground. When family members sought to purchase a plot there, they were refused, although the cemetery was not full: Billy Terry was black, and Elmwood was for "whites only." With the help of the Legal Defense and Education Fund of the National Association for the Advancement of Colored People (NAACP), Terry's widow and mother successfully brought suit against the cemetery, and on January 3, 1970, the soldier's body was moved from the "colored only" Shadow Lawn Cemetery and reinterred, with full military honors, at Elmwood.

The life, death, and burial of Corporal Terry illustrate a number of Vietnam-era issues. The war was the first major military conflict in which U.S. combat forces were racially integrated. Ironically, although integration of the armed forces had long been a goal of African Americans, it became a reality in a war that many white youths sought to avoid. The question became whether fighting in Vietnam was an opportunity for young black men to gain public respect and perhaps begin a professional military career or whether service in the war was a burden placed on underemployed and undereducated minority youth who did not have access to legal ways to avoid the draft. The racist policy of the cemetery also dramatized that blacks who served in Southeast Asia, whether casualties or surviving veterans, returned to racial discrimination and humiliation in civil society despite their often willing and patriotic sacrifices.

David L. Anderson teaches the history of U.S. foreign relations and the history of the Vietnam War at the University of Indianapolis in

From the *Indianapolis Recorder* Collection, C8136. *Courtesy of the Indiana Historical Society*

Indiana. He is the author of *Trapped by Success: The Eisenhower Administration and Vietnam, 1953–1961* (1991) and the editor of *Shadow on the White House: Presidents and the Vietnam War, 1945–1975* (1993) and *Facing My Lai: Moving beyond the Massacre* (1998).

The fourth of nine children, Bill Henry Terry Jr. was born February 23, 1949. His family lived on the south side of Birmingham, Alabama, at 501 First Street South, about ten or twelve blocks from Elmwood Cemetery. Billy was educated in Our Lady of Fatima Catholic School and public schools and completed the eleventh grade at Ullman High School. Rather than enroll for his senior year, however, he enlisted in the army and entered active duty on September 23, 1968.

For the nineteen-year-old Terry, the decision to choose the service over school made sense in his circumstances. Although he could have avoided being drafted for another year if he had remained in school, he faced a high probability of being called up as soon as he had his diploma. Going to college and thus obtaining a further educational deferment was out of the question. He could not afford college, and furthermore, he had other financial responsibilities, for he was married in June 1968 and had a son, Patrick, in August. To support his young family, he worked at odd jobs as a laborer, in a clothing factory, and at a service station. He also made some money as an unlicensed barber, a trade he had learned from his father, Bill Sr. Consequently, with a young wife and a baby to support and facing the draft if he did not return to school, Terry enlisted.

Although his enlistment was, in part, "draft induced," that is, prompted by the likelihood of conscription because of high Vietnam War draft calls, Terry had additional reasons for volunteering. He intended to make a career in the military, following in the steps of his older sister, who was already in the army. He believed the service offered genuine opportunity for a young African American to finish his education while also providing income and benefits for his family. It would also enable him to fulfill a desire to see the world.

For most recruits in 1968, however, the opportunity for world travel meant a trip to Vietnam, and in this, Terry was no exception. He went first to Fort Polk, Louisiana, for basic and advanced individual training (AIT), and on February 14, 1969, he completed the AIT infantry course. The notation on his training certificate read "RVN Oriented," which indicated that he was destined for combat duty in the Republic of Vietnam. He commenced his tour of duty in Southeast Asia on March 6, 1969.

Terry was an infantryman in Company D, Second Battalion, Third Infantry Regiment, 199th Light Infantry Brigade. Ironically, the brigade commander was Brig. Gen. Frederic E. Davison, only the third African American general in the history of the army and the first to lead an infantry brigade in combat. At the time he received his well-earned star in September 1968, Davison had declared that he wanted "his men to go home feeling they have done something and that black and white alike they have been treated fairly by the army."[1] On June 19 the brigade moved to the area around Xuan Loc in Long Khanh Province. After less than four months in combat, Terry was killed in action on July 3 during a search-and-destroy operation. His wife received the standard telegram of notification and sympathy four days later. In its bureaucratic formality, the wire said only that her husband was killed "while on a combat operation when a hostile force was encountered."[2] No death certificate was issued, and his family never learned the precise place or circumstances of his death. Three other standard forms eventually were given to the family: DD Form 1300 Report of Casualty (a minimal statement confirming Terry's death and length of service), a posthumous promotion to the rank of corporal, and a certificate of honorable service.

According to military unit records now available, the fighting in which Terry died was intense. At about 11:40 A.M. on July 3, his company was moving through dense forest toward a helicopter pickup zone northwest of Xuan Loc. They literally walked into the middle of a well-concealed North Vietnamese Army base camp and immediately came under heavy fire from machine guns, automatic weapons, and snipers. U.S. casualties mounted quickly. Company C of the Second Battalion worked its way through the jungle to provide covering fire for Company D. Both companies then pulled back about 250 meters, allowing U.S. tactical aircraft and artillery to pulverize the enemy camp shortly before 9:00 P.M. Terry and several other soldiers were reported missing and possibly killed during the fighting, and it was not until noon the next day that their bodies were recovered. Company D suffered nine men killed and twenty-two wounded in the battle.

Corporal Terry's body arrived back in Birmingham under military escort about a week after his death. Elmwood Cemetery had been advertising plots for sale, and after going to Vietnam, Terry had written his family that, if he was killed, he would like to be laid to rest in this beautiful and prestigious burial ground. His wife, Margaret Faye Terry, later recalled that "at the time we all thought of it as being a joke, something to pass the time, to make a letter longer." Sometime in June, however, another letter arrived from her husband, saying that "if I should die over here in Nam I want to be buried in Elmwood."[3] When that tragic possibility became reality, the family tried to make the arrangements. They knew that the cemetery was for whites only, but they went to Elmwood, accompanied by the military escort officer, in the belief that their situation surely would be different. The Elmwood manager turned them away, saying that racial covenants in the deeds of the other plot owners legally prevented him from selling to the Terry family.

Interment took place with full military honors on July 19 in the all-black Shadow Lawn Cemetery, but soon afterward, Billy Terry's widow and his mother, Jimmie Lee Terry, went to see the parish priest, Fr. Eugene Ferrell. "I just didn't feel right about it," Margaret Terry recalled. The white minister of a predominantly black congregation, Ferrell described his reaction: "It seemed a really very simple thing. He had died for his country, and he should have the right to be buried wherever he wanted."[4]

Father Ferrell contacted the NAACP Legal Defense and Education Fund, which helped the family file a class-action suit in federal district court. The plaintiffs asked the court to order Elmwood to sell burial plots in its public cemetery to any citizen, regardless of race or color, and to declare null and void the racial covenants in the existing lot deeds. Such a ruling would be precedent setting. In a previous incident in 1966, the public cemetery in the small community of Wetumpka, Alabama, had refused to bury Jimmie Williams, an African American and a Green Beret paratrooper killed in Vietnam. The white elected officials of the town declared that the black sections of the only cemetery in town were full and suggested a pauper's grave as an alternative. Williams's mother responded that her son "did not die a second class death" and "he didn't die a segregated death and would not be buried in a segregated cemetery."[5] He was laid to rest with full military honors at the nearest integrated burial site, the Andersonville National Military Cemetery in Georgia.

In death, Billy Terry had been thrust into the front lines of the civil rights struggle then under way in the United States, even though, as a friend of his remembered, "Billy never really got too much interested in the marching and the other civil rights things. He was always working at some job or another and never had much time for that, I guess."[6] His case attracted national press coverage. Catholic priests, organized by Father Ferrell, held prayer vigils in Birmingham and Washington, D.C., and Ferrell also led a group of clergy who asked President Richard Nixon to urge Elmwood to change its policy.

Because both sides acknowledged the facts, the briefs submitted in the case of *Margaret Faye Terry, etc., et al. v. the Elmwood Cemetery, et al.* and the judge's ruling focused on the Thirteenth Amendment and the Civil Rights Act of 1866, which declared African Americans free and entitled to the same rights of property as white citizens. The plaintiffs' brief cited precedents from cases involving property, discrimination, and grave sites. The defendants' response simply quoted Elmwood's rule, established in 1954, that "cemetery lots shall be owned only by human beings of the white and/or Caucasian race and the said lots shall be used only for burial of human bodies of the white and/or Caucasian race." The defendants further denied that "refusal to grant interment rights at Elmwood Cemetery constitutes a badge and incidence of slavery" unlawful under the Thirteenth Amendment and the Civil Rights Act of 1866.[7]

The constitutional arguments clearly favored the plaintiffs, and the cemetery's attorneys almost seemed to welcome a court ruling that would free Elmwood from an untenable legal position. The seventeen-page memorandum of opinion issued by Judge Seybourn H. Lynne, as prepared by his clerk Robert L. Potts, was a virtual history of civil rights legislation. Lynne decided entirely for the plaintiffs, declaring that Elmwood was legally obligated to sell burial plots without regard to race or color. The cemetery agreed to comply voluntarily with the ruling, and thus, no injunction was issued.

On January 3, exactly six months after Terry's death, his body was exhumed from Shadow Lawn and reinterred, with full military honors, in Elmwood. The ceremonies included a brief memorial service in Our Lady of Fatima Church, where he had been confirmed at age twelve and where his mother was an active parishioner. The flag-draped coffin was then transported in a hearse to Elmwood, followed by twelve hundred mourners singing "We Shall Overcome." Many residents of Terry's poor neighborhood watched from their yards and porches as the procession passed. At the cemetery a ten-man military honor guard led by a white chaplain and a black major fired the salute, played taps, folded the flag, and presented it to the widow. "This is not really a funeral march," Father Ferrell exclaimed in his eulogy. "This is a victory march for Billy and for truth and right."[8] The priest captured the symbolism of the moment when he observed: "We, the white race, have a lot of atonement to make to this young man, for we have discriminated against him from the cradle to the grave. . . . When he had done his best for his country, his country was still doing its worst for him."[9]

Tragic ironies such as the case of Bill Henry Terry Jr. pervaded America's war in Vietnam. Lyndon Johnson and other U.S. leaders repeatedly justified military intervention there as necessary to defend hallowed American principles of freedom, democracy, and self-determination. Yet for Americans at home as well as for the Vietnamese, the U.S. attempt to force its will on Vietnam undermined these noble ideals. Among the threats to America's governing principles, racism and economic discrimination in U.S. wartime policies were especially troubling.

Some racial and economic groups in the United States appeared to pay an exorbitantly high share of the personal costs for the war.

Selected government statistics suggested that the percentage of Hispanics among the fifty-eight thousand American war dead far exceeded that group's percentage of the population, and African American deaths early in the Vietnam War were reported to be double the relative proportion of blacks in the population. Conversely, middle-class and college-educated whites were greatly underrepresented both in the casualty totals and among the force of two million American servicemen who went to Vietnam.

Paradoxically, the inequities in Vietnam military service emerged just as the civil rights movement was beginning to remove some of the legal and social discrimination that had long oppressed African Americans. The connection between the war and the black struggle for equality appeared so clear to Martin Luther King Jr. that he joined the antiwar movement and declared the war's conduct to be a grave injustice and danger to black citizens. As soon as President Johnson launched an American ground war in Vietnam in 1965, it was evident that the military escalation threatened LBJ's ambitious domestic program—the Great Society. The president saw this peril clearly and lamented, in his earthy style, "If I left the woman I really loved—the Great Society—in order to get involved with that bitch of a war on the other side of the world, then I would lose everything at home. All my programs. All my hopes to feed the hungry and shelter the homeless. All my dreams to provide education and medical care to the browns and blacks and the lame and the poor."[10] Still, Johnson plunged the nation into the carnage of Vietnam, believing that the world's most powerful democracy had to oppose communist totalitarianism in Asia. Speaking for the intended beneficiaries of the president's domestic plans, King's Southern Christian Leadership Conference (SCLC) charged that the "promises of the Great Society top the casualty list of the conflict."[11]

The SCLC's use of the casualty metaphor was pointed. Even as the $20 billion annual expenditure on the war drained resources from poverty programs and saddled all Americans with growing inflation, young black men were dying in large numbers in combat. In 1966, *Parade* magazine reported that 50 percent of the men in the airborne and other elite fighting units were black soldiers. Although Department of Defense officials could not immediately confirm the racial composition of individual units, they did acknowledge that 15 percent of all the soldiers in Vietnam were black. Other reports showed that 20.7 percent of the army's 1965 casualties were black. At that time, blacks made up only 11 percent of the U.S. population and 13.5 percent of the 19- to 25-year-old segment, so the death rate clearly posed a disturbing issue of "representativeness."[12]

Because of the attention given to the 20 percent black casualty rate early in the fighting, that figure was cited repeatedly even after the war. If accurate, it would mean that 11,000 names on the Vietnam Veterans Memorial are those of black GIs. (In fact, the total is 7,257, or 12.5 percent of all deaths throughout the war.) In 1966 the percentage of black deaths was 20.8, but that number dropped to 13.4 in 1967 and was below 10 for each year after 1970. The high initial numbers reflected the nature of the army in 1964 and 1965. Elite combat units, the first to be deployed, were primarily composed of regular enlistees, not draftees. Many of these soldiers were minorities who, like Terry, saw the military as providing a better economic opportunity than civilian society. At the time of Terry's death the reenlistment rate for blacks was twice as high as that for whites in all the services and three times higher in the army, indicating the career orientation of minority troopers. Meanwhile, the dramatic rise in draft inductions, from 106,000 in 1965 to 339,000 in 1966, changed the racial composition of the combat units. Although there were racial and social inequities in the draft itself, the larger manpower pool and the assignment of 45 to 50 percent of draftees to Southeast Asia eventually brought the racial percentages in the units in Vietnam into closer proximity to the composition of the general population.

Statistics for Hispanic GIs somewhat paralleled those for blacks. Some authors claimed that Spanish-surnamed soldiers made up almost 20 percent of all Vietnam casualties. In fact, however, only about 4.9 percent of the names on the Vietnam Veterans Memorial are distinctively Spanish, which approximates the 4.4 percent of the 1970 census that was Latino.[13] Still, the 20 percent figure, which was derived from an analysis of war dead from California, Texas, New Mexico, Arizona, and Colorado, was close to correct for those states and almost double the percentage of Hispanic citizens in that region.

The high number of blacks in the army before draft calls were increased and the even higher number in the all-volunteer army in the post-Vietnam years presented two related possibilities: (1) that the military offered more attractive socioeconomic opportunities to minority youth than did society at large, and (2) that the army was largely a poor man's institution. Even with high wartime draft calls, this pattern persisted. Assuming that a college degree indicated middle-class status or a potential for middle-class income, it was significant that only 4.9 percent of enlisted men at the end of 1969 had degrees. College students received draft deferments, but few entered the service after graduation. Only 2 of Harvard's 1,200 graduates in 1970 went to Vietnam, for example, and only 56 went into the service at all.

Statistics alone do not tell the whole story. Using quantitative analyses, many sociologists support the contention made in Pentagon studies that discrimination in the military was more often socioeconomic rather than racial and that poverty, not race, was the dominant characteristic shared by most Vietnam casualties. This generalization must be used with care because race consciousness remained strong among the minority poor, who suffered under the twin burdens of poverty and color. Puerto Rican congressman Herman Badillo from New York found it "repugnant and fallacious" to contend that economic incentives made "the risk of injury or death so overwhelmingly attractive to young Blacks and Puerto Ricans" that they would want to be "the white man's killer."[14] Other minority observers questioned the use of statistics to define fairness because that suggested quotas, which bureaucrats had often applied in the past to limit minority access to opportunity. Despite the "concern" she heard professed about the high percentage of poor and blacks in the military, black congresswoman Shirley Chisholm perceived a possible racist fear "of a whole army of black men trained as professional soldiers."[15]

The historical record resounds with the rhetoric of black voices condemning the racism that permeated American society, including the military. In Vietnam, minority spokespeople contended, black men fought to impose "democracy" on a nonwhite Asian people while the black GI was denied the full benefits of democracy at home. The emphasis on the race of the enemy was new, but the rest of the complaint was old and all too familiar. During the Civil War, former slave Frederick Douglass proclaimed that he would willingly "march to the battle field" if he would have "a government that recognizes my manhood around me, and a flag of freedom waving over me!"[16] "The American Negro . . . is more than willing to do his full share in helping to win the war for democracy," W. E. B. Du Bois wrote during World War I, "and he expects his full share of the fruits thereof."[17]

These pleas went unheeded, and black veterans suffered at home under the same burden of Jim Crow segregation and racial oppression as others of their race. From the early days of the Republic, it was standard military policy to use black troops primarily to meet wartime manpower needs, to assign them to support (not combat) roles, to place them in segregated units under white officers, and to deny them command of white troops. In World War II, this institutionalized racism remained entrenched. Blacks fought valiantly in segregated units, yet no black GI received the Medal of Honor during the war (although there had been black recipients in earlier wars). The brutal racism of the Nazi enemy, the postwar rhetoric about freedom versus communist tyranny, and the insistent demands for justice from black leaders, however, finally brought change. In 1948, President Harry Truman ordered the integration of the armed forces. The process started slowly, but by the early 1960s, as the civil rights movement battered down barriers at lunch counters, bus terminals, and polling places, the U.S. military was the most integrated institution in the nation. And by earning high efficiency ratings, many blacks had achieved positions of genuine authority, especially as noncommissioned officers.

In 1965 Johnson's land war in Vietnam brought the first truly integrated conflict in U.S. history. Terry went to Southeast Asia when the American deployment was at its peak of 540,000 troops. Blacks constituted 10.7 percent of that number and 13.5 percent of the combat deaths in 1969. In the initial troop buildup, black fighting men seemed to follow the traditions of their predecessors in earlier wars. They were eager to prove their manhood and their patriotism. One young marine, Pfc. Reginald "Malik" Edwards, later recalled that he enlisted in the service for a job but chose the corps because "the Marines was bad." Once in training, he encountered racial slurs, but that did not deter his desire to fight the Vietcong: "I knew Americans were prejudiced, were racists and all that, but, basically, I believed in America 'cause I was an American."[18]

Edwards served in Vietnam with valor, reenlisted, and rose to the rank of sergeant, but in 1970 the corps booted him out with a bad conduct discharge for repeated fighting in retaliation for what he considered racial harassment. He joined other black veterans in the Black Panthers. "We figured if we had been over in Vietnam fighting for our country, which at that point wasn't serving us properly, it was only proper that we go out and fight for our own cause," he explained.[19] This embittered Blood, as black GIs began to call themselves in Vietnam, expressed forcefully a spreading black belief that the war was not their war. In a 1970 poll, 57 percent of black respondents favored U.S. withdrawal from Vietnam, compared to 37 percent of whites.

Initially, black leaders were reluctant to break openly with Johnson on the war because he was a valuable ally in their struggle for civil rights legislation. They also hesitated to appear disloyal in wartime and thus reverse their hard-earned gains in civic respectability. King expressed doubts about the war as early as March 1965, but he finally decided "to break silence" on April 4, 1967. In a stirring address at the Riverside Church in New York City, this Nobel Peace Prize laureate lamented the casualties, underfunded poverty programs, and recent outbreaks of urban violence. He joined his hallmark appeal for nonviolence at home with a plea for peace abroad. Declaring himself a brother to the poor of America and Vietnam, he castigated the U.S. government for brutalizing the downtrodden of both nations while defending a corrupt regime in Saigon. The United States was on the wrong side of the world revolution and needed, he urged, to make "a positive thrust for democracy."[20]

King's voice added stature to the growing antiwar movement, which, in 1967, many Americans still considered a radical fringe. Some journalists suggested that the minister had fallen under communist influence, but King's rhetoric was relatively mild. He stopped short of terming the war overtly racist and did not call for a communist victory, as did some white extremists. Black moderates Ralph Bunche and Roy Wilkins criticized King for merging the peace and civil rights movements. Black Power advocate Stokley Carmichael of the Student Nonviolent Coordinating Committee (SNCC) welcomed King's speech, but he, too, rejected a coalition with antiwar activists. SNCC leaders viewed the peace movement as "basically all-white" and something to which they could not relate. Carmichael's racial separatism led him to characterize the draft, for example, as "white people sending black people to make war on yellow people in order to defend the land they stole from red people."[21]

Shortly before his murder in 1968, King reflected on the "tragedy" of military service for young black men. He expressed faith in the initial sincerity of the proponents of the Great Society. But he believed the war prevented its realization, and that failure left closed many doors to education, training, and dignity for the poor. Meanwhile, young black males risked death in the military because "life in the city ghetto [or] life in the rural South almost certainly means jail or death or humiliation. And so, by comparison, military service is really the lesser risk." America was not a venal nation, King argued, but it was complacently blind to "habitual white discrimination." "Was security for some," he asked, "being purchased at the price of degradation for others?"[22]

In 1966 the Johnson administration created a remarkable program—Project 100,000—that addressed the tragedy of which King spoke. Its implementation, however, validated the minister's concern about equity. As touted by Secretary of Defense Robert McNamara, the program was designed to "salvage the poverty-scarred youth of our society" for military service and "for a lifetime of productive activity in civilian society."[23] The plan called for inducting 100,000 men a year (through the draft or enlistment) out of the 600,000 who failed annually to qualify under previous mental and physical induction standards. These men were some of the nation's poorest, least-educated, and most disadvantaged youth, but the Pentagon claimed the project would benefit them because it would "spread more equitably the opportunities and obligations of military service."[24] The plan also expanded the available manpower pool for the war—a fact readily admitted in military circles but not specifically designated as a program objective.

Project 100,000 was schizophrenic. Ralph Nader's Center for Study of Responsive Law termed it hypocritical in a report entitled "How the Great Society Went to War."[25] The initiative was simultaneously a Great Society effort to rescue "the subterranean poor" and a guise for filling the ranks in an increasingly questionable war with men who had little voice and few means to resist. McNamara and Clark Clifford, who became defense secretary in 1968, boasted that 40 percent of the men in the program were black, 60 percent had less than a high school education, and over half were unemployed or earning less than sixty dollars per week when inducted. Other statistics showed that 96 percent of them graduated from basic training (compared to 98 percent for all troops), and that, after the first sixteen and a half months, 91 percent of those in the army had received excellent conduct and efficiency ratings. Billy Terry fit this profile. The underside of Project 100,000 was revealed in an October 1967 *Washington Post* article: "Secretary of Defense McNamara has ordered the armed forces to accept some misfits and dropouts . . . so President Johnson won't be forced to widen the draft or call up the reserves during the 1968 election year."[26]

From the outset of the war, Johnson had purposefully sought to contain political repercussions by relying on the draft and enlistments rather than a mobilization of reservists, but his motive for developing Project 100,000 was not simply political expediency. The administration's leaders were part of the generation that had promoted the integration of the military as being good for the nation. Moreover, Johnson's personal stamp was on the civil rights laws of 1964 and 1965. McNamara had established federal civil rights protection for service personnel when outside military installations, and Clifford had been one of Truman's advisers who helped craft the executive order integrating the armed forces. Thus, these officials saw military training as beneficial to young black men, and each had personally aided in the African Americans' fight for the right to fight.

Respected social scientists in the 1960s also championed the benefits of military service for minorities. The planners of Project 100,000 drew explicitly on the work of Daniel Moynihan, the sociologist who, with Nathan Glazer, coined the term *ethnicity* in his studies of New York City. As assistant secretary of labor, Moynihan helped produce influential socioeconomic studies on young men disqualified for military service and on the black family. These reports argued that the young black male stood only to gain in self-esteem and skills from military service. Separate research outside the government similarly concluded that integration of the armed services had brought about "a marked and rapid improvement in individual and group achievement."[27]

These strong theoretical arguments make it difficult to characterize Project 100,000 as purposefully exploitative, but other studies conducted at the time and later revealed that the plan was a mistake of large proportions. "The main thing Project 100,000 seems to have done," Representative Chisholm observed, "was to ease the pressure of the draft among the white middle class."[28] In 1967, as the Pentagon began full implementation of Moynihan's recommendations on recruiting poor and minority soldiers, the National Advisory Commission on Selective Service issued a report entitled *In Pursuit of Equity: Who Serves When Not All Serve?* This investigation confirmed the high black casualty percentages. It also found that blacks accounted for only 1.3 percent of local draft board members but made up 16 percent of draftees. Minorities faced serious institutionalized racism, not just the socioeconomic hurdles that Moynihan highlighted.

The armed forces had data, especially from World War II, that also predicted many problems with Project 100,000. Candidates for the program had an Armed Forces Qualifying Test (AFQT) rank of Category IV, indicating a score of 10 to 30 out of 100 on the preinduction mental examination. (Billy Terry had an AFQT score of 20.[29]) Although a few Category IV new standards men (NSM)—as they were called—were later found to be retarded, most scored low because of a lack of education. Many read at or below the sixth-grade level. Experienced military trainers knew that it was inadvisable to try to make soldiers of such men, especially during wartime.

Project 100,000 ended in 1972 as military manpower needs declined and the program experienced mounting problems. Many NSM never received the remedial help, especially with reading, that the program had promised. Those training centers that did attempt to accommodate the needs of the NSM experienced marked cost increases. The NSM also had a high rate of recycling through training and of medical discharges. Commanders found a high absence rate among low-ability soldiers, and in the army, there were twice as many disciplinary actions and courts-martial in this group as among other men. In 1974, President Gerald Ford established a clemency board for draft and military absence offenders, and almost one-third of the military applicants were Category IV men, who would not have been in the service without Project 100,000. A follow-up study of the NSM, completed in 1990, found them worse off in terms of employment, education, and income than disadvantaged youth who never served.

William P. Bundy, one of Johnson's officials who helped shape Vietnam policy, has advised historians to compare the chronologies of the Great Society and the Vietnam War. This juxtaposition reveals the difficulty inherent in the Johnson administration's attempt to expand citizenship rights to more Americans at the same time that combat service was increasing citizenship costs. Yet the traditional linkage between military service and citizenship rights remained strong in the Pentagon rhetoric about a young man's military obligation and even in the arguments of some minority spokespeople. As late as 1971, with the war continuing and with growing controversy surrounding casualty figures and Project 100,000, the NAACP complained that AFQT scores were still being used to deny blacks "opportunity" in the armed forces.

For military service to convey civic opportunity, however, the mission assigned the armed forces must itself be honorable. This reality was central to King's indictment of American purposes in Vietnam. He could not join with Douglass and Du Bois and argue that for blacks, the risks of combat were a high but reasonable price to pay for respect. King contended that black casualties and the demise of the Great Society were unacceptable consequences of an immoral policy in Asia. In his view, the Vietnam War was a violent colonial conquest unbefitting the democratic principles of the United States.

Although the overall casualty figures for blacks and Hispanics were not as extraordinarily high as some critics claimed, minority opposition to the war mounted faster than did that of the white majority. The explanation rests, in part, on the fact that some inequities did occur, as reflected in the high percentage of black deaths early in the war, the high casualty rate among Hispanics from the U.S. Southwest, and the dashing of hopes raised by the Great Society. Project 100,000 illustrated the problem. Johnson's aides initially congratulated themselves on the number of poor blacks being helped by the program even as black leaders saw it as the latest example of minority manipulation by the white power elite. Combined with a history of discrimination, these realities caused minorities to perceive that they bore an unfair burden, regardless of what the actual data revealed. Adding to the distrust was the violence of the war itself, in pursuit of vague objectives in a place little understood by most Americans. The Vietnam War did not necessarily produce the tension and distrust within the United States, but the pressures of this controversial military operation revealed the depth of such preexisting pathologies.

The leaders of the Athenian democracy "adopted bad policies at home and in the empire," Thucydides recorded twenty-five hundred years ago during the Peloponnesian War, and "this failure did harm to the city in the conduct of the war."[30] The Vietnam experience underscores a timeless reality that foreign policy and all good public policy must serve the domestic interests and internal welfare of the nation and all of its citizens.

Bill Henry Terry Jr. was a good citizen. He came from a close-knit, churchgoing, hardworking family. Despite his youth and his humble circumstances, he was trying to be a good husband and father and a responsible adult. He was caught in a social web of race and class that actually made volunteering for almost certain assignment to a brutal and dangerous war appear to be a good choice. His gamble cost him his life, but in death, he still contributed to society and his family. Through the courage of his wife and mother and the responsiveness of Father Ferrell and the legal system, Terry's simple request for a dignified burial helped end one of the morbid legacies of Jim Crow racism—segregated cemeteries. It was also a significant step in giving African American soldiers proper recognition of their service and sacrifice. In later years Billy Terry's veteran's benefits enabled his son Patrick to attend college. Terry's short life left a lasting legacy.

Notes

1. Clipping from *Chicago Tribune*, September 16, 1968, in "Scrapbook," Box 2, Organizational History, Second Battalion, Third Infantry, Records of the United States Army Vietnam, Record Group 472, National Archives, College Park, Maryland.

2. The author thanks Margaret Terry for her generous assistance in providing copies of this telegram and other personal documents related to her husband's military service.

3. Margaret Terry, letter to author, March 2, 1998.

4. Quoted in James T. Wooten, "Black Soldier Buried among Whites," *New York Times*, January 4, 1970.

5. Quoted in James E. Westheider, *Fighting on Two Fronts: African Americans and the Vietnam War* (New York: New York University Press, 1997), 73.

6. Quoted in Wooten, "Black Soldier Buried among Whites."

7. Answer of Defendant, the Elmwood Cemetery Corporation, in case file of *Margaret Faye Terry, etc., et al. v. the Elmwood Cemetery, et al.*, Records of Alabama, North District, Records of District Courts of the United States, Record Group 21, National Archives—Southeast Region, East Point, Georgia.

8. Quoted in Wooten, "Black Soldier Buried among Whites."

9. Quoted in Westheider, *Fighting on Two Fronts,* 74.

10. Quoted in Doris Kearns, *Lyndon Johnson and the American Dream* (New York: New American Library, 1976), 263.

11. Quoted in David J. Garrow, *Bearing the Cross: Martin Luther King, Jr., and the Southern Christian Leadership Conference* (New York: Morrow, 1986), 470.

12. *Congressional Record*, House, 89th Cong., 2d sess., July 18, 1966, 15232–33.

13. The analysis of the Vietnam Veterans Memorial is my own count of distinctively Spanish surnames, in *Vietnam Veterans Memorial Directory of Names* (Washington, D.C.: Vietnam Veterans Memorial Fund, 1989). About

2,900 of the 58,219 names on the memorial are Spanish. Of the 2,900, about 1,800 were from the five southwestern states and represented 17.3 percent of the deaths from those states. Some of those with Spanish surnames were tribal American Indians. See Tom Holm, "Forgotten Warriors: American Indian Servicemen in Vietnam," *Vietnam Generation* 1 (Spring 1989): 58.

14. U.S. Congress, House Committee on Armed Services, *Extension of the Draft and Bills Related to the Voluntary Force Concept and Authorization of Strength Levels: Hearings before the Committee on Armed Services,* 92d Cong., 1st sess., February 23–25 and March 1–5, 9–11, 1971, 600.

15. Ibid., 670.

16. Frederick Douglass, "Pictures and Progress: An Address Delivered in Boston, Massachusetts, on 3 December 1861," in *The Frederick Douglass Papers,* ed. John W. Blassingame, 5 vols. (New Haven: Yale University Press, 1985), ser. 1, 3:468.

17. Quoted in Bernard C. Nalty and Morris J. MacGregor, eds., *Blacks in the Military: Essential Documents* (Wilmington, Del.: Scholarly Resources, 1981), 88.

18. Wallace Terry, *Bloods: An Oral History of the Vietnam War by Black Veterans* (New York: Random House, 1984), 6, 8.

19. Ibid., 13–14.

20. Martin Luther King Jr., "A Time to Break Silence," in *A Testament of Hope: The Essential Writings of Martin Luther King, Jr.,* ed. James Melvin Washington (New York: Harper and Row, 1986), 231–44.

21. Quoted in Charles DeBenedetti, with Charles Chatfield, *An American Ordeal: The Antiwar Movement of the Vietnam Era* (Syracuse, N.Y.: Syracuse University Press, 1990), 158–59, 172–73.

22. Martin Luther King Jr., "A Testament of Hope," in Washington, *A Testament of Hope,* 326–27.

23. Robert S. McNamara address to the National Association of Educational Broadcasters, November 7, 1967, "DOD Integration 1967" file, Office of the Secretary of Defense Historical Office, Washington, D.C. (hereafter cited as OSD Historical Office).

24. Office of Assistant Secretary of Defense (Manpower and Reserve Affairs), *Description of Project One Hundred Thousand,* April 1968, OSD Historical Office.

25. Paul Starr, with James F. Henry and Raymond P. Bonner, *The Discarded Army: Veterans after Vietnam* (New York: Charterhouse, 1973), 185–97.

26. *Washington Post,* October 23, 1967.

27. Charles C. Moskos Jr., "Racial Integration in the Armed Forces," *American Journal of Sociology* 72 (September 1966): 132–48.

28. House Committee on Armed Services, *Extension of the Draft,* 671.

29. Bill H. Terry Jr., Enlisted Qualification Record (DA Form 20), courtesy of Margaret Terry.

30. Thucydides, *The Peloponnesian Wars,* trans. by Benjamin Jowett, revised and abridged with an introduction by P. A. Brunt (New York: Washington Square Press, 1963), 83.

Suggested Readings

In addition to the sources cited in the notes, information on the demographics of those who served in Vietnam is found in Lawrence M. Baskir and William A. Strauss, *Chance and Circumstance: The Draft, the War and the Vietnam Generation* (New York: Vintage, 1978); Gilbert Badillo and G. David Curry, "The Social Incidence of Vietnam Casualties: Social Class or Race?" *Armed Forces and Society* 2 (May 1976): 397–406; and Neil D. Fligstein, "Who Served in the Military, 1940–1973," *Armed Forces and Society* 6 (Winter 1980): 297–312. For statistics on minority participation in the war, see Martin Binkin and Mark J. Eitelberg, with Alvin J. Schexnider and Marvin M. Smith, *Blacks and the Military* (Washington, D.C.: Brookings Institution, 1982); Ralph Guzman, "Mexican American Casualties in Vietnam," *La Raza* 1 (1970): 12–15; and U.S. Department of Defense, *U.S. Casualties in Southeast Asia: Statistics as of April 30, 1985* (Washington, D.C.: Government Printing Office, 1985).

III

Americans Struggle against the Vietnam Quagmire

On November 15, 1969, thousands of Americans, mostly young, marched through the streets of Washington, D.C., chanting, "One, two, three, four, Richard Nixon stop the war" and other antiwar slogans. Although the president had asserted in a nationally televised speech on November 3 that a "silent majority" of Americans still supported the war, the voices in the streets, public opinion polls, newspaper columns, and other signs pointed to the contrary. Americans wanted out of the Vietnam quagmire. For most citizens, however, just how that could be accomplished was unclear. The nation had entered the Vietnam era with a confidence in U.S. power and moral rectitude gained on the battlefields of Europe and the Pacific during World War II. But the horrific violence of the Vietnam War, the inability of national leaders to give clear meaning to that violence, and the prospect of more of the same without some fundamental change of policy had dissipated support for interventionism. Many Americans still wanted to believe Nixon's assurance that a peace with honor was attainable, but more and more people were demanding that, somehow and in some way, the burden of Vietnam be lifted from the country.

In August 1964, at the time of the initial U.S. bombing of North Vietnam, Congress had authorized the president to use military force in Southeast Asia. It had passed the so-called Gulf of Tonkin Resolution unanimously in the House of Representatives and with only two negative votes in the Senate. Congress, the press, and most citizens had accepted White House assertions that the U.S. defense of South Vietnam was a manageable and necessary commitment. As the war lengthened, however, public skepticism and opposition mounted. Critics challenged executive branch explanations for continuing the war. After the Tet Offensive of 1968, many Americans were saying that, regardless of the rationale, the war simply was not worth the price it extracted in terms of American lives, treasure, and internal discord.

In the later years of the Vietnam era, the war produced enormous domestic tension in the United States. Despite official allegations that some of the radicals were part of an organized conspiracy to subvert the U.S. government, thousands of Americans spontaneously participated in largely ad hoc antiwar protests. Many young men openly defied the patriotic tradition of military service by refusing to be drafted or by deserting rather than obeying orders to go to Southeast Asia. Even more startling was the unprecedented condemnation of the war by some of the returning soldiers. Morale within the military plummeted and was damaged even further as many citizens harassed or pointedly ignored veterans returning from terrible experiences in Vietnam, mistakenly thinking that these mostly conscripted troops were themselves responsible for U.S. policy in Vietnam.

Although some Americans dared to defy tradition and the law and resisted the war, others felt that love of country required them to attack the critics. Law enforcement authorities at all levels restricted the civil liberties of protestors, and many families were deeply divided as children and parents clashed over the war. Adding to the tension was the simultaneous upheaval created by the African American struggle for civil rights and the counterculture's hippie lifestyle of unkempt appearance, drug use, and sexual freedom.

Of the many examples of domestic conflict, one of the most tragic was the incident at Ohio's Kent State University on May 4, 1970. Nixon's announcement on April 30 that U.S. combat forces had launched offensive operations from South Vietnam into Cambodia touched off hundreds of protests of this seeming expansion of the war. A small group of demonstrators at Kent State set fire to the Reserve Officers' Training Corps building, and the governor sent the Ohio National Guard to patrol the campus. After a couple of tense days and for some never discovered reason, guardsmen fired into a group of students, killing four and wounding nine. Some of the victims were simply bystanders. Although many Americans were horrified by news of the killings and launched further protests, others expressed satisfaction that some of the disloyal bums who were disrupting the nation's colleges had gotten what was coming to them. The huge chasm in attitudes created by the war could not have been more evident.

Most Americans were neither radicals breaking laws nor sheep willing to be herded in whatever direction the government chose. The chapters that follow offer accounts of four individuals who courageously tried to change or stop the U.S. military intervention in Vietnam. All four were reputable professionals; none were hippies or youthful extremists. David Shoup, a Marine Corps general with his service's highest rank and honors, became one of the most outspoken dissenters within official circles (Chapter 9). Otto Feinstein was a college professor who labored at the grass roots to oppose the war through the political process, specifically in the campaign of Sen. Eugene McCarthy to unseat President Johnson (Chapter 10). Daniel Ellsberg traveled the full journey from being a Pentagon expert who designed strategy for the war to a rebel who leaked the secret Defense Department history of the war, the Pentagon Papers, in a effort to end the U.S. involvement (Chapter 11). Peter Arnett was one of several young journalists who went to Vietnam to cover the war and then became ardent critics as they reported the facts as they saw them (Chapter 12).

Many historical oversimplifications emerged after the Vietnam War. Some analysts blamed the disastrous conflict on one or a few U.S. decision makers, such as Secretary of Defense Robert McNamara or President Johnson. Others claimed that the United States could have "won" the war if only the press, the protestors, or even the presidents had not limited the full application of U.S. might. But as the efforts of these four earnest and loyal opponents of the war revealed, the problems and limitations of the U.S. military operation in Vietnam were not so simple. The Vietnam War was America's war and America's failure. The American people shared in the Cold War thinking and ignorance of Asia that produced the war. They also shared in the burdens of the war and in the agonizing struggle to escape the quagmire in which they found themselves.

9

David Shoup
Four-Star Troublemaker

Robert Buzzanco and Leigh Fought

There were always Americans who questioned U.S. involvement in Vietnam. During the French Indochina War, some of the most pointed cautions came from American military leaders who doubted the strategic value of the region and who could foresee major tactical, logistical, and political obstacles to fighting a ground war in Asia. During the 1950s, however, as Vietnam became more strongly identified as an important outpost in the containment of global communism and as U.S. military doctrine became more reliant on air power than on ground forces, the earlier doubts receded into the background. In the cherished American tradition of the military's deference to civilian leadership, professional officers loyally attempted to fashion effective military support for South Vietnam.

When the U.S. war in Vietnam expanded in the 1960s, Robert Buzzanco and Leigh Fought argue, a group of senior military men—many with high-level experience dating back to World War II and Korea—began to re-pose the old questions. Marine general David M. Shoup was a World War II Medal of Honor winner who later served as commandant of the Marine Corps. By the time of Lyndon Johnson's major escalation of the war, Shoup had retired from active duty and felt at liberty to offer brutally blunt assessments of U.S. policy. Joined by some other senior officers of his generation, notably Gen. James Gavin and Gen. Matthew Ridgway, he became a vehement opponent of U.S. intervention in Vietnam. Indeed, his indictment went beyond Vietnam policy to charge that American government, business, and military leaders had fallen victim to a militarism that belied the nation's historical identity.

Given the credibility associated with four-star generals, Shoup and his like-minded colleagues often made the front pages of national newspapers with their pointed critiques of the war and of American society. These were not upstart journalists or hippie flower children but unimpeachably loyal and knowledgeable citizens. Their informed opinions offered a counterpoint to the charge from some that the military was not being allowed to win the war. Shoup argued that increasing the military commitment would only aggravate the strategic and moral blunder that had already been committed.

Robert Buzzanco is an associate professor of history at the University of Houston in Texas. He is the author of *Masters of War: Military Dissent and Politics in the Vietnam Era* (1996), which received the

Courtesy of U.S. Marine Corps

Stuart Bernath Book Prize from the Society for Historians of American Foreign Relations. He has also received SHAFR's Stuart Bernath Lecture Prize (1998). His newest work is *Vietnam and the Transformation of American Life* (1999). He earned a Ph.D. at Ohio State University. Leigh Fought is a Ph.D. candidate at the University of Houston and is completing a dissertation on Louisa McCord and gender in the antebellum South. She is an instructor in the Houston Community College system.

Images of antiwar protests have become staples of the historical record of the 1960s. As presented in textbooks or in the popular media, such images usually include photos of longhaired demonstrators in hippie clothes, campus radicals burning their draft cards, or mainstream dissenters, such as Sen. J. William Fulbright or Sen. George McGovern. Invariably, scholars, journalists, and polemicists fail to discuss those within the military who demonstrated against American involvement in Southeast Asia. Yet active-duty soldiers and former soldiers, such as the members of the Vietnam Veterans Against the War (VVAW) and the Winter Soldier Organization, most of whom had served in Vietnam, played an important role in the resistance against the U.S. war in Indochina. Several influential retired officers also spoke out forthrightly against the war but none more so than Gen. David Monroe Shoup. He was certainly not a typical protestor. Medal of Honor winner in the Pacific theater in World War II and later the commandant of the Marine Corps, he broke ranks with the military establishment in the 1960s to become a vitriolic public critic of the Vietnam conflict, of the military-industrial complex, and of U.S. Cold War policy in general. He became a four-star troublemaker.

From a boyhood of poverty in rural Indiana to a seat of influence at the Pentagon and national acclaim as an antiwar spokesperson, Shoup remained a unique and iconoclastic individual and a man of contradictions. He was sensitive and rough, patriotic and angry at his country. All told, these complexities created a memorable character, making him one of the more important, albeit neglected, individuals in the public sphere in the 1960s. Defenders of the war in Vietnam could unfairly deride young protestors as communist dupes or traitors or fools, but they could not credibly level such charges against a senior officer who had become the chief of his military service.

Shoup was born in the appropriately named town of Battle Ground, Indiana, in 1904 and considered himself an "Indiana plowboy" for the rest of his life. He attended DePauw University, where he worked his way through school doing a variety of blue-collar jobs; he enrolled in the ROTC program because it paid nine dollars a month, precisely the amount of his rent. While a senior at DePauw, he attended a conference at which the famed marine commandant John Lejeune encouraged ROTC members to write to him requesting a commission, which Shoup did. On graduating in 1926, he entered the army reserves—again, primarily because he needed the money—but was then called to duty by the U.S. Marine Corps. He accepted a commission as a second lieutenant and was assigned, of all things, to play football, a task he disdained.

Fortunately for Shoup, who would never be confused with football legend Red Grange, he was rescued from the gridiron with his first overseas assignment. Serving in China in 1927 and 1928, he kept a journal—which he sardonically titled *The China Expedition Which Turned Out to Be the China Exhibition*—that offers some insight into the motivation for his activities in the Vietnam era. Though accepting some of the racial assumptions prevalent in the West about Asians, he nonetheless criticized American missionaries, businesspeople, and diplomats who exploited the local population for their own gain. He likewise castigated his fellow soldiers for their patronizing and often cruel treatment of the Chinese. While in China, Shoup recognized the growing power of Chinese nationalism as a political force, a lesson which he would draw on again when the United States began to wage war in Vietnam several decades later.

After a variety of assignments in the 1930s, Shoup became a hero in World War II. Serving as operations officer for the Second Marine Division in the Pacific theater, he won two Purple Hearts, but the high point of his service came in November 1943 at the Tarawa atoll in the Gilbert Islands. There, he led the marine assault on the Japanese stronghold on the island of Betio. After four bloody days of battle, the marines emerged victorious, and for his efforts, Shoup received the Medal of Honor. Following the war, he steadily progressed up the leadership ranks of the Marine Corps. His most notable assignment came in 1956 when he investigated the deaths of six recruits at Parris Island, South Carolina, and then spearheaded efforts to reform marine training.

In 1959, while serving as the commander at Parris Island, Shoup received word that President Dwight Eisenhower had appointed him commandant of the Marine Corps, and he assumed that position in January 1960. As commandant, he was concerned with reforming and restructuring marine training, using marine resources and manpower with less waste, and coordinating the marine component of the new "flexible response" strategy of the Kennedy administration. He received public attention because he made the swagger stick—to him a symbol of colonialism and cruelty—an optional piece of equipment for his men. He also had a public feud with Sen. Strom Thurmond, who complained that Shoup was not adequately indoctrinating his troops in anticommunism. "I'm teaching them how to fight," he responded, "not how to hate."[1]

Shoup also developed clear opinions on two of the most crucial foreign affairs issues of the day: U.S. policies toward Cuba and toward Vietnam. The commandant warned against the ultimately disastrous Bay of Pigs invasion of Cuba in April 1961 and against an armed American response during the October 1962 missile crisis. Bringing a map overlay of Cuba into a policymaking meeting to show just how large the island was and how difficult it would be to invade, Shoup urged his associates to avoid a violent confrontation with Fidel Castro. With regard to Vietnam, his critique was more developed, and it eventually made him a national figure in the anti-war movement.

Shoup was always wary of U.S. involvement in Indochina. In 1961, as a communist insurgent group, the Pathet Lao, threatened the American-supported government in Laos, he rejected calls for armed intervention; he later stated that the military only wanted to "find . . . some way to stop [the deteriorating Laos situation] and get out." At the same time, he began to warn against expanding the American role in Vietnam. He deployed a helicopter squadron— Task Unit Shufly—to the Saigon area in 1962 only because the Joint Chiefs of Staff directed him to do so. Later that year, in October, he briefly toured Vietnam and, as he sarcastically put it, "came back an expert." After his trip, he roundly criticized the U.S.-sponsored Strategic Hamlet program that was removing Vietnamese peasants from their home villages and relocating them to "safe" areas that resembled concentration camps. Believing that American efforts to train the Vietnamese military had produced only negligible results, he continued to oppose any plans for combat in Vietnam "with no qualms whatever" and added that "every responsible military man to my knowledge" was against war in Vietnam, as well.[2]

By the early 1960s, David Shoup was also developing a comprehensive analysis of U.S. foreign policy that would lead him to the forefront of the national debate over the war in Southeast Asia and America's global role. Though he had become a favorite of President Kennedy, the commandant had serious reservations about the administration's commitment to preparing American forces for counterinsurgency warfare in the Third World. To Shoup, U.S. soldiers were not well suited to respond to the contentious political climates in less developed countries, where nationalist and communist uprisings were common. As he saw it, military solutions to wars of national liberation or revolutions were not feasible. U.S. leaders, he warned, had to realize that nationalist movements could not be dismissed and opposed as communist-inspired and could not be thwarted by force of American arms. To attempt to do so, he contended, would require American troops to fight on various fronts against nationalist-communist forces around the world, with great risk to and sacrifice by U.S. military services, especially the marines.

Because of Eisenhower's warnings about the military-industrial complex and after the Bay of Pigs disaster, Shoup began to fear the influence of government agencies such as the CIA and the power of big business in the making and execution of foreign and military policy. Industry, he argued, had its own agenda and often pursued goals that discouraged freedom and democracy; simultaneously trying to overthrow a government in Cuba and prop up one in Laos, the CIA was virtually unchecked and ran its own operations without adequate oversight. As he saw it, American soldiers were in peril of being deployed to areas where they would be in great danger because nonmilitary institutions were wielding undue influence over U.S. national security decisions.

Although already skeptical of American actions abroad but believing that to oppose them would be disloyal, Shoup did not publicly critique U.S. policies while he was commandant. After retiring in late 1963 and observing the growing American role in Vietnam, however, he began to speak out, and by the mid-1960s, he was a virulent opponent of the war. As early as the 1964 debate over the pivotal Gulf of Tonkin Resolution, Sen. Wayne Morse of Oregon, one of only two senators to oppose giving the government a blank check to wage war in Indochina, had wanted to call Shoup and other military dissenters—including Gen. James Gavin, Gen. Matthew Ridgway, and Gen. J. Lawton Collins—to testify against the measure. The move was stifled by Sen. J. William Fulbright, the chair of the Senate Committee on Foreign Relations, who would ironically become a supporter of Shoup's actions in later years.

In May 1966, Shoup decided he could no longer suppress his opinion on Vietnam, and he publicly attacked the growing war in harsh terms. Speaking at the World Affairs Day for junior college students in Los Angeles, the former commandant blasted the American obsession with communism, observing that the majority of Vietnamese were nationalists who had historically challenged foreign interference in their affairs. Furthermore, he said, Indochina was in no way vital to America's global interests. "The whole of Southeast Asia," he indelicately observed, "was not worth the life or limb of a single American." Even more remarkably, Shoup saw the war as an act of American aggression. "I believe that if we had and would keep our dirty, bloody, dollar-crooked fingers out of . . . these nations so full of depressed exploited people," the general angrily charged, "they will arrive at a solution of their own [not one] crammed down their throats by Americans."[3]

Shoup's rhetoric was striking, but he was not alone among retired military brass in condemning the U.S. war. That same year,

many other senior officers (most notably, the influential and deco-
rated Generals Gavin and Ridgway) began publicly to question and
criticize the war, as well. In February 1966, Senator Fulbright, who
had turned against the war, invited Gavin, a three-star general and
past ambassador to France, to testify at the televised Senate Vietnam Hearings, where Gavin challenged the Johnson administration's rationale for and optimism about the U.S. intervention in
Southeast Asia. American involvement, Gavin believed, had already
grown "alarmingly out of balance" because the region was not vital
to the national security and the war was sure to require a vast commitment without a likelihood of victory. As Gavin saw it, the United
States would have to discover political, not military, solutions to the
crisis in Vietnam, but "it may be far too late for that now," he feared
in early 1966.[4]

General Ridgway had replaced Douglas MacArthur as the commander of United Nations forces in Korea and then served as army
chief of staff in the 1950s. In 1966, he, too, publicly disparaged the war
in Vietnam. Earlier, during the 1954 Dien Bien Phu crisis, he had
forcefully rejected attempts to intervene in Indochina to bail out the
French. Over a decade later, he still believed that the United States
had little to gain from involvement there. In his view the war was
hurting the nation's image and influence globally, was undermining
hopes for arms control, was exacerbating tensions with the Soviet
Union, and was limiting America's ability to respond to foreign policy
needs elsewhere. Ridgway further blasted the administration's justi-
fications for the war—preserving self-determination, extending freedom, and restoring law and order—as little more than "admirable
slogans" and asserted that the United States had no military strategy and goals in Vietnam. He thus called on President Johnson to "spell
out, more specifically and pragmatically, our immediate and long-
range political objectives" while firmly rejecting any goals that would
require an undue military effort. Even more, he described those objectives that the administration had established, such as gaining "freedom" for the Vietnamese people, as "theoretically noble, realistically
disingenuous, and pragmatically fallacious." Those who claimed that
American security was at stake in Vietnam, he added, "strain the
credulity of the most naive believer."[5]

The opposition of retired officers such as Shoup, Ridgway, and
Gavin in the mid-1960s, then, had a significant impact on national
discussions of the war. As the liberal journal *The Nation* pointed out,
it was "difficult to cast doubt on the patriotism of a military man,
and doubly so when he has Shoup's record of gallantry and leadership." The former commandant, Rep. Don Edwards further observed,
"cannot be dismissed as a misguided idealist, or a military novice.
For forty years he has fought for the principles of democracy."[6] Antiwar groups, especially those composed of soldiers and veterans,

often referred to Shoup and the other military dissenters in their own literature about the war. A wide spectrum of the media—including *The Nation, New Republic, Time, Forbes,* and *National Review*— reported favorably on the generals' activities. In addition, Shoup and retired army general Hugh Hester supported and spoke at rallies sponsored by the VVAW. By publicly attacking the war, the brass thus contributed to a national chain of opposition to Vietnam, as politicians and journalists time and again cited the officers' views to strengthen their own criticism of the conflict. The government, too, showed an interest in Shoup and the others, going so far as to have the Federal Bureau of Investigation conduct surveillance on some of the retired generals.

By 1967 the dissident officers were a vital part of the antiwar movement, though not associated with it in a formal manner. Shoup continued his public assault on the war, and in various media appearances, he developed an even more comprehensive appraisal of it. When President Johnson asserted that American troops were in Vietnam to stop the communists before they threatened U.S. territory, Shoup was incredulous and called such alarmist claims "pure, unadulterated poppycock."[7] With Gavin in agreement, he also rejected the domino theory as an excuse for the war, instead arguing that myopic anticommunism had pushed the biggest domino, the People's Republic of China, into the enemy camp.

Moreover, the generals warned, should America fail to limit the war, it could find itself in a terribly expanded conflict. In 1966, Gavin felt "quite uneasy about an overresponse in Vietnam" that might provoke Chinese intervention. In fact, the brass believed that America's continued involvement in the war actually helped the PRC and Soviet Union. Gavin explained that those two communist powers could pursue expansive foreign policies because the United States could not challenge them while tied down in Vietnam. Although some hawks argued that China was too weak and unstable to intervene in Vietnam, especially with its internal Cultural Revolution then under way, Gavin believed that undue escalation could "bring order to the Chinese situation, with a prompt and militant response to the aid of Hanoi." Shoup agreed and also scored American relations with the PRC, complaining that the alienation of Mao Zedong might be Washington's "greatest blunder . . . unless the final results from our Vietnam commitment overshadow it."[8]

Shoup called on the United States to withdraw from Indochina, plaintively wondering, "Why can't we let people *actually* determine their own destiny?" The marine general believed America was, in fact, harming the people of Vietnam, the very individuals that the leaders claimed to be helping. Shoup maintained that the enemy forces—the National Liberation Front and the Vietcong—were much more popular among the Vietnamese populace than the fictive government of South Vietnam, and he observed that the opposing forces were actually "99 percent South Vietnamese," with the United States involved in a civil war on the wrong side. General Gavin agreed with Shoup, arguing that most VC fighters and supporters were not really communists but victims of government and elite oppression who had revolted as nationalists. Even the North Vietnamese leader Ho Chi Minh, they maintained, was a nationalist (albeit a communist, too) and would never be a puppet of the other communist powers, the Soviet Union and China. Indeed, the generals argued that China's Mao did not dominate Ho, and thus, they urged the United States to deal with Ho as a "free agent," as Gavin put it. Shoup agreed and accordingly described the war as a struggle between "those crooks in Saigon" and Vietnamese nationalists seeking a better life, free of foreign domination. Consequently, the military critics argued for recognition of the NLF in any negotiations concerning Southeast Asia.[9]

The dissenting generals also offered a strong condemnation of U.S. strategy in Vietnam, especially the air war. To many hawks inside the United States, a totally unrestrained air war against North Vietnam was the key to victory. Thus, from early 1965 forward, the United States conducted a massive bombing campaign against the North, known as Operation Rolling Thunder. Between August and December 1967 alone, for instance, American pilots bombed almost every target of military and economic importance in North Vietnam, flying over fifty thousand sorties and dropping over one hundred thousand *tons* of ordnance. Despite such massive firepower, as Gavin, Ridgway, and Shoup realized, the American air war had not measurably reduced the enemy's will or production. The idea of victory through the air was thus "one of the great illusions of all time," Ridgway said. He further observed that "Korea . . . taught us that it is impossible to interdict the supply routes of an Asian army by air power alone," and Shoup believed that American bombing actually was helping North Vietnam by bringing its people closer together and hardening their commitment. He felt it was "ludicrous" to try to stop the flow of materiel by bombing and referred to the communists' main supply route as the "Ho Chi Minh Autobahn."[10]

The generals called for an immediate halt to the air war. In a statement that brought, as the *New York Times* put it, "one of America's most prestigious military figures into the national debate" on Vietnam, Gen. Lauris Norstad, onetime Allied commander of the North Atlantic Treaty Organization, urged a cessation of all U.S. hostilities and called for an unconditional bombing halt in November 1967. Gavin simultaneously called for a "strategy of sanity" and observed that, since the North did not bomb the South, President Johnson should not expect Ho to reduce his commitment as a quid pro quo sign of good faith. The air war had to be halted, Shoup, Gavin, and the others insisted, because it was counterproductive and ineffective.[11]

The antiwar officers also contended that the air campaign was morally repugnant. General Gavin charged that American bombs were turning all of Vietnam into a "parking lot" and asserted that the bombing was isolating America in the community of nations. He pointed out that the United States had already dropped millions of tons of bombs on Vietnamese noncombatants and declared that "just bombing a city . . . for psychological reasons" was an illegitimate and unethical use of power. After Lt. William Calley's conviction for war crimes in the murder of villagers at My Lai, Gavin went so far as to observe that it was "tragic when a lieutenant in the infantry gets convicted and officers flying bombers don't." Marine colonel James Donovan, a close associate of Shoup's, also noted that the "lavish fire-power" used by the air force had devastated an already "hapless" nation and "created desolation and called it pacification."[12]

Worst of all, the generals believed, the air war could trigger hostilities or even a nuclear exchange between the United States and the PRC or the Soviet Union, which could have genocidal consequences. General Ridgway stated that a victory involving nuclear arms would be the "ultimate in immorality," adding that "there is nothing in the present situation . . . that requires us to bomb a small Asian nation 'back to the stone age.'" Gavin also warned that the use of nuclear weapons would produce a horrific situation in which hundreds of millions of Asians might die, America would be responsible for the ravaged survivors, and Southeast Asia's economy would be laid flat. Shoup agreed, stating that the air war had to stop "unless we want to commit ourselves to genocidal actions."[13]

On a more practical level, the dissident generals also felt that the war was taking a tremendous economic as well as moral toll on the United States. By early 1966 the military critics realized that America had taken over the Vietnam War, prompting Gavin to ask: "Is Vietnam . . . worth this investment . . . with all the other commitments we have? . . . Are we not losing sight of the total global picture?" Shoup likewise observed that American interests had suffered because of the war, and he doubted that, whatever the United States might gain in Indochina, "no matter how greatly it may be embellished, will ever equal one one-thousandth of the cost."[14]

American preoccupation with Vietnam, the generals also realized, was causing the government to "grossly neglect"—in Gavin's words—other public needs. In 1968, Gavin published a book, *Crisis Now*, in which he explored the crises of Vietnam and decay in American society. At home, he pointed out, while Washington was spending upward of $25 billion on the war, violence and pollution grew more severe, authorities were becoming more repressive, and millions of citizens lacked health care, employment training, and housing and educational facilities. He noted, however, that many Americans remained wealthy, and he cautioned that they "cannot live in an enclave of affluence" while billions of others lived in poverty around the globe. The nation deluded itself by thinking that it could add to its own prosperity while ignoring other countries because such inequality created a "worldwide discontent" with which the United States would ultimately have to contend. President Johnson's attempt to build the Great Society would never be realized if America shut out the rest of the world.[15]

With such a comprehensive, public indictment of the war, the generals attracted more attention as the conflict dragged on. In 1968, after the enemy's massive Tet Offensive, Shoup appeared before the Senate Committee on Foreign Relations to give his latest appraisal of the war. Though President Johnson and his military advisers were claiming that U.S. forces had dealt the NLF-VC troops a heavy blow during Tet, the former commandant had a much different opinion. As he saw it, the fact that the enemy could launch such a huge offensive—striking virtually every center of military and economic importance in South Vietnam in a coordinated attack during a holiday cease-fire and even invading the grounds of the U.S. embassy in Saigon—revealed the depth of America's problems in Vietnam. On top of that, the military's request for 200,000 more troops, to be added to the 540,000 already in the country, indicated that conditions were worse than ever. Just to protect the areas hit during Tet, Shoup told the assembled senators, would require at least 800,000 U.S. soldiers, and to take an offensive role would necessitate far more. Indeed, he believed that the United States would never be able to measure the enemy's capabilities and response and thus would never be certain of the number of troops it would need. "You can just pull any figure out of the hat," he lamented, "and that would not be enough." U.S. officials, he complained, had assigned American soldiers a task that was "impossible for them to perform." Given his indigenous support in the South, Ho Chi Minh could match American efforts without straining his North Vietnamese forces. "If I had to go through another of those Tet Holiday winning streaks," Shoup sarcastically concluded, "I didn't know whether I could take it or not." James Gavin agreed: "There will be no victory in Vietnam. Only more victims. This is the difficult and unfortunate truth we have to understand."[16]

As a result of Tet, millions of Americans turned against the war in Indochina. Just months before the offensive the U.S. commander in Vietnam, Gen. William C. Westmoreland, had given optimistic predictions of future success, finally seeing a light at the end of the tunnel. By spring 1968, as Shoup and many others realized, the United States was no closer to victory, and the American public was rapidly tiring of the destructive war. The Johnson administration understood that the situation in Vietnam had changed and accordingly began to take measures that would eventually de-escalate the war. First Johnson and then his successor, Richard Nixon, began the policy of "Vietnamization"—shifting the burden for fighting away from American troops and onto the South Vietnamese—and the incremental withdrawal of U.S. forces began. At the same time, however, Nixon increased the pace of the air war and geographically expanded the fighting into Cambodia and Laos. Shoup and other military critics thus continued to oppose the war and to receive even more public notice after 1968.

In 1969, General Shoup and his friend and fellow marine officer Col. James Donovan expanded their critique of the war beyond U.S. actions in Vietnam. They indicted the role of the military in American society. In an article in the *Atlantic Monthly* titled "The New American Militarism," they laid out a series of comprehensive charges concerning the militarization of American culture. As they saw it, the United States was becoming aggressive and imperialist because of "militarism." In the throes of the Cold War, Washington was taking military approaches to international problems that might be more appropriately handled by seeking common ground for political solutions. American leaders, Shoup observed, had become "pugnacious and chauvinistic." Military voices carried more weight in national policy discussions, and groups such as the Veterans of Foreign Wars were propagandizing for the armed forces establishment. The American people, the general charged, were likely to buy into such militarism because the U.S. education system was discouraging independent thought while stressing obedience.[17]

Shoup and Donovan also complained that the military's own structure had encouraged the war. Every officer obviously sought promotions, and service in battle offered the best opportunity for rising up through the ranks. Too many officers, they contended, were pushing for war, obscuring the actual mission of the military to defend the national security and drawing the services more deeply into political games. At the same time, the four branches of the military—army, navy, air force, and marines—were engaged in competition to be the first, fastest, and most effective branch in wartime. In the process, the various services exaggerated their own capabilities, and military advisers manipulated information to make their own branches look best. Expanding on the ideas in his article with Shoup, Donovan charged in a book titled *Militarism U.S.A.* that the armed forces "participated in what may not have been exactly a conspiracy, but was at least a well-organized readiness—indeed, an inclination—to get into the war."[18]

Shoup and other officers took on the military-industrial complex, as well. In 1960, Eisenhower had warned that the major corporations that produced weapons and military equipment possessed great power in developing national policy, and Shoup shared his fears. The United States, the former commandant contended,

> did not have and does not have . . . a national security policy . . . and I have always thought that that was the genesis of the military-industrial complex, simply because here were the chiefs sitting down there wondering what armed forces should we have to meet the requirements of the Commander-in-Chief and our nation? When actually it should be the other way around. There should be a national security policy that tells the armed forces what to be able to do. So this annually rolled up into obviously hundreds of millions of dollars that the armed forces said they needed because they didn't have any directive.[19]

The military-industrial complex, many officers believed, was not balanced between the two sectors. The industrial component essentially determined the nature of the American economy; the military, though it controlled the technique of war, did not hold effective power. In fact, General Gavin had observed in the 1950s that "what appears to be intense interservice rivalry in most cases . . . is fundamentally industrial rivalry."[20] Shoup and other brass also recognized the vital role of big business in determining policy and joined the Business Executives Move for Peace in Vietnam—a coalition of military and financial interests opposed to the war. Clearly, the antiwar officers recognized the interdependent and intricate nature of the military-political-economic state and concluded that victory in Southeast Asia, even if possible, was neither cost effective nor moral. This convergence of military and economic forces had again demonstrated the difficulties involved in advocating a military solution in Vietnam.

Such a critique of American militarism would likely have been dismissed in earlier years, but by the late 1960s and early 1970s the critical views of a group of distinguished officers could not be easily ignored and were an integral part of mainstream opposition to the war. In an op-ed piece for the *New York Times,* General Ridgway lamented that success in Vietnam "is not now and never has been possible under conditions consistent with our interests." The Nixon administration, he concluded, had to "repudiate once and for all the search for a military solution." Gavin similarly testified before the Senate that America was irrevocably "suffering a grievous strategic defeat" in Indochina. After touring Vietnam for two weeks and then meeting with National Security Adviser Henry Kissinger, Rear Adm. Arnold True also attacked Nixon for "shoring up the dictatorial regime" of South Vietnam's president, Nguyen Van Thieu.[21]

In April 1970, Nixon expanded the war by invading Cambodia and thereby prompted more military criticism, along with renewed public outrage and international condemnation. The Cambodia "incursion," as Nixon termed it, "startled" Gavin, and he feared that Nixon might venture into North Vietnam, as well. Army general William Wallace Ford also attacked the administration; if Cambodia had a "friend like us," he wondered, "what is the meaning of an enemy?" General Hester added that Nixon had invaded Cambodia while allegedly winding down the war with his policy of Vietnamization, which amounted to a cynical ploy to wage war by proxy and was "more criminal and immoral" than a direct American slaughter of the Vietnamese. To Hester, Vietnamization meant that the United States was "hiring Asians to kill, maim and wound other Asians for the profit of the U.S. military-industrial complex." Gavin contended, furthermore, that Vietnamization undermined America's stated aims because it was a substitute for withdrawal when, in fact, a commitment to plans and dates for leaving was needed. American money and energy, he insisted, should only be used "for the extrication of our forces."[22]

General Shoup called on Nixon to set a date for a "complete pullout" from Vietnam, and he believed that all U.S. forces could and should withdraw by the beginning of 1971. As he saw it, Vietnamization was "never devised to end the war" but was being used to continue the conflict with South Vietnamese "mercenaries" while co-opting public criticism by reducing casualties. Such a disengagement, Shoup added, was costly. Even with an American pullout, "it would take millions of dollars, just to keep the [South Vietnamese army] equipped to fight to whatever level they fight, and to steal and thieve to whatever level they desire." General Ford likewise found little comfort in America's program for withdrawal. Vietnamization, he complained, was not possible if it was dependent on developing a stable government and army in the South, something that the United States had been unable to do since the early 1950s. Writing in the influential journal *Foreign Affairs* in July 1971, Ridgway also found it difficult to reconcile the reality of disengagement with Nixon's promise that the war would end soon. As long as any American forces remained in Indochina, he feared, "the war will drag on." Thus, the general urged the United States to help build up the Southern military to adequate strength for "say . . . six to nine months" and then proceed to phase down "forthwith [and] expeditiously to completion" until all forces had left Indochina.[23]

By mid-1971, however, Vietnamization—which had not ended the war—had helped to quiet the American public's outrage over the war, and the generals' criticisms did not have the impact they had had a few years earlier. Still, the military critics had made a substantive impact on the antiwar movement. Ridgway was one of the Wise Men called on by President Johnson to advise him about a war that the general considered "the most egregious mistake any U.S. government has ever made." Many top Republicans, fearful that Ronald Reagan might get their party's presidential nomination in 1968, approached General Gavin about running for the office himself, and four years later the Democrats approached him about being their vice presidential candidate. Shoup became a Washington favorite, too, with Senators Fulbright, Morse, Symington, and others urging the White House to listen to and heed his words.[24]

Shoup's opinions, however, may have been too frightening for the establishment to consider seriously. Although his opposition to the war in Vietnam was not unique, his broader cultural and political attack on American policy and American institutions went well beyond the views of other mainstream critics. By joining his appraisal of Vietnam with a critique of politics, militarism, the Central Intelligence Agency, the military-industrial complex, and the American educational system, the former commandant offered a remarkable and comprehensive analysis of the way America operated in the global arena. Like another "maverick marine," Gen. Smedley Butler—who spoke out against U.S. imperialism in the early twentieth century—Shoup took seriously American rhetoric about democracy, self-determination, and freedom from his earliest days in China through the Vietnam era. It was thus easy for him to blast the war in Vietnam. For Shoup, it was simply un-American for the United States to try to crush Vietnamese nationalism and to use the military for purposes that did not involve national security.

Today, more than a generation after the Vietnam War's end, too few Americans know about Gen. David Monroe Shoup, yet military officers, whether aware of him or not, follow his example. During the 1980s, for example, many top-level service officials opposed the Reagan administration's violent interventions into Latin America, and others criticized the Bush administration's invasion of Panama and the Gulf War. The U.S. military was wary of plans to intervene in Haiti, Somalia, and Bosnia. If he were still alive, David Shoup would surely be smiling as he reads reports of the military's reluctance to use U.S. armed power abroad in areas where political understanding and diplomacy, not warfare, are most needed. In addition, he would just as surely still be calling for the establishment of a humane and democratic foreign policy.

Notes

1. Shoup quoted in Howard Jablon, "David M. Shoup, U.S.M.C.: Warrior and War Protestor," *Journal of Military History* 60 (July 1996): 513–38.

2. Robert Buzzanco, *Masters of War: Military Dissent and Politics in the Vietnam Era* (New York: Cambridge University Press 1996), 134–35.

3. David M. Shoup speech at Junior College World Affairs Day, Los Angeles, May 14, 1966, in U.S. Congress, Senate Committee on Foreign Relations, *Present Situation in Vietnam,* 90th Cong., 2nd sess., 1968, 47.

4. John Gavin in U.S. Congress, Senate Committee on Foreign Relations, *Supplemental Foreign Assistance, Fiscal Year 1966—Vietnam,* 89th Cong., 2nd sess., 1966, 243 (hereafter cited as *The Vietnam Hearings*).

5. Matthew Ridgway, *The Korean War* (Garden City, N.Y.: Doubleday, 1967), 232, and idem, "Indochina: Disengaging," *Foreign Affairs* 49 (July 1971): 586.

6. *The Nation,* April 17, 1967, 483–84; and Don Edwards in *Congressional Record—Extension of Remarks,* March 18, 1968, p. 6911.

7. Robert Buzzanco, "The American Military's Rationale against the Vietnam War," *Political Science Quarterly* 101 (Winter 1986): 565.

8. Gavin in *The Vietnam Hearings*, 236, 262; Gavin in Senate Committee on Foreign Relations, *Conflicts between Capabilities and Commitment,* 90th Cong., 1st sess., 1967, 4; Gavin in Senate Committee on Foreign Relations, *Moral and Military Aspects,* 91st Cong., 2nd sess., 1970, 60–61, 66; and Shoup in Senate Committee on Foreign Relations, *Present Situation in Vietnam,* 1968, 48.

9. Transcript of Shoup interview with Rep. William Ryan, December 19, 1967, David M. Shoup biographical file, Marine Corps Historical Center, Washington, D.C. (hereafter cited as MCHC).

10. Matthew Ridgway, "Pull-Out, All-Out, or Stand Fast in Vietnam?" *Look,* April 4, 1966, 81–89, and transcript of Shoup interview with John Scali on *ABC Scope,* August 6, 1967, in Shoup file, MCHC.

11. Buzzanco, "The American Military's Rationale," 572.

12. Gavin in *The Vietnam Hearings,* 228, 238, 317–18; and James Donovan, *Militarism U.S.A.* (New York: Scribner's, 1970), 173–74.

13. Ridgway, "Pull-Out," 84, and transcript of Shoup interview with Ryan, MCHC.

14. Gavin in *The Vietnam Hearings,* 239, and Shoup in Senate Committee on Foreign Relations, *Present Situation in Vietnam,* 19.

15. James Gavin, *Crisis Now* (New York: Random House, 1968), 8–9.

16. Shoup in Senate Committee on Foreign Relations, *Present Situation in Vietnam,* 15–17, and Gavin, *Crisis Now,* 39.

17. David Shoup and James Donovan, "The New American Militarism," *Atlantic Monthly,* April 1969, 51–56.

18. Donovan, *Militarism U.S.A.,* 100.

19. Shoup in Jablon, "David M. Shoup," 513–38.

20. James Gavin, *War and Peace in the Space Age* (New York: Harper and Row, 1958), 256–57.

21. Ridgway in *New York Times,* March 14, 1970; True in *New York Times,* July 18, 1969; and Gavin in Buzzanco, "The American Military's Rationale," 567.

22. Ford in *New York Times,* February 18, 1971; Hester in *New York Times,* April 10, 1970, and April 3, 1971; and Gavin in Buzzanco, "The American Military's Rationale," 570.

23. Shoup in Senate Committee on Foreign Relations, *Legislative Proposals Relating to the War in Southeast Asia*, 91st Cong., 2nd sess., 1970, 489–92; and Ridgway, "Indochina: Disengaging."

24. Ridgway in Buzzanco, "The American Military's Rationale," 564.

Suggested Readings

In addition to the sources listed in the notes, see Matthew B. Ridgway, *Soldier: The Memoirs of Matthew B. Ridgway* (New York: Harper and Row, 1956), and Mark Perry, *Four Stars* (Boston: Houghton Mifflin, 1989).

10

Otto Feinstein, the McCarthy Campaign in Michigan, and Campus Activism during the Cold War*

Melvin Small

Like the unanticipated Tet Offensive and the killings at Kent State, another traumatic incident of the Vietnam era that deeply troubled Americans was the violence surrounding the 1968 Democratic National Convention in Chicago. In front of a worldwide television audience, the Chicago police—supported by the Illinois National Guard—followed the edict of law-and-order mayor Richard J. Daley to tolerate no disruption of the convention by protestors. Although admittedly taunted by some radicals in the crowd, the police overreacted in an orgy of beatings and mass arrests far out of proportion to the provocation. As gripping as the street scenes were, an equally fundamental drama was occurring inside the convention hall. Internal divisions within the Democratic Party paralleled the fissures in American society and revealed the inability of the political process to respond effectively to the challenge that the war presented.

Attending the Chicago convention was an alternate delegate from Michigan by the name of Otto Feinstein, who supported Sen. Eugene McCarthy as a peace candidate for the Democratic presidential nomination. Feinstein was the leader of the McCarthy Democrats, or the Concerned Democrats in Michigan, from 1966 through 1969. A refugee from Nazi Austria, he became involved in reform democratic or social democratic politics at the University of Chicago, where he founded the journal *New University Thought (NUT)*. He then taught at Wayne State University in Detroit, where he became involved in Michigan politics. In the fall of 1967, he was one of those people most influential in convincing Senator McCarthy to run for president as an antiwar candidate, and he was central to the successful insurgent effort in Democratic Party politics in Michigan. The national McCarthy campaign failed to nominate its candidate, but, as Melvin Small explains, the political changes that Feinstein and other McCarthy Democrats effected were significant. Amid the many accounts of hippies, radicals, and SDS anti-warriors, the story of adult, liberal, mostly college-related reformers

*Chris Johnson, Tim Kiska, Lynn Parsons, Sarajane Miller-Small, and John Weiss assisted in the preparation of this chapter.

Courtesy of Melvin Small

such as Feinstein reveals much about reform politics within the Democratic Party.

Melvin Small is a professor of history at Wayne State University in Detroit, Michigan, and past president of the Council on Peace Research in History. His Ph.D. is from the University of Michigan. Among his many publications are *Johnson, Nixon, and the Doves* (1988), *Covering Dissent: The Media and the Anti-Vietnam War Movement* (1994), *Democracy and Diplomacy: The Impact of Domestic Politics on U.S. Foreign Relations, 1789–1994* (1996), and *The Presidency of Richard Nixon* (1999).

The anti–Vietnam War movement was centered on college campuses where professors and graduate students provided leadership to undergraduates who marched, rallied, leafleted, petitioned, and sometimes committed acts of civil and uncivil disobedience to demonstrate their opposition to the conflict. At no time in American history had academics figured so prominently in the creation of a political movement. They reached their peak of influence and genuine power during Sen. Eugene McCarthy's campaign for the 1968 Democratic presidential nomination.

Most of the millions who participated in the movement to end the war were liberal Democrats committed to working within the system to improve the prospects for peace and justice at home and abroad. Although the media often presented the antiwar movement as dominated by left-wing, countercultural, even anti-"Amerikan" young people, many of those who worked most effectively to end the war were middle-class adults who wore coats and ties and dresses and heels and saluted when the flag passed. They were normal people contending with critical issues that affected their personal, professional, and civic lives on individual, community, institutional, social, and cultural levels. Prof. Otto Feinstein of Wayne State University in Detroit was one of the national leaders of the McCarthy drive and executive director of the McCarthy campaign in Michigan. He was committed to working through the system, and his many earlier campus-based political activities prefigured his involvement in the attempt to nominate a Democratic presidential candidate who would end the war in Vietnam and preserve the New Deal coalition.

Feinstein was born in Vienna in 1930, the son of Abraham Feinstein and Bella Silber, both of whom came from Hasidic Jewish families. Born in the Austro-Hungarian Empire, Abraham came from Bukovina, which later became part of Romania, and Bella was from Galicia, which would become part of Poland. After serving in World War I and graduating from law school, Abraham became a successful and influential banker and commodity trader, with his business centered in Bucharest. Because of the 1929 pogroms in Romania, he moved his wife to Vienna for safety. Their first child, Otto, was born in the Austrian capital.

Otto grew up in a well-to-do household. Although his parents did not follow their families' Orthodox traditions, they were practicing Jews. At a very young age, he became aware of the anti-Semitism that he and his family confronted in a variety of ways. He also remembers well the intense political conflicts between the Left and the Right in the political cauldron that was Austria during the depression.

Four months after the 1938 Anschluss—the Nazi annexation of Austria—Abraham, a Romanian citizen, was able to obtain the aid of the Romanian consul in Vienna in escaping with his wife and two children to Zurich. He had read Adolph Hitler's *Mein Kampf* and had made careful preparations to leave any area controlled by the Nazis. Having begun public school in Vienna, Otto continued his education in 1938 and 1939 in Zurich and Lausanne. His father moved the family to London in 1939; there, after spending one day in school, Otto and his younger brother, Alfred, were evacuated to Cornwall.

Fearing a German invasion of England, Abraham arranged for his family to travel to the United States on tourist visas to see the New York World's Fair. (The U.S. immigration quota for European Jews was very small.) By the time the Feinsteins arrived in New York in May 1940, the fair and their visas had only three days until expiration. They could have been turned away at Customs, but a kind immigration official let them enter the country. Ultimately, American relatives helped the Feinsteins obtain immigrant visas.

In New York, Otto attended public schools in Jackson Heights and Manhattan before the family took up permanent residence in 1941 in Forest Hills, located in the New York City borough of Queens. By the time that he entered Forest Hills High School in 1944, he had attended nine grade schools in four countries and had been taught in three different languages. His father had established himself in the export-import business, which provided the family with a comfortable lifestyle, albeit not as comfortable as that to which it had been accustomed in Europe.

Although his father had never been involved in sectarian politics, political discussions always dominated the family meal times. Abraham read four newspapers daily and listened avidly to radio commentators, which was not surprising during World War II for a person concerned about the rest of his family in Europe. In the years immediately after the war, Otto traveled to the Continent with his father to search, generally in vain, for relatives who survived the Holocaust. For the rest of his life, the Holocaust would remain a central experience for him, as it did for many European—

and American—Jews. His advocacy of citizen activism to promote social justice and to maintain a healthy democratic system had its roots in that experience.

At Forest Hills High School, Feinstein played on the soccer and chess teams, sang in the chorus, and excelled scholastically, although he was not Americanized enough to care about such things as the prom. He remembered that his main political ambition as a freshman was to join the U.S. Army and "get even" with the Nazis. After winning a New York State Regents scholarship in 1948, he tried to obtain admission to Columbia University but was told by a Jewish interviewer that the "quota for intelligent students had been filled." When he ran into similar indications of not-so-veiled anti-Semitism at Cornell and Syracuse, he decided (along with his brother, who had caught up with him in school) to go to the University of Chicago, which had no quota and offered an attractive general education curriculum. Under the university's Hutchins Plan, it was also possible to graduate in two years, which Otto did in 1950.

While at Chicago, Feinstein almost immediately became involved in protests against racism at the university hospital and against Illinois's anticommunist Broyles Bill. He joined the Young Progressives of America during his first semester and soon became an officer of that wing of the Henry Wallace presidential campaign, for which he served as a poll watcher in the 1948 election. He also played on the university's soccer team, and his teammates elected him their representative to protest the Broyles Bill at a demonstration in Springfield.

Feinstein developed a lifelong interest in grassroots politics while working on local political issues in the depressed neighborhoods surrounding the university. Within the school, he became an activist in the more progressive of the two main student parties— the party involved in activities beyond the campus. Interestingly, Sander Levin, whom he would meet in Michigan Democratic Party politics twenty years later, was a leader of the more conservative student party at the University of Chicago. In 1950 the university's student council elected him to be an observer at the epochal Prague conference of the International Union of Students, an organization that could not survive the dark days of the early Cold War as an independent institution. The experience in Prague, mingling with students from both blocs, gave him firsthand exposure to the nature of the Cold War that had descended on Europe.

Throughout his years as a student, Feinstein saw a direct connection between his interest in the social sciences and political life outside the academy. He knew from the first that he would pursue a scholarly career that dealt with social issues. After graduating in 1950, he went on to the Institute des Hautes Études in Geneva, where he spent three years studying for a licentiate in international relations. At Geneva, he became active in the Swiss Federation of Students and the Swiss Union of Jewish Students and was vice president of the Association of Anti-Colonial Student Unions.

In 1953, he was drafted into the U.S. Army. During his two years at Camp Kilmer, Fort Dix, and Fort Meade, he "broadened his understanding of people from different classes and regions of the country." Using the GI Bill, he returned to the University of Chicago in 1955 to work on a Ph.D. In Geneva, he had studied traditional international relations; now, he concentrated on economic development and cultural change in the Third World. Completed under Bert Hoselitz in 1956, Otto's thesis dealt with the economic, social, and political role of foreign investment in Venezuela. As a graduate student, he also resumed his activity in campus politics, again representing his party in the student council.

Distressed with the way in which "old ideological positions developed in a different era" continued to dominate political discourse, Feinstein and a group of friends set out to publish a journal of opinion in 1959. They wanted, as they noted in their first issue, "to develop a coherent way of looking at society which can provide a rational basis for a political program for the '60s and '70s." The first issue of *New University Thought* appeared in the spring of 1960 and featured articles by Linus Pauling, David Reisman, Feinstein, and several other members of the editorial board. Published quarterly through the late 1960s, *NUT* offered nonsectarian, eclectic approaches to the problems of war and peace, race, and economic development. It boasted a *"radical* mode of analysis, radical in the original sense of going to the root."

The editors were mostly young scholars looking for ways to create a broad intellectual community in which they could use their expertise to develop new solutions to societal problems. Colleagues involved with *NUT* nationwide not only contributed to the journal but also formed study groups on their campuses to consider the issues raised in the journal. Feinstein never forgot about the "submission of the universities and academics" to fascism in the 1930s and maintained throughout his career that the "universities had a social role critical for democratic societies." Not surprisingly, *NUT* became an essential vehicle for sharing information about the war in Vietnam and, later, about the McCarthy campaign. In its front-page article on September 16, 1960, the *Times (London) Literary Supplement* offered "an especially warm welcome" to the first volume of *NUT*, noting that Feinstein's article on Latin America deserved a "worthy place in any educated European's library."

With a press run of five thousand copies, *NUT* relied on subscriptions and a growing network of supporters in over twenty colleges, including the University of California, Berkeley, and Columbia University. The editors ran twenty thousand copies for one special 1962 issue on peace. Among the contributors to that issue were Seymour Melman, Arthur Waskow, Rep. William Fitts Ryan (D–NY), and Todd Gitlin. The journal's call for new paradigms in 1960 resembled the Students for a Democratic Society's Port Huron Statement of 1962. Both organizations were similarly dissatisfied with the contemporary political debate, but the people at *NUT* were of an older generation and were willing to work within the system, liberal warts and all.

In the fall of 1960, Feinstein took a job at Monteith College in Detroit's Wayne State University, and in December 1961, he married fellow *NUT* editor Nicolette Margaret Cecelia Carey, who was also an assistant editor of the *Bulletin of Atomic Scientists*. (Although it took Feinstein two years to make it through the University of Chicago, Carey used the Hutchins Plan to graduate in one year!) Founded in 1958, Monteith was an experimental college that employed the general studies model of the University of Chicago. In fact, several of its faculty had attended or were recruited from Chicago.

In the 1960 presidential campaign, like many of his colleagues, Feinstein did not work *for* John F. Kennedy but *against* Richard M. Nixon. In 1962, he became a Democratic Party precinct delegate and soon organized fellow delegates into the Wednesday Evening Club, a discussion-action group interested in promoting new ideas within the party. Their goal was not to take over or "subvert the party" but to invigorate its debate and move it in new and more promising directions. (Of course, party regulars did not always see things that way.) When Feinstein became vice president of the Thirteenth Congressional District Democratic Party in 1964, he established an important base from which to operate.

Open housing and the establishment of the Wayne County Community College system were among the key issues during the early 1960s in which Feinstein played a leading role. He and several colleagues also produced a local, seventeen-part public television series, *The Balance of Fear*, on the nuclear arms race, and after the Partial Test Ban Treaty was approved in 1963, other public television stations aired one of the segments in fifteen cities. The budget for the series was $180.

Feinstein was a leader of the Committee for a Sane Nuclear Policy (SANE) and a friend of its longtime director, Sanford Gottlieb, who also contributed articles to *NUT*. When Feinstein determined that the local Detroit chapter of SANE was too involved in internecine conflict with the national office, however, the tireless and always creative organizer founded Wayne SANE, which soon recruited twenty-three faculty members for its speaker's bureau. He also became one of the founders of the Center for Teaching about Peace and War (later the Center for Peace and Conflict Studies), an organization devoted not only to studying such issues in Wayne State University but also to bringing them to the community. The organization was one of the first peace and conflict centers in the United States.

In a related venture, Feinstein traveled to Columbia University to help organize the Universities Committee on the Problems of War and Peace in February 1963. In their founding document, which resembled *NUT*'s first editorial, the committee's leaders announced that they intended "to make specific use of the special talents of academic people in discovering, developing and articulating information and suggestions relating to the problems of war and peace." Feinstein was elected executive secretary of the organization, whose sponsors included Kenneth Boulding, Richard Falk, S. I. Hayakawa, Herbert Kelman, Guenter Lewy, and David Reisman. Feinstein and his wife edited the newsletter of the organization that went out to nine thousand academics on 250 campuses. The committee's membership and newsletter overlapped with those of *NUT*, but unlike the magazine, this organization was concerned exclusively with war and peace issues.

During this period, Feinstein published a flurry of articles on disarmament and international relations in *NUT*, the *Bulletin of Atomic Scientists*, the *Saturday Review of Books, Current History*, and other journals, and he edited a book on development, *Two Worlds of Change* (1964). As a student of the developing world, he was well aware of the colonial war fought by the French against the Vietnamese and the American acceptance of the French burden in Vietnam in 1954. He worried as the United States became more and more involved in Southeast Asia and doubted President Lyndon Johnson's explanation of the 1964 Gulf of Tonkin incident that led Congress to pass the Gulf of Tonkin Resolution. He was concerned about Johnson's policies in Vietnam, but he was far more worried about the prospect of Sen. Barry Goldwater's (R–AZ) election in 1964. That concern led him to organize the Republicans and Independents for Johnson in Detroit. Feinstein compared Johnson to Truman as a president with laudable domestic programs who had been led by others into dangerous Cold War policies, in part because he did not know much about international relations.

After Johnson began the sustained bombing of North Vietnam in February 1965, Feinstein and his colleagues at Wayne and throughout the *NUT* and the Universities Committee networks immediately began to hold meetings and workshops on college campuses. The bombing was the catalyst that sparked the antiwar movement in the United States and throughout the world. The

Universities Committee declared March 4 a national "Vietnam Day," during which faculty, students, and community people participated in meetings and lectures on over 100 campuses, anticipating what soon came to be called "teach-ins." Feinstein and his Wayne colleagues kept in close contact and shared strategies with like-minded faculty members at the University of Michigan, some forty miles away in Ann Arbor—particularly with history professor John Weiss. It was not surprising, then, that the University of Michigan's famous teach-in of March 24–25, 1965, resembled the conference held on Wayne's campus on March 4. During that frenetic early spring, on the weekend of April 8–9, Feinstein was among the more than 100 mostly East Coast faculty members who traveled to Washington to lobby over 60 legislators on the war.

In its summer 1965 issue, *NUT* led with an article entitled "Vietnam: The Bar Mitzvah of American Intellectuals." The journal had questioned American involvement in Vietnam as early as August 1962. Now, three years later, the editors wrote that "the most significant aspect of the recent ferment and action in academia has not been the actions themselves . . . but the potential change in what academics do and how they see their role in society." For the first time "American academics have begun to feel that they have the competence and the right to pass judgment upon our policy, to express this judgment, and to work actively in a variety of ways to make this judgment felt." They were speaking out publicly against U.S. policies in Vietnam at precisely the time in American history when "the universities and the faculty and researchers attached to them as individuals and as a class are becoming increasingly important and powerful in the functioning of our society."

The editors were pleased that "academics are beginning to learn how to use the mass media to communicate their ideas" and how to establish relationships with government officials. In the end, they predicted that academics might even form a sort of "shadow cabinet" to "evaluate present programs and propose new ones from the highest level of competence." Feinstein and his colleagues called for a careful and patient nurturing of the antiwar activities on campuses, building them into something that might lead to profound changes in the nature of the relationship of the once insular academic community to the national political culture. In the spring of 1965, that community was moving in the direction called for when *NUT* editors first presented their agenda in 1960.

In addition to bringing out the seminal *NUT* issue on the war, Feinstein helped organize antiwar meetings and petition drives. These included the "Citizens' Hearings on Vietnam" on the Wayne campus, led by two Michigan congressmen, Republican William Broomfield and Democrat Charles C. Diggs, on August 6 and 7, as well as the International Conference on Alternate Perspectives on Vietnam, held in Ann Arbor from September 14 to 18, 1965. Among those presenting papers at the Ann Arbor conference was the distinguished French scholar Jean Lacouture.

On March 13, 1966, Feinstein, Weiss, and other antiwar Democrats established the Council for Democratic Action within Michigan. They had worked with friends in the Women's International League for Peace and Freedom (WILPF) to identify Democratic precinct delegates who desired to change administration policy at home and abroad. As its first order of business, the new council sent the Michigan Democratic State Committee its Vietnam program, which called for an end to the bombing, negotiations, and free elections open to all factions in South Vietnam. The state committee summarily rejected the proposals, but a formal process for developing opposition to the national party's policies had begun in the Detroit metropolitan area.

One outgrowth of this activity was the formation of reform caucuses in several districts, most notably the Liberal Conference in the Seventeenth Congressional District. In May 1967, Feinstein and his colleagues, now calling themselves the Conference of Concerned Democrats, announced a meeting to be held in Detroit on Wayne's campus on June 10. As many as 350 people came to hear Zoltan Ferency, the antiwar Michigan Democratic State Party chair, Detroit mayor Jerome Cavanagh, state senator Coleman Young, and Rep. John Conyers. A highlight of the meeting was a rousing speech by Wayne history professor Lynn Parsons. He urged the Concerned Democrats to elect precinct delegates, "to speak up, to work hard, to sacrifice long hours in travel and in meetings," and to work "through the political party which for most of the century has led the nation in meeting its most serious problems." The Michigan Conference of Concerned Democrats, which grew out of this gathering, served as a model used by Allard Lowenstein, Sanford Gottlieb, Bella Abzug, and others to develop a nationwide Concerned Democrats organization at a meeting in Washington later that month.

By August, the Concerned Democrats had organized units in all but two of Michigan's nineteen congressional districts. In December seven hundred Concerned Democrats attended a rally in Detroit featuring Julian Bond, John Conyers, Zoltan Ferency, and television actor Robert Vaughn, better known as "The Man from U.N.C.L.E." They responded enthusiastically to a call to action: "The time has come to proclaim the American Dream of Equality for all as the priority of our nation. For an all-out war on poverty and racism. To recognize that Vietnam has become . . . a symbol of the 'arrogance of power' and 'the major roadblock to the realization of the American Dream.'"

In office since 1963, Ferency was one of the few party chairs to oppose Johnson's reelection in 1967. His "disloyalty" came to a head at a meeting of the Michigan Democratic Central Committee in Port Huron in the early fall, when he found himself virtually the only state Democratic official unwilling to support the president's bid for a second term. Ferency decided to resign in order to help an antiwar candidate who would challenge Johnson. Drifting even further to the left after Hubert Humphrey won the Democratic nomination, Ferency founded the Human Rights Party in 1969, a third party that enjoyed very limited success in Michigan through the 1970s. Characteristically, even after disappointments in 1968 and 1969, Feinstein remained a loyal Democrat.

He and other Michigan insurgents who wanted to convince President Johnson to change his policies in Vietnam had to deal with the United Automobile Workers (UAW), the single most influential group within the state Democratic Party. The UAW was committed to many of the same progressive domestic programs as the Concerned Democrats but, nonetheless, was reluctant to criticize Johnson because it feared for the survival of those programs. Moreover, UAW president Walter Reuther practiced a form of democratic centralism in his organization that made it difficult even for his brother, Victor, an early opponent of the war, to get his voice heard either within the executive board or among the rank and file.

By virtue of his office in the Thirteenth Congressional District, Feinstein had been appointed to the Resolutions Committee of the 1966 state convention. Although Feinstein received support from a majority of delegates in all of Michigan's counties for a resolution mildly critical of U.S. involvement in South Vietnam, Reuther, Sen. Phil Hart, Feinstein's old University of Chicago classmate Sander Levin, and other party regulars muscled through their own motion in support of the president. At one point, clever party parliamentarians prevented Feinstein from speaking even during an open debate.

Generally realistic in his approach to politics, Feinstein cannot understand to this day why the UAW would not meet his group halfway and why "they never talked to us as human beings." He was not interested in sharing power or "infiltrating" the party; he wanted only to work with all of its factions to refocus its foreign policy. The UAW was leery of groups that appeared on its left, however, and among the emerging leadership of the Concerned Democrats were a handful of former (or maybe even current) members of the Communist Party who had crossed swords with the UAW during the 1940s.

On the surface, the differences between those who supported Johnson and those who called for a change in Vietnam policy appeared slight. Both Johnson and his opponents among the Concerned Democrats called for a negotiated end to the war. The president pointed over and over to his many offers to the North Vietnamese to come to the peace table and bargain in good faith. The chief difference was that the Concerned Democrats contended that the administration had to halt the bombing before serious negotiations could begin. That was the position taken by Hanoi, as well.

Feinstein never became involved directly in the organization of the major mass demonstrations that were held, generally twice a year, from 1965 through 1971. Like many others in the leadership of the antiwar movement, he wondered about the resources and energy expended on these activities. Accepting a division of labor within the movement, he spent most of his time working on campus and within the Michigan Democratic Party on electoral politics.

It was one thing to form the Concerned Democrats. It was quite another to identify a candidate willing to run against Johnson in 1968. At some time in late 1966, Feinstein came to the conclusion that Johnson was not going to be sufficiently affected by the antiwar movement to search for a viable way to end the war. Even worse, it was clear that the Democratic Party, "the only practical vehicle for social change," was on the verge of coming apart over the war issue. From Feinstein's perspective, only New York senator Robert F. Kennedy could hold together the cumbersome New Deal coalition that stood for progressive reform in the United States. Throughout 1967, he therefore worked on both the local and the national level to try to convince Kennedy to challenge Johnson. On one occasion, prodded by David Reisman, he traveled to Boston to present his analysis of the 1968 election to John Kenneth Galbraith and other Kennedy advisers.

Even after Kennedy clearly indicated he would not throw his hat into the ring, Feinstein hoped for his candidacy because no other Democrat could keep the party together. Indeed, he was still a Kennedy man when Minnesota senator Eugene McCarthy made his important visit to Detroit on November 10, 1967, to speak at a party dinner in the Second Congressional District—and to test the political waters. James Harrison, the public relations director for Michigan's Democratic State Central Committee, had already set up the first McCarthy for President Committee in the nation.

McCarthy supporters asked Feinstein, who had connections to the Sheriff's Department because of his position in Wayne County's Thirteenth District, to work with them to organize a small McCarthy-for-president rally at Detroit Metropolitan Airport. McCarthy had not yet announced his candidacy but was leaning toward running. The idea was to encourage him with an impressive show of grassroots support at the airport.

Still favoring Kennedy, Feinstein refused to get involved until he was convinced to take action by his wife, who saw McCarthy as the only viable option. Thus it was that he asked friends and colleagues to show up at the airport to greet the senator with handwritten placards calling for "Peace with McCarthy" and proclaiming "We Want Gene." This rally turned out to be one of the major early expressions of popular support for McCarthy covered by the media. Encouraged by the Michigan event and the enthusiastic response to his appearance in Berkeley, McCarthy formally announced his candidacy on November 30, 1967.

Several weeks later, Ferency asked Weiss to become chair of the Michigan McCarthy campaign and replace the Lansing-based Harrison. Feinstein became executive director of the organization and actually ran the operation from that position. An early leader in the national McCarthy campaign, Ferency had met in October with Allard Lowenstein and Prof. Arnold Kaufman of the University of Michigan in Ann Arbor to launch the formal "Dump Johnson" movement in Michigan.

Although they established headquarters for the Michigan McCarthy campaign in a residential area of the city away from the Wayne State campus, many of those who worked at the McCarthy office were faculty, spouses, and young people connected to the university. Much of the important financial planning was handled by several faculty wives, who were of that generation of women who stayed home with the kids. The Michigan McCarthy campaign raised more money for the candidate than any other McCarthy organization in a state without a primary election. With few exceptions, the campaign workers were white and middle-class, a reflection of McCarthy's inability to connect with African Americans, a core Democratic constituency in Detroit.

Feinstein's leadership did not go unchallenged. Phil Moore, a representative from McCarthy's national headquarters, reported back from Michigan on July 1, 1968, that the candidate's people in Ann Arbor had set up their own statewide splinter group supporting the senator, and another group in the Detroit suburbs also had chosen to go it alone "because of disagreement with the leadership of Otto Feinstein." Moore also claimed that "the abrasive style of the McCarthy state-wide organization headed by Otto Feinstein . . . has alienated most of the party leadership." Unwilling to roil the waters, however, he recommended to the national headquarters that Feinstein, who would be "very good in the precinct delegate races, and with particular groups such as the Blacks," be supported as the official state McCarthy chief but that the splinter groups be permitted to do their own thing, as well. Moore also recommended sending actor Paul Newman to Michigan because there were "two

woman delegates who have said they will go for McCarthy if Newman calls."

A congenitally genial and gentle bear of a man, Feinstein admits
that he and his people may have been "abrasive"—but only "to the
national McCarthy guys," in part because they focused so narrowly
on the delegate count while he and his colleagues were more interested in building a permanent progressive coalition within the
Democratic Party. The McCarthy group in Michigan was involved in
party politics, candidate-centered politics, and movement politics;
the regular Democrats and the national McCarthy people had more
narrow agendas.

NUT's January–February 1968 number was devoted to the
Campus Concerned Democrats and contained a lead article by
Richard Place, a friend of Feinstein's and another Wayne historian,
entitled "Why McCarthy?" Place understood that many of his colleagues felt McCarthy had no chance of winning, that he was too
professorial, and that he was "a one-issue candidate." Place contended, however, that whether or not McCarthy could win, "he has
provided a nucleus around which those of us who despair of the
entrenched leadership of both national parties can organize and
show our strength as a bloc." McCarthy's candidacy was also a way
to raise the question of "how to divide our resources between our
world commitments as a super power and our commitment to create
a viable and just society in America." Finally, although there was a
chance that McCarthy might really win the nomination, Place
insisted that we "can win through 'losing,'" by making "our votes,
money, and actions amount to something on the national political
level."

The article then listed the presidential primaries and their
dates, followed by a page full of addresses and phone numbers for
the national and state McCarthy headquarters. The second article,
written by George W. Shepherd Jr. of the University of Delaware,
dealt with the nuts and bolts of how to elect delegates to the national convention, followed by the names and addresses of Campus
Concerned Democrats, which, at the time of publication, were at universities in more than thirty states. The Campus Concerned Democrats organization, of which Feinstein was executive secretary, was
formed on December 3, 1967, after McCarthy had appeared at the
national convention of the Concerned Democrats.

In the same *NUT* issue, Feinstein's article entitled "What You
Can Do" began with his by-then common theme of how "the University reaches into all corners of our society, often having wider and
deeper contacts than the political parties themselves." He described
how to organize on every campus an Issues and Politics 1968 conference. At these conferences, faculty and students would present

papers that would be released to the media, and thereby, it was hoped, "the political climate in the community can be affected." Feinstein was especially interested in developing speaker's bureaus on campuses that would send academics to talk to unions, social and religious groups, and parent-teacher associations about the war and domestic politics. Considering the growing number of "Concerned" faculty members, he hoped to create two thousand such groups. Although he fell well short of his goal, faculty and graduate students on many campuses did appear before community groups and—as important—in print and on electronic media to try to win the battle for the hearts and minds of Americans. John Weiss, for one, remembers making presentations in Michigan communities and elsewhere every other week for one year.

The special issue of *NUT* concluded with a useful article by Sanford Gottlieb of SANE explaining community organizing, followed by a long list of materials available to McCarthy campaigners. Considering that McCarthy declared for the presidency less than a month before and that his supporters built the organization from scratch, the level of activity and wide range of resources made available in *NUT* was impressive and a tribute to the mostly academic activists behind it. Although readers with experience in politics did not need the simple instructions on how to operate within the party system to effect change, many of those in the McCarthy campaign were inhabitants of "ivory towers" who knew little if anything about grassroots politics. It was also important to spell out in detail a common strategy for the campaign. Involved in such activities since high school, Feinstein understood those subjects quite well.

The Michigan McCarthy organization helped raise money to send nine thousand young people, including high school students, to primaries in New Hampshire, Wisconsin, and Indiana. Feinstein recruited Peace Corps veterans who had the maturity necessary to lead their younger comrades and who were experienced at operating in "foreign" environments. Ferency himself went with McCarthy to New Hampshire to show the poet-politician how to campaign at plant gates. According to Ferency, the candidate was "not really in tune with politics." In fact, he had not considered making a run for the presidency—only a symbolic protest against the war—until he did well in New Hampshire and "got the fever."

After McCarthy almost won in New Hampshire, Robert Kennedy declared his candidacy on March 16, 1968, four days after the primary. Some in the McCarthy camp immediately joined Kennedy, but Feinstein and Ferency felt a certain loyalty to the Minnesota senator and his many young supporters who resented Kennedy's late and seemingly opportunistic candidacy. Thus, Feinstein decided to stick with McCarthy even though Kennedy was

more likely to defeat Johnson and unite the party. Making the difficult decision to stay with their candidate suggested a strain of
quixotic idealism—or perhaps morality—among the McCarthy
people that is rare in the political game. But their dual strategy of
keeping both men in the race to gain enough votes to deny Humphrey the nomination on the first ballot at the national convention
in Chicago and then convincing McCarthy to release his delegates to
Kennedy on the second ballot might not have been so quixotic after
all. Despite the hard feelings that existed between the McCarthy
and Kennedy groups in Michigan, leaders of the McCarthy camp
were able to present unity slates of delegates from district conventions, who were elected to the August 30–31 state convention.

For these leaders the main and insurmountable problem in
Michigan was that those who would elect the delegates to the national convention had been chosen in 1966. Consequently, the May
1968 precinct elections and the county, district, and state conventions, in which the newly elected McCarthy delegates would com-
pete, could only have an indirect impact on who would represent
Michigan in Chicago. If the McCarthy people made significant gains
throughout the state, Feinstein reasoned, the party regulars could
not, in all conscience (or political wisdom) ignore them—that is, if
they *had* a conscience. Certainly, they had to be impressed by such
events as the Tiger Stadium rally at which at least twenty-five thousand people turned out to hear McCarthy on July 27, 1968, the
largest political rally in the state that year. Prominent Ford family
member William Clay Ford, who owned the Detroit Lions, helped
pay for the event, and Detroit mayor Jerome Cavanagh, an antiwar
Democrat, provided buses.

McCarthy and Kennedy people were able to pass resolutions
favorable to their cause in many district conventions. Typical was the
Seventeenth Congressional District of Johnson loyalist Rep. Martha
Griffiths, where one of the leaders of the Liberal Conference Caucus,
William Broadhead, went on to become a long-term member of Congress from the district. Twenty percent of the winners in the 1966
district elections were favorable to the McCarthy-Kennedy cause. In
the 1968 elections, that number rose to between 45 and 51 percent.
Thus, the Concerned Democrats had achieved one of their main goals
and were on the verge of having enough influence in the party to
affect its domestic and international policies.

Feinstein helped organize a petition drive that attracted more
than 100,000 registered voters. The petition asked the state Democratic Party to acknowledge the influence of the McCarthy forces
and award their leaders an appropriate share of the 24 at-large
seats in the Michigan delegation. That delegation had 94 votes, or
100 delegates, at the national convention, of which 76 had already
been elected at district meetings in May.

New party chair Sander Levin told Feinstein to negotiate with Sam Fishman, the powerful head of the UAW's Community Action Program (CAP), about obtaining a "fair portion" of the at large delegates. An old-line anti-Stalinist who Feinstein claims was "still fighting the battle of the Barcelona Post Office," Fishman rejected Otto's plea for recognition for his group, even after Feinstein promised that the ten thousand paid-up members of the McCarthy for President organization would join the Democratic Party. (At the time, the entire paid-up membership of the state party was only two thousand.) Feinstein, however, would not promise to support Humphrey on the second ballot as a price for those seats. Ultimately, the state party grudgingly agreed to give the McCarthy forces two at large seats. From Feinstein's perspective, the decision by the UAW and the state politicos to refuse to treat his people with generosity helped to weaken the Michigan Democratic Party and later paved the way for the Republicans to make statewide gains.

Feinstein attended the Chicago convention as an alternate delegate from his district. He did not expect McCarthy to win the nomination but thought that he and his colleagues might be able to move Humphrey and the rest of the party closer to their positions on the war and civil rights. Mayor Richard J. Daley's cordoned off convention center reminded him of a concentration camp, but he felt even more ostracized by the convention organizers who marginalized the members of his delegation, even to the point of housing them in a motel far from the main action. Feinstein returned to Detroit one day before the convention ended to try to keep a lid on the protests that were simmering among his supporters over the police riot in Chicago. He addressed rallies and meetings, explaining that it was still necessary to support the party, considering the alternative. He felt that he helped to "avoid a major confrontation and contained the anger." Other parties, especially those in New York and California, suffered far more fragmentation and internal warfare than the one in Michigan.

The McCarthy-Kennedy forces controlled almost a majority of the votes of delegates to the state convention in August, two weeks after the national convention—demonstrating just how far they had come in Michigan in 1968. Many who attended wore black armbands in mourning for Chicago. The state convention dropped unit rule, censured Mayor Daley and the Chicago police, and adopted the minority plank on Vietnam that the national convention had rejected. In a close vote, 1,100 to 1,000, the state convention also defeated a resolution that would have condemned the Democratic National Committee's handling of the national convention and vowed never to hold another convention in Chicago as long as Daley remained mayor.

Although the McCarthy forces were not welcomed as a group in the state Humphrey campaign, many members worked individually for the candidate. McCarthy himself was extremely slow to endorse Humphrey. Feinstein met with him and William Clay Ford when the senator was in Detroit for the 1968 World Series in early October. He was disappointed to hear McCarthy explain that he was withholding his support from Humphrey as a way to compel him to move toward his own position on the war. Ultimately, McCarthy endorsed Humphrey at the eleventh hour, when it did the Democratic standard-bearer little good. Humphrey carried Michigan nonetheless, in part because the unions convinced hundreds of thousands of their members to switch their allegiance from third-party candidate George Wallace.

After the election, many insurgents dropped out of Democratic Party work. Some were disappointed and disillusioned by what they had witnessed during the year. Campus-based activists returned to their research and teaching, concerned once again about tenure and promotion. As party pros had predicted, they were one-issue activists who, after failing to stop the war, no longer were interested in the tedious and unglamorous work of local politics. Feinstein, by contrast, was in the struggle for the long haul and did not lose faith, even after the election of Richard Nixon. In fact, supported by new activists he had helped to bring into his party, he ran for state Democratic Party chair in 1969. He was a reluctant candidate, but the Concerned Democrats could not find anyone else who was willing to enter the race.

According to his campaign literature, Feinstein was the "only candidate who has worked intensively with the new forces that have come into the Party . . . the young people, the professionals and intellectuals, the urban and rural poor, the various minority and ethnic groups. We need these people in the Party—if it is to win"; he was described as "uniquely qualified to provide the kind of leadership that can unite the disparate forces in the Party." Otto came in second on the first ballot at the January 1969 state convention with 21 percent of the vote, and an ally who finished fourth took another 10 percent. It was not a bad showing for an amateur politician—an academic with a slight foreign accent (both New York and European) who was confronting the savvy party regulars dominated by labor. Further, Feinstein won two of the nineteen congressional districts (his own Thirteenth and the Liberal Conference–dominated Seventeenth) and received 29 percent of the votes in the Detroit metropolitan area. The main problem, as he pointed out in his own February 4, 1969, postmortem, was that "we have been particularly weak in the more outlying counties." An attempt by sectarian forces to reconfigure the Michigan Concerned Democrats and to impose a far more bureaucratic structure on the organization caused Feinstein to resign from his position as executive secretary in March. Paradoxically, some of those who led the attempt to restructure the organization were the same people—formerly old leftists—who had once caused party power brokers such as Sam Fishman to see red.

Like so many other academics involved in leadership roles during those heady days, Feinstein never again participated so directly in party politics, although he remained a precinct delegate and did heavy campaigning in 1972 and 1976. It had been a remarkable moment in history when college professors and sometimes even graduate students negotiated almost as equals with senators, mayors, and party chieftains over issues that dramatically affected American politics. Although he would not again enjoy such a position, he continued his lifelong effort to develop mechanisms and institutions that would involve the academy with social problems. In 1971, he was the prime mover behind the creation of the Southeast Michigan Ethnic Heritage Studies Center, which was devoted to ethnic conflict resolution. In 1973, he became director of Wayne's innovative University Studies and Weekend College Program, which, in eighteen months, enrolled thirty-six hundred adult students. Among other activities, the new college produced one thousand broadcast programs for its telecourses, making it the second largest telecourse producer in the world. Feinstein's To Educate the People Consortium, which grew out of the program modeled on England's Open University, adapted the Wayne model to thirty-five other universities and ultimately, with support from the United Nations Educational, Scientific, and Cultural Organization (UNESCO), branched out into the European Community.

Feinstein also organized the City-University Consortium in Detroit, which sponsored joint city-university projects, often involving students, on key urban issues. Finally, in his own department, he developed the Civic Literacy and Urban Society module for the basic introductory political science course, which, among other things, offered students the opportunity to participate in voter registration projects in Detroit.

From those early days at the University of Chicago in the late 1940s to the present, Otto Feinstein has never relinquished his dream of creating a university community closely tied to the outside world, a community in which scholars would offer their special talents and expertise in practical ways to improve the chances for peace and justice at home and abroad. The failure of the McCarthy campaign was only one transitory, if bitter and enervating, setback for Feinstein in an admirable career of creating valuable programs and institutions that affected the quality of life for tens of thousands of students and faculty and the millions of citizens of the national and international communities with whom they interacted.

Author's Note

Unless otherwise noted, all Otto Feinstein quotes are the product of a series of interviews I conducted with him over several months during the fall of 1997. Quoted material from Democratic Party documents and broadsides comes from Feinstein's personal archive as well as the personal archive compiled by Pat Thornton for the Liberal Conference, which is in my possession. Zoltan Ferency's observations about Eugene McCarthy are quoted from Zoltan Ferency Oral History, July 15, 1988, p. 40, Walter P. Reuther Library of Labor and Urban Affairs, Wayne State University, Detroit, Michigan.

Suggested Readings

For the McCarthy campaign, see George Rising, *Clean for Gene: Eugene McCarthy's 1968 Presidential Campaign* (Westport, Conn.: Praeger, 1997); Eugene J. McCarthy, *The Year of the People* (Garden City, N.Y.: Doubleday, 1969); Jeremy Larner, *Nobody Knows: Reflections on the McCarthy Campaign of 1968* (New York: Macmillan, 1969); and Ben Stavis, *We Were the Campaign: From New Hampshire to Chicago for McCarthy* (Boston: Beacon Press, 1969). For discussion of media images of the antiwar movement, see Melvin Small, *Covering Dissent: The Media and the Anti-Vietnam War Movement* (New Brunswick, N.J.: Rutgers University Press, 1994).

11

Daniel Ellsberg
The Man Who Uncovered the War

John Prados

"In war," the Greek writer Aeschylus declared, "truth is the first casualty." During the Vietnam era, Americans became focused on issues of truth and credibility—and especially on the lack of both. Strategists such as Robert McNamara, Dean Rusk, Walt Rostow, and Henry Kissinger often asserted that the United States had to stand firm in Vietnam to show the world that America's promises to support its allies could be trusted. In essence, they were arguing that honest representation was a mainstay of national security. Among the American people, ironically, the very issue of their leaders' honesty and credibility became a major element of the antiwar indictment. Many citizens were outraged by what they perceived as the overt lies told by their own government.

On Sunday, June 13, 1971, the *New York Times* began a series of articles based on a hitherto secret history of Vietnam War decision making prepared within the Department of Defense. The Nixon White House attempted unsuccessfully to block the publication of these Pentagon Papers by various legal means. The documents, which disclosed political secrets, not military ones, provided fuel for the already growing fire of public distrust and disillusionment about the war. Although far from definitive, the Pentagon Papers contained evidence of the shallow and politically self-serving reasoning that went into the decisions to fight the war.

A former Pentagon insider named Daniel Ellsberg was the central figure in the delivery of the secret documents to the *New York Times* and other media outlets. During the course of the war, he made a complete metamorphosis from ardent war supporter to antiwar activist. Early on, he labored at the RAND Corporation on Vietnam research projects for the Defense Department, and even wrote a segment of the Pentagon Papers; later, he was prosecuted by the U.S. government for leaking those very documents. Nixon administration efforts to nail Ellsberg led to the formation of a White House infiltration unit, eventually known as the notorious Plumbers, and thus contributed significantly to the Watergate scandal and the demise of an entire presidency. Daniel Ellsberg had a front-row seat as many Vietnam decisions were made within the Pentagon, and, as he grew more concerned about what he saw, he followed Mark Twain's advice: "When in doubt, tell the truth."

Courtesy of Daniel Ellsberg

John Prados is a historian of national security affairs and international security, as well as a designer of strategy board games. With a Ph.D. in international relations from Columbia University, he is the author of many books and articles, including *The Sky Would Fall: Operation Vulture, the U.S. Bombing Mission, Indochina, 1954* (1983); *Valley of Decision: The Story of Khe Sanh* (1991), with Ray W. Stubbe; and *The Hidden History of the Vietnam War* (1995). His many board game credits include the award-winning classic *Third Reich*, now in its fourth edition.

Daniel Ellsberg's epiphany began on the day of the alleged second incident involving United States Navy destroyers in the Gulf of Tonkin. August 4, 1964, happened to be his second day of full-time work at the Department of Defense, in the storied Pentagon on the Virginia bank of the Potomac River, across from Washington, D.C. Five years later, it was Ellsberg who began to reproduce and disseminate the Pentagon Papers, a top secret Department of Defense study of Washington's conduct of the Vietnam War from 1945 to March 1968. Revelation of the Pentagon Papers transformed the domestic public debate over the war, providing critics with evidence from the U.S. government's innermost councils that long-standing charges about the conduct of the conflict were substantially correct. The record established in the Pentagon Papers would be the accepted version of events in Vietnam until the government released official records a decade later. Thus, in terms of its impact on the political debate over Vietnam in the United States, Ellsberg's 1971 leaking of the Pentagon Papers to the American press stands as one of the single most important events. Here, an individual's actions literally shaped history. Who Daniel Ellsberg was and how he decided to declassify unilaterally the Pentagon Papers must be of considerable interest in any balanced appraisal of the Vietnam War and what it wrought in America.

On August 4, 1964, two days after the destroyer USS *Maddox* was targeted by Vietnamese torpedo boats in the Gulf of Tonkin, the *Maddox* and another destroyer *C. Turner Joy,* were back in the gulf asserting a U.S. presence. During the night the ships' crewmen believed themselves under attack again because they received a series of anomalous sensor readings—radar and sonar returns—and some intercepted radio messages. Whether an attack—a second incident in the Tonkin Gulf—actually occurred has been disputed ever since. Hanoi denied making any such moves, and a 1968 investigation by the United States Senate concluded the evidence *for* the attack was outweighed by that *against* it. In subsequent years, navy pilots who had flown above the destroyers that night, as well as officials of the Central Intelligence Agency and the National Security

Agency, disputed either the claims of an attack or the meaning of the intercepted radio traffic, showing that the messages received on board the destroyers referred to the situation during the first Tonkin Gulf incident two days earlier.

The evidence in postwar Vietnamese commentaries, from no less a source than the commander in chief, Gen. Vo Nguyen Giap, is that no attempt was made to attack any American ship on August 4; in contrast, the sea battle of August 2 was very real, carried out on orders from the local naval authorities at Thanh Hoa. Giap personally supplied these facts to Robert S. McNamara, the American secretary of defense at the time of the Tonkin Gulf incident, during a meeting between the two in 1995. Two years later, the substance was repeated for the record at a conference in Hanoi between American and Vietnamese delegations, a meeting that included another encounter between McNamara and Giap. McNamara now asserts that he is convinced a second Gulf of Tonkin incident never happened.[1]

Coincidentally, only days after the end of the 1997 conference in Hanoi, the U.S. government declassified and released tape recordings of President Lyndon Baines Johnson's telephone conversations on August 4, 1964. Included among them was Johnson's talk early that morning with Secretary of Defense McNamara, hours before Washington had any detailed knowledge of events in the Tonkin Gulf. President Johnson demanded that the Pentagon prepare a list of targets to be struck by U.S. bombers in ostensible retaliation; Secretary McNamara responded that the targets had already been selected. Similarly, the actual execution of the bombing raid, code-named Pierce Arrow, was ordered on the basis of the president's instructions *before* an evening meeting of the National Security Council at which a final decision in the matter was supposed to be reached.

Actually, even before President Johnson and Secretary McNamara went ahead with the Pierce Arrow bombing, questions were already being raised regarding the reality of the second incident. During the night and only very shortly after sending the original reports that his ships were under attack, Capt. John J. Herrick, the officer leading the American destroyers in the Tonkin Gulf, had had second thoughts. At 1:25 P.M. Washington time, he cabled that sensor readings appeared doubtful, hence, he wrote, "SUGGEST COMPLETE EVALUATION BEFORE ANY FURTHER ACTION."[2] The Joint Chiefs of Staff's order to execute the bombing was nonetheless dispatched long before such an evaluation was made. Moreover, McNamara and Johnson both went before the press and assured the public there was no question the dastardly attack against the American ships occurred. McNamara repeated these assurances to the Senate Foreign Relations Committee as it considered passage of the Tonkin Gulf Resolution. This measure, which took wing as a simple affirmation of support for Johnson's retaliatory bombing, would eventually be stretched by the administration into a justification for the entire Vietnam War.

Daniel Ellsberg—just two days into his job at "the Building," as its denizens call the Pentagon—observed firsthand the rush to judgment about the Tonkin issue. As special assistant to John T. McNaughton, McNamara's assistant secretary for international affairs, he witnessed the entire process—and it sickened him. It was his awakening to the fact that high policy in Washington did not always flow from careful consideration and principle.

Injury piled on insult as Ellsberg saw the lengths to which Pentagon authorities and the United States Navy went to build a case for their version of the alleged Tonkin Gulf incident of August 4. Over the months and years, as more and more observers and then participants expressed doubts about the events of that day, his initial misgivings only intensified.

Who was this man who would sit among the best and brightest of the U.S. advisers in the Vietnam years? Born in Chicago on April 7, 1931, Daniel Ellsberg was a quintessential product of the "can-do" thinking pervasive among the generation that fought World War II. His father, Harry, an engineer, was a key manager in some of the largest construction projects of that day, including such sensitive national security endeavors as the Willow Run plant—the largest war materials factory in the world at that time, which mass-produced the then secret B-29 "Superfortress" heavy bomber. After the war, he worked on the Hanford nuclear plant. Harry Ellsberg took his son to see some of the projects and imparted to him many practical precepts from his trade. Daniel became a teenager at the height of World War II, a great and heroic struggle that was so markedly different from the Vietnam imbroglio. Both his principles and his patriotism were strong. Indeed, in 1987, when an interviewer asked him to compare himself with Oliver North, a marine officer in Vietnam who, for self-professed patriotic reasons, became enmeshed in the Iran-Contra affair of the 1980s, Ellsberg replied, "We didn't start all that far apart."[3]

Intellectually brilliant and an academic performer from an early age, Daniel attended the Cranbrook School in Bloomfield Hills, Michigan, as a full scholarship student. There, he earned awards for academic excellence and won a Pepsi Cola scholarship that enabled him to go to Harvard College. At Harvard, Ellsberg was elected to Phi Beta Kappa, and his bachelor's degree in economics was awarded summa cum laude. After graduating in 1952, he spent a year at King's College of Cambridge University as a Woodrow Wilson Fellow.

These were the years of high Cold War tension and a time before the inception of all-volunteer armed forces in the United States (initiated in 1973). Every male American had a military obligation: He could choose to serve voluntarily or submit to the draft, which might or might not call him up. Because enlistees, unlike draftees, could select service and branch, Ellsberg opted to become a marine and enlisted voluntarily. Although he had expressed no earlier interest in the military, he felt he had a duty to do something about his obligation as soon as his temporary deferment for graduate school in economics ran out.

The United States Marine Corps believed that Ellsberg represented real officer material and accepted his application for officer candidate school at Quantico, Virginia. He also needed special medical permission to enter the marines, for he had badly injured his knee in a 1944 automobile accident that left his leg in a cast for a year. (His mother and sister had died in the tragedy, a trauma that had spurred him to some of his academic accomplishments.)

Never again able to bend his knee fully, Ellsberg was excused from learning to shoot from a kneeling position, and he also failed to qualify the first time he tried with the .45-caliber automatic pistol. Building on this failure and a line he remembered from James Thurber's short story "The Secret Life of Walter Mitty," in which the incompetent protagonist fantasizes a claim to have been able to murder someone with a gunshot using his bad hand, Ellsberg determined to overcome his difficulties. In the end, he attained expert proficiency with the pistol with both hands, and he was rated a sharpshooter with a rifle. While he was in training, France's Vietnam war was climaxing at the battle of Dien Bien Phu. In fact, an American marine battalion waited aboard ships off the Vietnamese coast, prepared to intervene on behalf of the United States. One day, Ellsberg recalls, his drill sergeant entered the room and said with impressive calm, "I hope your rifles are clean—Dien Bien Phu just fell!"[4]

Neither he nor the U.S. Marines went to Vietnam immediately after the French defeat, but as a second lieutenant, Ellsberg was put in command of a marine rifle platoon. He had earlier married Carol Cummings, the daughter of a marine general, and had two children. Lieutenant Ellsberg was considered a "comer" among marine officers, and he was selected to command a rifle company, unusual because a unit of this size is typically led by a captain. He extended his marine active duty for a year to go with his unit on a Mediterranean deployment with the U.S. Sixth Fleet, although he would not remain with the troops after being reassigned as a battalion operations officer.

In the meantime, he had become attracted to game theory, a sophisticated formula for determining choices that was considered useful in economics, and in the 1950s, he was championed by analysts who had much to do with U.S. national defense. Ellsberg's undergraduate thesis at Harvard had focused on game theory, and he had met Oskar Morganstern, who, along with John Von Neumann, was a primary innovator of game theory. He hoped to study game theory when, still a marine, he applied for admission to the Society of Fellows of Harvard University. He was accepted as a junior fellow in June 1956, but that invitation coincided with his departure for the Mediterranean. He declined the fellowship at that time, but Harvard went out of its way to leave the door open, telling him he could reapply. He left the marines in 1957 and, as a member of Harvard's Society of Fellows, began preparing for a career in defense analysis work.

The accomplishments that ultimately brought Ellsberg to national attention were his contributions to improving the efficiency of the U.S. national defense. In 1959, his work with game theory as a technique of defense analysis led to an invitation to give the prestigious Lowell Lectures, sponsored by Harvard's Society of Fellows, at the Boston Public Library. One of the half dozen lectures had the title "The Art of Coercion: The Role of Threats in Diplomacy, Economic Bargaining, and War." Another, "The Theory and Practice of Blackmail," took as its example Adolf Hitler's Germany in the 1930s, in the period leading up to the Munich crisis of 1938.

Ellsberg spent the summer of 1957 at Stanford and toward the end of that stay visited the RAND Corporation in Santa Monica, where he met Alain Enthoven and Charles J. Hitch. They were key economists for RAND, which performed contract consultant work for the U.S. military services, especially the air force, and for the Department of Defense. Hitch invited Ellsberg to spend the next summer at RAND as a consultant. It was the beginning a long association. Daniel Ellsberg was a RAND employee from 1958 to 1964 and then again between 1967 and 1970.

At Santa Monica, he became involved in a variety of projects concerned with nuclear warfare and central issues of national security. Although he had loved the Marine Corps, RAND became a real home to the intellectually restless, precocious young man. He collaborated with some of the leading strategic thinkers of the age—Albert Wohlstetter, Andrew Marshall, Fred Hoffman, and Herman Kahn—and he communicated directly with key national security analysts in the Kennedy administration. He also had access to top secret nuclear data, from which he articulated tough questions about the nation's basic national security plan—questions he posed to the staffs of the National Security Council and the air force's Strategic Air Command. The information he developed challenged existing war plans that had been based on the faulty premise of a "missile gap" between the United States and the Soviet Union. There was, in fact, no such gap, but many planners had proceeded as if America were lagging behind the Soviets in missile technology. Ellsberg's questions led to a new understanding of how many millions of lives throughout the world would be lost if existing U.S. war plans were ever executed. Discussions resulted in a new basic war plan in 1962 and the announcement by Secretary of Defense McNamara that the United States was shifting away from targeting enemy cities and instead was working on a "counterforce attack" against enemy military targets. It was Ellsberg who compiled the final draft of McNamara's announcement.

Whatever else one might say about McNamara, he clearly took seriously the dangers of nuclear war. In that area, he was impressed by the systems analysis of efficiency experts such as those at the RAND corporation—the best and the brightest, including Daniel Ellsberg. With the Cuban missile crisis of late 1962, Ellsberg's services were again placed at the disposal of senior groups of U.S. officials, in particular the planning task forces headed by Paul Nitze (for the Pentagon) and Walt W. Rostow (for the State Department). Largely on the strength of his performance in these matters, Ellsberg was asked to join the staff of assistant secretary of defense for international security affairs, John McNaughton. Ironically, little of his work as special assistant to McNaughton in 1964 and 1965 would concern nuclear weapons.

Ellsberg's first involvement with Vietnam came in the fall of 1961 while he was at RAND. The Santa Monica researchers had a contract for a study of Pentagon practices in the development of novel weapons and equipment. A RAND evaluation team that included Ellsberg went to South Vietnam, which, at that time, was being touted as a "laboratory" for the kinds of gear and ideas suitable for such low-intensity conflicts as guerrilla wars. Observing the fragility of the Saigon government, its intransigence in the face of its own political shortcomings, and the intractability of official Vietnamese-American relations, he quickly concluded that Vietnam would be a bad place for RAND. The result was an internal recommendation that the company avoid taking on contracts for work in Vietnam or on issues related to the conflict there. Neither RAND nor Ellsberg himself took that advice: War work became a substantial portion of the company's cash flow, and Ellsberg soon found himself in the Pentagon nerve center for the Vietnam War.

The August 1964 incidents in the Tonkin Gulf marked the beginning of Ellsberg's Vietnam nightmare. The new right-hand man of one of the Pentagon's top officials witnessed successive events in which the U.S. government said one thing and did another. As Lyndon Johnson, who had succeeded the assassinated Kennedy in

November 1963, campaigned for election in 1964 on a platform of avoiding an Asian war, Ellsberg, working inside the Pentagon, saw the simultaneous creation of JCS target lists for Vietnam, complete with estimates of the number of aircraft sorties necessary to destroy each site mentioned. He had stayed away from shoptalk about Vietnam before 1964, but in McNaughton's shop, that proved impossible. Because his boss was impressed with his work, Ellsberg was given portfolios in McNaughton's most important area of concern—Vietnam. At the time, he considered himself an uncompromising Cold Warrior, dedicated to the fight against Russia, but Vietnam would change that. He was also the president's man and convinced that the public did not understand policy and that Congress was made up of a bunch of yokels or, worse yet, parochial, shortsighted troublemakers. Vietnam would change that viewpoint, as well.

His work in the Pentagon proved to be exhausting and endless. In February 1965 the Vietcong shelled an American air base at Pleiku in Vietnam's Central Highlands. Washington used the attack to justify bombing the North and quickly expanded its effort from a simple retaliatory strike to a sustained air campaign. Ellsberg worked in the Pentagon through the night of the Pleiku attack, frantically putting together data on the available options. Scarcely a day later, there was another Vietcong bombing of a multinational barracks at the Vietnamese port town of Qui Nhon. Ellsberg was at his desk in McNaughton's office when a colonel entered to announce the news. Though he now recalls having a computerlike memory in that period, at the time of this incident, he suddenly could not, for the life of him, remember what had happened at that other place, Pleiku. The lapse in memory was no doubt due to fatigue, but his memory would not be improved when, on the night of the Qui Nhon incident, everyone in his office again stayed up, on an open line to Saigon to gather any details of terrorist incidents over the preceding thirty days that McNamara could use with President Johnson in justification of new bombing. People around Ellsberg were just as tired as he was. Decades later, he puzzled over how he and the others could have thought themselves capable of making rational decisions under these conditions.

Soon called Operation Rolling Thunder, the bombing of North Vietnam was another shock for Ellsberg. Both he and McNaughton opposed the sustained bombing, but it was the assistant secretary, not he, who attended White House meetings on the subject. Ellsberg had a catbird's seat, however, because each time McNaughton returned from a session of the National Security Council or one of President Johnson's fabled "Tuesday lunches," he would detail the goings-on so his subordinates could properly follow up on the decisions made. In those days, Ellsberg now recalls, it seemed as if

President Johnson was the moderate on Vietnam, edging toward small commitments of ground troops as an alternative to bombing. Yet barely a month later, in March 1965, the president went ahead and committed ground troops without making any effort to end or circumscribe the bombing. The episode became another benchmark in Ellsberg's growing doubts about Vietnam.

The initial deployments of U.S. ground forces to South Vietnam involved relatively small units—two marine battalions—but even this modest commitment concerned Ellsberg. Assistant Secretary McNaughton was convinced that putting U.S. Marines into Vietnam sent the wrong signal about intervention and that army troops might be less provocative. He and Ellsberg spent a full day and night trying to substitute the army's 173rd Airborne Brigade, then located on Okinawa, for the marines slated to land at the Vietnamese ports of Da Nang and Chu Lai. As it transpired, McNaughton could not get the army on board at that late date, and the marines wanted their walk in the sun. The marine landings took place as anticipated.

Meanwhile, Ellsberg's personal life was in turmoil, for his marriage was falling apart. He and his wife, Carol, agreed to divorce in early 1964. When he later met a new woman, she turned out to be an opponent of the war; in fact, their first date was at a march circling the White House. He worried that television cameras might show his face, in the crowd, which would have had dire consequences for his Pentagon job.

Oddly enough, Vietnam itself seemed to offer Ellsberg a way to get around his personal problems and his doubts about policy. Washington had put together a new team of specialists to be dispatched to Saigon as a full-time brain trust for the pacification side of the Vietnam War. He volunteered for the mission, which was led by Gen. Edward G. Lansdale under State Department auspices. Going to Saigon thus meant shifting out of the Pentagon, though Ellsberg kept his senior pay grade as a State Department employee.

Working in the field completed his disillusionment with the U.S. effort in Vietnam. For one thing, the Lansdale team was handicapped because Washington had a greater interest in conventional military operations, and Lansdale, with a colorful reputation as a loose cannon, had plenty of enemies in both the U.S. embassy and the military chain of command. Ellsberg originally favored the ground force commitment, but before the end of 1965 he had seen much of Vietnam, spoken to the best Americans there, and came to see that the war was a stalemate: Not only was the United States not making progress, it was not even near the point at which progress was possible.

Ellsberg and others identified a series of things that could be done to stimulate Saigon's political and military effort, but there were insurmountable obstacles, as well. For example, most American advisers with South Vietnamese army units could identify people in those groups who would be much more effective combat leaders than the Vietnamese commanders. Like those advisers, Ellsberg wanted command changes that never happened. Finally, he realized that political affinity for the Saigon leaders, not military savvy, was the criterion for promotion in the South Vietnamese army. The situation proved identical with regard to district and province chiefs.

One American on his short list of people to see in South Vietnam was John Paul Vann, a former army officer who had become a pacification adviser in Hau Nghia Province and then in the Mekong Delta as a whole. Ellsberg saw Vann in company with Lansdale in the fall of 1965, went back alone a month later to spend more time in Hau Nghia, and then accompanied Vann on a trip throughout the delta. That excursion marked the beginning of the extended tours Ellsberg would make across South Vietnam, eventually covering thirty-eight out of forty-three provinces. His detailed report on Hau Nghia's problems, he later told reporter Neil Sheehan, was among his best wartime writing.

Finally convinced that the United States was in trouble in Vietnam, he concluded it made a difference *how* Washington fought the war. In the spring of 1966, given the political troubles brewing in Saigon, the political-religious crisis with the Buddhists, and the stagnation of the war effort, he saw Vietnam as a total mess. It was then that he began working with George G. Jacobsen, one of Washington's oldest Vietnam hands, on a set of recommendations for tactics and techniques designed to smooth the edges of the U.S. war effort. They proposed restricting indiscriminate artillery fire and bombing, getting U.S. units to use more patrols and fewer large search-and-destroy operations, and making a whole series of other changes. The military never accepted their well-intended recommendations.

As the Jacobsen group completed its work, Ellsberg experienced more distress in his personal life. His antiwar girlfriend, Patricia, went to South Vietnam to visit him twice, but after quarreling over his continued war work, Ellsberg broke off the relationship (although they would get together again years later and have been happily married since the war). At the same time, his divorce became final. He was anxious to visit his two children in Los Angeles, but he had put off taking family leave on the advice of colleagues who needed his help on Saigon political matters; then, he discovered he was no longer entitled to a home visit. Ultimately, the efficiency expert was reduced to begging White House staffer Robert Komer to call him to Washington for consultations so that he could see his children on the way.

This October 1966 trip home led to the high point of Ellsberg's bureaucratic career. He was asked to cut short his home leave to join Nicholas de B. Katzenbach, the new undersecretary of state, on a familiarization trip to Vietnam. Katzenbach was accompanying McNamara on one of the defense secretary's periodic visits. Ellsberg brought with him over two hundred pages of his best Vietnam memos, and when he found himself seated on the plane across from his old boss, John McNaughton, he showed him his Hau Nghia paper and other writings. McNaughton read the papers with furrowed brow and passed them to McNamara, who had consumed the entire stack of materials before the plane landed.

A week or so later, McNamara offered Ellsberg a seat on his plane returning stateside. As their plane approached Andrews Air Force Base near Washington, Ellsberg was summoned to McNamara, who was deep in argument with Bob Komer. McNamara was saying that the situation in Vietnam was really bad, and Komer was maintaining that things were improving. The secretary of defense turned to Ellsberg. "You're the expert on this," he said. "I want you to settle this for us." Ellsberg stuck to his analysis that there had been no progress in the war and that conditions in Vietnam were unchanged. "See," McNamara shot back to Komer, "that's just what I've been saying—we've got a hundred thousand more troops over there and there's no progress—it's worse!"[5]

A few minutes later the Air Force KC-135 plane was on the ground at Andrews, where Secretary McNamara faced the glare of television lights and the microphones of the press. He proceeded to talk about how optimistic he was and how many indicators showed progress in the Vietnam War. Ellsberg marveled at McNamara's quick change, although he did not get to see the secretary's post-trip memorandum to President Johnson, which was, in fact, pessimistic. Once again, he was struck by the divergence between what was said and done inside government and what the country's leaders were willing to tell the American people.

In due course, Ellsberg returned to Saigon. He labored there through the summer of 1967 until he was struck down by hepatitis amid frantic preparations for the South Vietnamese presidential elections. On his way to the airport to leave the country, he stopped by the embassy to get the most recent monthly pacification reports covering each of South Vietnam's provinces. He planned to use the reports in Washington to bolster his message that the Vietnam War was stalemated.

In a renewed effort to get out the truth about Vietnam in Washington, Ellsberg briefed McNamara again, as well as Katzenbach, top negotiator W. Averell Harriman, White House speechwriter Harry McPherson, and Johnson's national security adviser, Walt W. Rostow. He had not seen Rostow since 1965, when the latter had confidently predicted to him that the U.S. bombing would bring Hanoi to heel and that "the Viet Cong are going to collapse within weeks." Now, in 1967, Rostow told him: "You don't understand. Victory is very near. I'll show you the charts. The charts are very good."[6] This time, Ellsberg had his province pacification reports to put up against Rostow's charts, but the White House aide showed little interest in information that contradicted his own viewpoint. Harriman also found Ellsberg too pessimistic and attributed his negativity to ill health.

That fall, Ellsberg was invited to speak to a luncheon of senior people from local television affiliates of the Columbia Broadcasting System (CBS). He reiterated themes he had presented in his many briefings—that a stalemate in Vietnam was irrevocable, that progress was an illusion, and that Washington needed to end U.S. involvement. Sen. Robert F. Kennedy addressed the same group and asked Ellsberg to drive back with him to Capitol Hill. During the ride, Kennedy questioned him about the experiences that had led him to his conclusions, and the senator seemed to have a passion and concern that was not to be found among the other officials with whom he had been dealing. It was the first of repeated private briefings that Ellsberg gave the senator, right through the Tet Offensive of early 1968. When Kennedy decided to run for the presidency, he asked Ellsberg to be his chief of research and statements on Vietnam. Ellsberg declined in order to be free to provide his views to any candidate who sought them, but he favored the senator and was deeply shocked by his tragic death in June 1968.

While continuing his efforts at consciousness-raising, Ellsberg participated in compiling the Pentagon Papers—the Defense Department study of America's Vietnam decisions whose leak would lead to his own notoriety. He merits some credit for giving McNamara the idea for this study, though the former defense secretary remembers that the concept came from Harvard professors during one of his appearances at the school. Wherever the idea came from, Ellsberg personally wrote the portion of the study that dealt with the escalation of the U.S. commitment early in the Kennedy administration. Indeed, one reason he had been eager to talk with Bobby Kennedy was to question the former president's brother on this subject.

Soon, Ellsberg realized that his own frustration with Vietnam was a product of the way policy had been made and that it was, in a sense, inevitable. Soured on presidents, the Building, and the system, he returned to the RAND Corporation, whose president, Henry Rowen, was a good friend. He maintained his security clearances, however, and got permission to read the full Department of Defense decision making study—forty-seven volumes of analysis and supporting documents that totaled over seven thousand pages. He would be one of the few officials, including both the Department of Defense people who had ordered and received the study and the analysts who had written it, to actually read the Pentagon Papers in their entirety. The record there revealed that the flaws he discovered in the early Kennedy years had, in fact, been present throughout the entire period covered by the Pentagon Papers, 1945 to 1967.

The truths Ellsberg found in the Pentagon Papers stunned him, but for a long time, he did nothing other than to try to pass along the insights Vietnam had brought him. The straw that broke the camel's back came on September 30, 1969, when he read in that morning's *Los Angeles Times* that the army was dismissing murder charges in the court-martial of a number of Special Forces men—popularly known as Green Berets. The men, including the Fifth Special Forces Group commander, Col. Robert Rheault, were accused in the death of a Vietnamese man who had been one of their own agents but who was suspected of also working for the Vietcong. The Green Beret affair involved the CIA, as well, and it proved highly controversial. The disposition of the case was a catalyst for Ellsberg, who came to the realization that the system he had been part of lied "automatically to conceal murders, from top to bottom, from the sergeant up to the Commander-in-Chief."[7]

Ellsberg determined he would no longer be part of that system. With the help of a former RAND analyst, Anthony Russo, and a photocopying machine, he created a duplicate set of the Pentagon Papers, one that did not reside within the vaults used to store secret documents. He took the purloined copy to the Senate Foreign Relations Committee but to no effect. In fact, he spent more than a year trying to get people in authority to pay attention to what the secret record told about U.S. policy in Vietnam. Finally, he took the documents to the press, specifically, the *New York Times* and the *Washington Post*. Both published extensive excerpts and histories based on the Pentagon Papers, and though the newspapers were briefly enjoined from proceeding by a Nixon administration lawsuit, the U.S. Supreme Court ultimately ruled against the government attempt to suppress these documents.

Revelation of the Pentagon Papers changed the terms of the debate on the Vietnam War. Richard Nixon was furious and went after Ellsberg, who became the target of White House political operatives. White House personnel actually participated in a break-in at the office of his psychiatrist, Lewis Fielding, seeking information that could be used to smear Ellsberg's reputation. Later the same individuals, by then working for the Nixon 1972 campaign organization, hired former and current CIA contract agents who beat up

Ellsberg on the steps of the United States Capitol after a rally on May 3, 1972.

The Justice Department prosecuted Ellsberg for possessing and somehow converting to his own use information related to the nation's security. It was a vague formulation of a charge under the espionage laws—a federal grand jury in Boston examined the leak of the documents but never brought an indictment under the espionage statutes or any others. He was not prosecuted for violating his secrecy oaths but only on the shaky ground of possessing secret material. Ellsberg's defense was that he had not violated any laws in the way they were interpreted by any previous precedent. The case was thrown out of court in 1973 after repeated revelations of governmental misconduct, including the break-in at Fielding's office, concealment of exculpatory evidence, illegal CIA actions, and an offer of the FBI directorship to the presiding judge.

Ellsberg's release of the Pentagon Papers had far-reaching effects. The Watergate scandal and the constriction of the U.S. government's freedom of action in the Vietnam War were, to some degree, directly attributable to his action in revealing the secret document. In government declassification policy, including responses to requests for war-related records under the Freedom of Information Act, there is another Ellsberg legacy—many classified documents have become public quickly because they or their substance had already become known in the Pentagon Papers.

A number of former military men and government officials continue to despise Ellsberg for what he did. McNamara, for example, says that although he admires the first American draft resister, who went to jail for his convictions, he has only contempt for Ellsberg, who broke his oaths. Ellsberg responds exactly as he did during his court case, stating that the Constitution is a higher authority than any political administration. To others, however—including a generation of younger Americans who tried to stop the Vietnam War and put right what had been wrought—he is a hero. For them, the example Daniel Ellsberg set as a man who acted on principle and changed history in the process may well have been as powerful as the impact of the Pentagon Papers themselves.

Notes

1. Author's notes from the conference on "Missed Opportunities? Revisiting the Decisions of the Vietnam War," June 20–23, 1997, Hanoi, Vietnam. In his Vietnam memoir, McNamara cited the doubts of others regarding the second attack, but he did not openly state a belief of his own. See Robert S. McNamara, with Brian VanDeMark, *In Retrospect: The Tragedy and Lessons of Vietnam* (New York: Vintage Books, 1996), 135–36.

2. Eugene G. Windchy, *Tonkin Gulf* (Garden City, N.Y.: Doubleday, 1971), 211.

3. David Sheff, "Daniel Ellsberg Interview," *Rolling Stone*, December 10, 1987, 221.

4. Daniel Ellsberg, interview with author, July 10, 1997.

5. Ibid. See also Neil Sheehan, *A Bright Shining Lie: John Paul Vann and America in Vietnam* (New York: Random House, 1988), 681–82.

6. Quoted in David Halberstam, *The Best and the Brightest* (New York: Random House, 1972), 637.

7. Jan Wenner, "Dan Ellsberg: The Rolling Stone Interview, Part II," *Rolling Stone*, December 6, 1973, 38. The first installment of this interview appeared on November 8, 1973, 38–56. Both parts are very informative, in particular on the Nixon administration. By this time, of course, Ellsberg was emerging from his battle with prosecutors. The best source on that subject is Peter Schrag, *Test of Loyalty: Daniel Ellsberg and the Rituals of Secret Government* (New York: Simon and Schuster, 1974).

Suggested Readings

The subject of Daniel Ellsberg's later actions, and a seminal documentary collection on the Vietnam War, the Pentagon Papers are of substantive interest to all students of the Vietnam experience. They are available in several versions. Most widely used is Neil Sheehan et al., eds., *The Pentagon Papers as Published by the* New York Times (Chicago: Quadrangle Books, and New York: Bantam Books, 1971). The Quadrangle Books edition contains useful excerpts of the legal briefs and the Supreme Court opinion rendered in the case. Offering the most extensive selection of the secret documents that were appended to the original study is *The Senator Gravel Edition—The Pentagon Papers: The Defense Department History of United States Decisionmaking on Vietnam*, 4 vols. (Boston: Beacon Press [1972]). The version organized along the same lines as the Department of Defense original was published by the House Armed Services Committee, *United States–Vietnam Relations, 1945–1967*, 12 vols. (Washington, D.C.: U.S. Government Printing Office, 1971). This set actually contains more extensive documentation on the French period in Vietnam, but it leaves out much of the key documentation on the American war. In the Pentagon Papers he leaked, Ellsberg omitted four volumes that focused on diplomatic contacts between the United States and North Vietnam. These were later released under the Freedom of Information Act and subsequently published. See George C. Herring, ed., *The Secret Diplomacy of the Vietnam War: The Negotiating Volumes of the Pentagon Papers* (Austin: University of Texas Press, 1983). U.S. government activities covered by the four volumes on negotiations were a major focus of the June 1997 Hanoi conference cited in the notes. For a report on this conference and six other meetings between former U.S. and Vietnamese officials, see Robert S. McNamara, James. G. Blight, and Robert Brigham, *Argument without End: In Search of Answers to the Vietnam Tragedy*, with Thomas J. Biersteker and Herbert Y. Shandler (New York: Public Affairs, 1999).

12

Peter Arnett
Reporting America's Wars
from Saigon to Baghdad

Clarence R. Wyatt

One of the historical cornerstones of America's democratic culture has been a free press. During the Vietnam era print and electronic reporters in Southeast Asia found themselves at the intersection between what official U.S. announcements claimed was the American role in the war and what the journalists were actually witnessing. Initially believing in Washington's rationale for U.S. intervention, many of these reporters became skeptical and ultimately cynical about the official line. After the 1968 Tet Offensive the eminent American television anchorman Walter Cronkite lamented that the public, too often disappointed by the optimism of American leaders, no longer had faith in claims that there were silver linings in the darkest of clouds. Although some officials and citizens deemed the press defeatist or even sympathetic to the nation's enemies, journalists in Vietnam felt compelled by professional ethics, patriotism, and their own consciences to criticize America's conduct of the war and call for a change in policy. It is difficult to identify any one reporter as representative of Vietnam War journalism, but Peter Arnett's long tenure in Southeast Asia and the breadth and depth of his reporting illustrate well the triumphs and the challenges of covering the longest war in U.S. history. His career after Vietnam, as Clarence Wyatt argues, also underscored the war's complex, controversial, and continuing legacy for the relationship between American journalism, the U.S. government, and the American people.

With other reporters such as David Halberstam and Neil Sheehan, Arnett developed a broad perspective on the before, during, and after of the massive U.S. military deployment in Southeast Asia. Born in New Zealand, he worked for the American wire service Associated Press (AP); as Sheehan has written, Arnett "counted" as an American because he shared the same attitudes as his American colleagues. They were gadflies biting at the horse of officialdom, and they did so at great personal and professional risk of being swatted. Arnett's story is part of the human tradition of the Vietnam era, and, like the other biographical sketches in this book, it has connections with the universal human tradition.

Courtesy of Centre College

Clarence R. Wyatt is an assistant professor of history at Centre College in Danville, Kentucky, and received his Ph.D. from the University of Kentucky. He is the author of *Paper Soldiers: The American Press and the Vietnam War* (1993), which was published in paperback in 1995.

During the 1991 Persian Gulf conflict, viewers of the Cable News Network (CNN) had a virtual front-row seat at the war via the reporting of Peter Arnett, one of the network's senior foreign correspondents. Arnett became known as "Baghdad Pete," and his reports from the Iraqi capital during U.S. air attacks on the city inspired the wrath of many Americans and the admiration of others. He had established his reputation as one of the premier war correspondents of the post–World War II era in Vietnam, however, long before his dramatic broadcasts from the roof of the Al-Rashid Hotel in Baghdad.

Arnett was born November 13, 1934, in Riverton, New Zealand, but he grew up in the town of Bluff, situated on, as he says, "the bottom end of New Zealand, which is at the bottom end of the world."[1] Nailed to a lamppost in Bluff were directional signs pointing to the great cities of the world, all thousands of miles away. "Those signs mesmerized me," he said, "and I would follow [them] and my dreams to the far reaches of the world."[2] Growing up on the edge of the world inspired him to explore and probably helped him develop the ability to be a detached observer, a characteristic that would serve him well as a journalist.

A run-in with authority turned Arnett toward journalism as a career. Kicked out of a local boarding school because of his passionate pursuit of a girl named Dawn, he joined the *Southland Times,* the local newspaper, in January 1951. The chief reporter, Albie Keast, was a terror as a boss, demanding tremendous volumes of work from his poorly paid reporters and flying into rages when they did not meet his expectations. Arnett credits Keast with giving him "the grit to face down characters far more venal than he would ever dream of being."[3]

Having determined that there was a much bigger world to cover than cat shows and school plays in Invercargill, New Zealand, Arnett soon left his first job for a position with the *Standard,* the weekly paper of the New Zealand labor movement. His skepticism of military leadership began during this time. In January 1956, he did his two weeks of military training, as was required of all young New Zealand males at the time. The antiquated equipment the troops used was unsafe, and their living conditions were so unhealthful that at least one trainee contracted polio. Arnett wrote a story about the experience, but his report was spiked by the military as a potential "breach of military security," prosecutable under New Zealand's Espionage Act.[4]

Disgusted by the episode, he left the *Standard* for a brief, undistinguished journalistic career in Sydney, Australia. While there, he became enamored of a young British woman, who, in March 1958, suggested that she and Arnett sail for Southeast Asia on a Dutch tramp steamer. The two fell in love with the region, especially with Bangkok, and each secured work, she with a United Nations agency and Arnett with the *Bangkok World,* one of the two English-language papers published in the city.

Although his romantic relationship withered under the pressures of work and the fleshly temptations of Bangkok, his journalistic career blossomed. The job of editor of the *Bangkok World* was literally handed to him: "You can have mine," the editor said to Arnett when the latter inquired about a reporting job. The *World* was owned and published by Darrell Berrigan, a restless Californian who had landed in pre–World War II Shanghai as a freelance reporter. Berrigan believed firmly in the Cold War mission of the United States in Asia. He also knew that aggressive reporting would offend any number of Thai officials, who could shut down the paper on a whim. But with a staff that amounted to Arnett, a Tamil Indian coeditor and office manager, and two Thai reporters, the *World* could do little original reporting. It offered instead international news from the Associated Press and United Press International (UPI) and covered local news through releases from U.S. agencies in Thailand. For all these reasons, Berrigan unashamedly made the *World* an outlet for the official line of the U.S. embassy.

As much as Arnett may have agreed with his Indian colleague that "basically what we're doing here is bullshit," he also understood that, through Berrigan, he had entered the closely connected worlds of American journalism and U.S. foreign policy.[5] As editor of the *World,* he was part of the American social and professional circuit in Thailand, for Berrigan's home and office were required stops for the heavyweights of U.S. journalism in Asia. Arnett saw that mainstream American reporters strongly supported U.S. foreign policy in the region. This experience was his first exposure to the Cold War consensus that generally existed in the 1950s and early 1960s among leadership circles in the United States and in the public at large, a consensus that Arnett would later challenge.

At first, he became more enmeshed in that consensus when he left the *Bangkok World* in 1960 to start up and manage a similar paper in Vientiane, the capital of the Kingdom of Laos. The United States sought to support a sympathetic government in Laos under Gen. Phoumi Nosovan through a large civilian aid program. A similarly large but covert U.S. military and intelligence effort stretched the spirit, if not the letter, of the 1954 Geneva accords that had declared Laos neutral.

Arnett gained entry into this clandestine world largely because he chose not to challenge it. He had come to enjoy the camaraderie of the American community in Vientiane, as he had in Bangkok. More important, he comprised the entire staff of the *Vientiane World*—publisher, editor, sole reporter, and copyboy—and he found the challenge of filling twenty-five columns with copy each week overwhelming. As in Bangkok, he was dependent on releases from the U.S. Information Service and on crumbs received from local officials.

He found at least a partial way out of this box by working as a stringer in Laos for the Associated Press. He made his initial splash on the world press stage when he was the first reporter to file a story on the escape of Prince Souphanouvong, leader of the leftist Pathet Lao. His scoop was easy enough to score: Not only was he working as the AP stringer at that time, but he was also covering for the UPI stringer who was visiting Bangkok and helping out the British news service Reuters until it could replace its departed reporter in Vientiane. The only other Western reporter posted in Laos, a stringer for Agence France-Presse, was out of the country on leave. Later in 1960, when Lao army captain Kong Le led a successful coup against the U.S.-supported government, Arnett was again first with the news, swimming across the Mekong River to Thailand to file stories when the military shut down the telegraph office and the airport.

Increasingly frustrated with the lack of independence of the *Vientiane World,* he sought a full-time position with the Associated Press. His determination and hustle in Laos on its behalf had impressed people at the wire service, and in 1961, he became the AP correspondent in Djakarta, Indonesia. In a little more than a year in Indonesia, Arnett firmly established his reputation as a reporter who was intolerant of official stonewalling and obfuscation. He traveled to the ends of the far-flung archipelago, reporting particularly on the famine spreading across the country. Earlier, he had angered the Indonesian foreign minister, who was a close friend of the AP's chief of world services. Concerned about access and about expanding their client base in rapidly developing Asia, superiors at the AP warned Arnett to take a lower profile for a time. He then produced another hard-hitting story on the Indonesian famine and President Sukarno's lack of response.

A few days later, on May 2, 1962, the government expelled him from the country, and Arnett for the first (but not the last) time became a symbol of freedom of the press. Reluctant to support him before, the AP now called his expulsion an outrage. The U.S. State Department declared its "attachment to the principle of freedom of the press" and stated that "in this context it is unfortunate whenever a journalist representing an American wire service is denied access to news."[6] These words would prove ironic in Arnett's next assignment—Vietnam.

When he arrived in Vietnam on June 26, 1962, he believed that his assignment would last just a year. With only relatively brief interruptions, however, he would devote the next thirteen years of his working life to Vietnam. In the process, he would become a major player in the controversy regarding the role of the press during the war and would secure his place as one of journalism's great foreign correspondents.

His arrival was a part of the early buildup in the American press corps in Saigon, mirroring the growing U.S. commitment to an independent, noncommunist South Vietnam. Like most of the other reporters stationed there, he found Saigon was a wonderful assignment. Its gardens and wide boulevards were filled with all of the sights, sounds, smells, and sensations that Southeast Asia could offer. The restaurants served excellent French, Chinese, and Vietnamese food, the night life was vibrant, and many male reporters waxed poetic about the charms of Vietnamese women and their traditional clothing, the *ao dai*.

Arnett took advantage of all of these pleasures. Like most members of the press corps, he was able to live quite comfortably in Saigon. Even on limited salaries and expense accounts and especially if they were willing to patronize the black-market currency exchange, reporters could live at the best hotels or rent places of their own. Arnett lived in an apartment above the AP bureau, and retained, for thirty dollars a month, an elderly Chinese woman to serve as cleaning lady and laundress. He ate every meal at one of the city's restaurants and did at least his share of barhopping. He later recalled one evening when he and his colleague Horst Faas "visited the Papillon Bar on the Catinat and got so carried away by the revels that we allowed ourselves to be locked inside with nine bargirls and a barman all eager to do business. Horst got into the spirit, consuming large quantities of Scotch and dancing on the bar. I stuck to 33 beer, a local potion that many believed was laced with formaldehyde."[7]

Arnett also quickly encountered the challenges associated with covering the situation in Vietnam. Working conditions were difficult, at best. The AP bureau was located on Rue Pasteur, not far from President Ngo Dinh Diem's official residence and the central business district on Tu Do Street. The one-room office, already cramped, now had to accommodate Arnett and AP regional photographer Horst Faas, both of whom had arrived in Saigon on the same day. Arnett soon learned of the vagaries of communications within South Vietnam and with the rest of the world, as he tried to negotiate the three phone systems and the Post, Telephone, and Telegraph Office, on whose international cables the press depended in order to file dispatches.

He also discovered the particular challenges of covering a war. He soon learned that the pressures of satisfying the demand for copy tied him down far more than he liked, making it difficult for him to get out into the countryside. Serving a variety of clients and operating on morning and evening news cycles across four time zones in the United States, wire service personnel worked almost constantly to gather, check, write, and transmit breaking news. Faas and the other photographers could roam the country at will, but Arnett lamented that he himself was "bound by the daily news grind, required to write a story or two each day."[8]

He finally covered his first combat incident, an assault on a Mekong Delta village in the middle of a suspected Vietcong base area on August 29, 1962. The helicopter assault was a nerve-racking experience. "I hung on for dear life as the helicopter pitched and corkscrewed its way to join the other dozen craft in a loose formation about a thousand feet above the ground. The hammering, jarring roar of the Sikorsky H-34 made thinking impossible."[9] Things did not improve when he leaped from the helicopter along with the South Vietnamese troops. "There was no escape from the thick, slimy swamp. The knee-deep mud beyond the clearing soon became waist-deep as we swam through the mangroves on the way to our first objective, a village a mile ahead." When the troops entered the village, they found evidence of a Vietcong presence—trenches, propaganda—but no soldiers, just one old man. The only shot fired in anger came from a sniper's gun.[10] Arnett learned much about himself and his work on this first combat mission: "I found that no briefing back at headquarters could compensate for the drama of actually being in the field of struggle. I discovered that I was neither repelled nor excited by the limited action I had seen; I felt detached from it all, observing. The best lesson of all was that, unlike the soldiers, I could leave any time I wished."[11]

As difficult as these conditions were, he soon discovered that the greatest challenge faced by the resident press corps came from the policies and actions of the South Vietnamese and U.S. governments. The regime of South Vietnamese president Diem tried to control foreign reporters just as it muzzled the South's press. "The authorities could not understand why we didn't champion the war effort as reporters had done in World War Two and Korea," Arnett said.[12] By the summer of 1962 South Vietnamese secret police were following reporters, ransacking their rooms, and tapping their phones. The Diem government also expelled reporters. These efforts "convinced us that the American Embassy was indifferent to press freedom and unwilling to call the regime on its increasing paranoia," he remembered.[13]

He was right. Committed to preventing South Vietnam's demise but concerned about making that goal too much of a public priority,

Kennedy was manipulated by Diem, who responded to his private pleas for social and political reform with threats to throw U.S. advisers out of the country. Thus, Kennedy had to give unqualified public support to Diem while playing down the degree of American involvement. To this end, his administration began to restrict and control information about the war. Kennedy directed that U.S. officials should not "grant interviews or take other actions implying all-out U.S. involvement," that the release of any information about the activities of American troops except from official sources be forbidden, and that "correspondents should not be taken on missions whose nature [is] such that undesirable dispatches would be highly probable." He also stressed that "articles that tear down Diem only make our task more difficult."[14]

This policy soon pitted the resident reporters against the U.S. military and diplomatic corps in South Vietnam, a situation totally in contrast to that which Arnett had known in Thailand or Laos. In addition to acquiescing in South Vietnamese actions against the press, U.S. officials, both in Saigon and Washington, took repressive steps of their own—declaring certain U.S. facilities off-limits to American reporters, denying journalists access to combat missions, and ordering that the expanding flow of supplies and equipment be brought into the country at isolated docks, away from the Saigon waterfront and reporters. American civilian and military personnel were instructed to dodge or dissemble in response to questions about a growing U.S. presence in the conflict.

Arnett soon felt the weight of all these various forms of pressure. Not long after arriving in South Vietnam, he did a piece challenging American and South Vietnamese claims of success for the Strategic Hamlet program, intended to relocate the rural population into secure villages. The South Vietnamese held up Operation Sunrise, a project some thirty miles north of Saigon, as a showpiece of the program's success. When he visited the area, however, Arnett found that only a few of the planned hamlets had been built and that the people residing in them resented having been uprooted from their homes. "I wrote . . . that the Operation Sunrise hamlets were becoming more trouble than they were worth [and] that the experimental hamlets had in fact become expensive internment camps."[15]

The reporting by Arnett and the rest of the resident press corps reflected a contrarian viewpoint not because of political or ideological bias, as some critics then and since have claimed, but rather because of the sources they were forced to use. Denied the information necessary to do their jobs by the stonewalling of U.S. officials and the outright hostility of the Diem regime, the reporters turned to the American military advisers. These men had themselves become increasingly frustrated with the Kennedy administration's refusal to acknowledge the problems of the Diem regime and the growing U.S. role in the conflict. In the absence of other sources of information, the advisers' concerns shaped the coverage coming out of South Vietnam.

The disaffection between the press and government officials became clear in the early days of January 1963. Lt. Col. John Paul Vann, senior adviser to the ARVN Seventh Infantry Division, had convinced the unit's commander to attack a major concentration of Vietcong in the northern Mekong Delta at Ap Bac. But the ARVN commanders failed to carry out the plans agreed on with the advisers, and the Vietcong escaped the trap; the enemy then inflicted heavy casualties on the ARVN and showed an ability to counter helicopter assaults by downing five choppers. Despite this outcome, Gen. Paul Harkins, the senior U.S. military commander in South Vietnam, arrived at the scene claiming that "we've got them [the Vietcong] in a trap, and we're going to spring it in a half an hour." Having already visited the area and seen the aftermath of the ARVN defeat, the reporters' opposite impressions were confirmed by Vann. "It was a miserable damn performance," he said. "These people won't listen. They make the same goddamn mistakes over and over again in the same way."[16] Ap Bac showed Arnett that "either the authorities were unaware of the full dimensions of the insurgency, or these dimensions were being concealed from us."[17]

The pressure exerted on Arnett by the South Vietnamese increased during the Buddhist crisis in the summer of 1963. The Buddhist clergy staged dramatic protests against government repression, with some monks even burning themselves to death in public. Many elements of South Vietnamese society and politics antagonistic to Diem came together around the Buddhists' actions. On July 7, Arnett was covering a demonstration when secret police trapped him in an alley and attacked him. They kicked him with their signature pointed-toe shoes until fellow journalist David Halberstam came to his rescue. Not long after this incident, the regime let the word pass to Arnett that his name was on an assassination list. In mid-August, Arnett filed a story on unrest in the coastal city of Nha Trang following the first self-immolation of a Buddhist nun and the disrespectful treatment given her body by authorities. A few days later, Dennis Warner, an Australian correspondent, warned him: "Peter, you're the top of the hit list now."[18]

Following the deaths of Presidents Diem and Kennedy in November 1963, Arnett decided to stay in Vietnam indefinitely. He had fallen in love with and soon married Nina Nguyen, daughter of the chief administrative officer of the South Vietnamese National Assembly. He had also fallen in love with Saigon and, most important, with the story of "the beautiful, sprawling sweltering city of Saigon, where there was more news per square foot than any place I had ever been."[19] By the time that President Lyndon Johnson dispatched U.S. ground troops to South Vietnam in the summer of 1965, Arnett had become one of the most respected reporters in Saigon, and his work during the height of the U.S. combat involvement reflected both the strengths and weaknesses of American journalism during the war.

His lengthening experience in Vietnam and his marriage into a Vietnamese family made him more sensitive to the various Vietnamese sides of the story than were most reporters for American news organizations. As U.S. troops flooded into the country, the dynamic of American journalism took over, and editors demanded a greater focus on the combat activities of U.S. soldiers and less emphasis on those of South Vietnamese troops. Arnett continued to try to ensure that the sacrifices of the soldiers and civilians of the South would not disappear from view, but he could not resist the pull of journalistic ethnocentrism. The Associated Press staff "kept the AP wires humming with 'hometowners,' aware that whatever we wrote about those men and women would be published at least in their hometown newspapers. . . . I understood the emphasis on the Americans, but regretted it."[20]

Arnett also pursued another kind of coverage that was relatively rare among the mainstream media, especially the wire services—analysis of larger questions and long-term trends of the war, particularly in terms of U.S. strategy. He wrote stinging criticisms of the use of big-unit sweeps to "find, fix, and fight" the North Vietnamese and Vietcong. The chief architect of this approach was Gen. William C. Westmoreland, commander of the U.S. Military Assistance Command in Vietnam. The strategy called for sending American troops out on patrol and essentially using them as bait to draw out the enemy, who would then be destroyed by superior U.S. firepower. Arnett argued in several long, thoughtful analyses that this strategy had a high cost to the Americans and to the people of South Vietnam. As he wrote in a January 1967 piece, in the three years since Westmoreland had been in command in Vietnam, the war "was fifty-seven times more costly per day [and] American casualties had increased fiftyfold." In the fall of 1967, he wrote that "thirty months of hard, inconclusive fighting in Vietnam has forced American military commanders to acknowledge a crucial fact, that unless the dispirited Vietnamese armed forces can be revitalized into a fighting army, United States troops will be tied down for at least a decade just holding the lid on the communists all over the country." In a story about fighting in the city of Ben Tre during the 1968 Tet Offensive, he detailed the devastation of the city. The great weight of American firepower had been unleashed on Ben Tre, an irony captured in Arnett's quotation from an unnamed U.S. major: "It became necessary to destroy the town to save it." He then questioned: "At what point do you turn your heavy guns and jet fighter-bombers on the streets of your own city? When does the infliction of civilian casualties become irrelevant as long as the enemy is destroyed?"[21]

As the war expanded, the main tasks of the Associated Press became providing clients with summaries of the previous day's military activity and covering particularly dramatic engagements. Arnett was a master of both. Producing the daily war wrap-up was a grinding task that required him to attend the briefings by the American and South Vietnamese authorities—the so-called Five O'Clock Follies—where he would pick up the reams of after-action reports and statistics churned out by the various government and military agencies and ask a few questions. He then raced back to the AP office and tried to pick the major story lines out of the material while working the hellish phone systems in order to get clarification about them from someone in the field. While writing the daily summaries, he worked nearly around the clock as he answered queries from AP editors and sought to provide updates for morning and evening news cycles twelve hours behind him.

Arnett's senior status in the bureau and his growing reputation enabled him, however, to continue following one of his fundamental principles as a reporter—to get out to where the story was. He continued to go out into the field, where he produced some of the most powerful stories of the war. The best example came from his coverage of the November 1967 campaign around the remote Central Highlands town of Dak To, particularly the battle for Hill 875—something that even thirty years later, he still termed "the most unnerving experience of my life."[22]

The North Vietnamese had laid a trap on the hills and ridges around Dak To. For weeks, they had moved men into the area, some twelve thousand in all, and dug an extensive series of trenches and bunkers designed to withstand direct hits from American air strikes and artillery. In early November 1967, soldiers of the U.S. 173rd Airborne Brigade and the Fourth Infantry Division began a terrible fight with the North Vietnamese. On November 18, three companies of the 173rd had been outflanked on the slopes of Hill 875, so named to denote its height in meters. The paratroopers were being hit from the top of the slope and from their right and left flanks. Eight helicopters had been shot down trying to get reinforcements in and wounded out, and twenty soldiers had been killed by a misdirected air strike.

Arnett was one of three reporters who accompanied a relief mission up the hill, arriving at the scene in late evening. He picked up a shovel to dig a foxhole for the night, "but the metal struck at human flesh, a body buried there by a bomb explosion. . . . I recoiled in horror and stepped back on something soft and discovered it was a detached arm from another corpse. I looked about me and felt ill. I was an interloper on desperate ground. I had been proud of a certain professional detachment, but now I felt ashamed of my neutrality, useless with my notebooks and cameras and water bottles."[23]

At first light the next morning the position came under intense mortar and rocket fire. When an air strike brought a brief respite, Arnett moved down the hill with the wounded and the dead to be choppered out. "I . . . scrambled aboard, lying on the floor as we lifted up and out, and I stayed that way for a while because I was crying." When he finally reached a telephone, he sent one of the most powerful dispatches of the war. "War painted the living and the dead the same gray pallor on Hill 875. The only way to tell who was alive and who was dead amongst the exhausted men was to watch when the enemy mortars came crashing in. The living rushed unashamedly to the tiny bunkers dug into the red clay of the hilltop; the wounded squirmed toward the shelter of trees that had been blasted to the ground. Only the dead didn't move, propped up in the bunkers where they had died in direct mortar hits, or facedown in the dust where they had fallen to bullets."[24]

Arnett's experience in Southeast Asia embodied the paradoxical relationship between U.S. journalists and the government and military, a relationship in which the official line could be challenged—but only within limits imposed both by official actions and by the dynamic of American journalism during the Vietnam War. From the beginning of the U.S. military escalation, Arnett's willingness to question the official claims of steady progress in the war or specific aspects of U.S. strategy was evident. Such independence earned him special attention from the authorities, including President Johnson. In late summer 1965 Johnson's press secretary, Bill Moyers, contended that reporting by Arnett and CBS correspondent Morley Safer was "irresponsible and prejudiced" and that those two journalists were particularly suspect because they were not Americans. The White House ordered an investigation of both men, seeking to tie them to the Vietcong.[25]

Such investigations and the ire of commanding officers did little to restrain Arnett. Instead, he, like the rest of the press corps, was far more controlled by the nature of the story and the characteristics of American journalism. As he went about his major work as a wire service correspondent, providing daily summaries of the war and spot news coverage of particular combat actions, he recognized that Vietnam presented particular challenges. Most of the combat there involved multiple encounters between relatively small units.

Also, the country's terrain, ranging from swamps to mountains to triple-canopy jungle, made it impossible to reach many actions.

Still, editors demanded stories of such combat every day—or several times a day in the case of Arnett's employer. To meet that demand, he and other reporters relied largely on official sources for the vast majority of the information they used to do their jobs and on military transportation to get them to the battlefield. The U.S. government and military took note of this dependence in the last days of the Kennedy administration, and President Johnson formally capitalized on it via a policy called Operation Maximum Candor soon after he came to office. This policy was designed to exploit the press's dependence in order to make the government's depiction of an event the first if not the only one reported. News organizations realized their problem and occasionally expressed concern about "undue reliance on centralized sources," but they could do little about the situation.[26]

A less well-known problem that reporters faced was pressure from their own employers. The AP, like other major news organizations, was a basically conservative institution. Its staffers on government and military beats depended on access to government officials, and reporters for an entire organization were often frozen out for varying periods of time if one of their colleagues raised the ire of the officials. The threat of such retaliation was always present. The AP was also a big business, with a market share to maintain and shareholders to satisfy. Reporting that consistently seemed too far out of the mainstream could jeopardize the corporate bottom line, especially in the case of organizations that owned broadcast properties subject to Federal Communications Commission regulation.

As a result, AP management periodically expressed concern about Arnett's tougher articles. In 1965, at the same time that Johnson ordered an investigation of the reporter, the AP's personnel chief asked managing director Wes Gallagher to call for more balanced coverage in light of Arnett's work. AP management also imposed limits on how its reporters could characterize the struggle. Throughout the war, Arnett said, "we were dissuaded by our editors from suggesting that the Vietnam conflict contained significant elements of a civil war, even though every Vietnamese knew the truth of that description." AP reporters could describe the strengths and weaknesses of American and South Vietnamese troops, but the enemy could only be spoken of negatively. "It would . . . have been professional suicide for us in the AP," he wrote later, "to suggest that the Vietcong insurgents and Hanoi's regular forces were generally superbly trained and well motivated and seemed to believe in their revolutionary cause."[27]

His worst experience with censorship at the hands of the AP came during the U.S.–South Vietnamese invasion of Cambodia in April and May 1970. On May 4, he joined an armored unit as it mounted an attack on the town of Snuol, occupied by well-dug-in North Vietnamese troops. Once the enemy had been cleared from the town, U.S. soldiers engaged in a frenzy of looting. His story and three photographs detailing the spree were killed by the AP foreign editor, whose message to the Saigon bureau read: "We are in the midst of a highly charged situation in the United States regarding Southeast Asia and must guard our copy to see that it is down the middle and subdues emotions. Specifically today we took looting and similar references out of Arnett copy because we don't think it's especially news that such things take place in war and in present context this can be inflammatory." The present context was, of course, the killing of students at Kent State. Arnett replied to AP headquarters, saying that he was "professionally insulted by New York's decision to kill all my story and picture references to the Snuol looting on grounds that it was inflammatory and not news. I was also personally upset by the suggestion of foreign editor Bassett that this was emotional reporting. To ignore the sordid aspects of America's invasion of Cambodia would surely be a dereliction of reporting to suit American political interests. I intend to continue to report the war the way it is and will leave the responsibility of suppressing the news with New York."[28]

Over the preceding eight years, Arnett had become identified with Vietnam War journalism. He had mastered the challenges and seized the opportunities of covering the biggest story in the world at the time. He had married a Vietnamese woman, and they had a son and a daughter. He had achieved material and professional success, winning the Pulitzer Prize in 1966. Yet in 1970, he had had enough. His constant work and his continued taste for the bachelor life had long been straining his marriage. And the pressure from U.S. officials and the second-guessing by AP management also began to take their toll.

In the end, however, it was the killing that finally got to him. In the summer of 1970, he sat on a park bench in Saigon with his old colleague Morley Safer, who asked him if he had become hardened to the killing. "No," he told his friend, "I was probably a reverse case. I took a hardboiled approach to the Vietnam War from the very beginning. . . . I've seen as many as 120 Americans on a battlefield at the Nha Trang Valley, and I've seen 200 at a time North Vietnamese just chopped to pieces by artillery, and I've always tried to look past that." His tolerance broke at the town of Snuol, however, where he had witnessed the looting by American soldiers. "We went in on the tanks the next morning and the enemy had fled," he told

Safer. Left in the marketplace were five bodies, a woman, looked like three kids, and a man, [who] had sort of been all fused together by napalm." It was at that moment, he said, that he had decided "I just don't want to see any more bodies."[29]

Arnett went to AP headquarters in New York, working first as a senior writer in the features department and then as a senior correspondent. He returned to Southeast Asia for seven months in 1972 and covered North Vietnam's Easter Offensive of that year. Late in 1972, he was the sole journalist to cover the release of three American prisoners of war to a group of U.S. antiwar activists in Hanoi. He returned again in March of 1975 to cover the last days of South Vietnam. Arnett knew the war was over when a Vietnamese photographer who had worked for the AP for ten years revealed that he was a Vietcong agent and escorted two North Vietnamese soldiers into the bureau office. The group shared sodas and pound cake.

Back in the States, Arnett chafed under the headquarters style in New York—"I didn't favor the button-down gray look of AP management." He realized that war reporting was still his calling, but his bosses tried to force him to do other stories. "I was busy but not happy," he remembered. "I was not being sent to the places where I really wanted to go: to Nicaragua, where the Sandinistas were fighting to overthrow the Somoza regime, to El Salvador, to Africa, where terrible conflicts were dragging in the big powers, to the civil war in Lebanon."[30]

In 1981, while covering the serial murders of young African American boys in Atlanta, he happened to encounter Richard Blystone, an old AP colleague now working for cable broadcaster Ted Turner's fledgling Cable News Network. After a couple of conversations and a quick camera test, Arnett decided to join the new venture. He left the AP "because of what I had learned [there]—the thrill of covering wars, for which there was no substitute."[31]

Soon, he was back at his beat, going to El Salvador, Afghanistan, and the Middle East. He quickly picked up his new medium. "I tried to compensate for our weaknesses with the hustle I had learned at the AP. I stayed with the crew to give guidance on stories. I endeavored to send an edited news package ready for use to our Atlanta headquarters every day from wherever I was. If I could, I used every inch of our cameramen's shots."[32]

Arnett went to Moscow in 1986 as CNN's correspondent there, covering the last throes of the old Soviet system as Mikhail Gorbachev unleashed his reform program. He even managed for old times' sake to get roughed up by police while covering a demonstration. He returned to the Washington beat in June 1988. A year later, he produced a series on southern Africa and covered the U.S. invasion of Panama, but he feared that his career was languishing.

Then, in August 1990, Iraqi strongman Saddam Hussein invaded and occupied the neighboring country of Kuwait. Tension mounted over the next months as the United States put together a coalition to face down Saddam or use force to expel the Iraqis from oil-rich Kuwait. Arnett had just arrived in Jerusalem as CNN's correspondent. Network management resisted his pleas to go to Baghdad until just before the January 15, 1991, deadline set by the United Nations Security Council for an Iraqi withdrawal. The city would soon be under intense attack, and the CNN crew in Iraq was contemplating leaving. Management realized that staying on the scene, however, and providing coverage from ground zero during a major war in the world's most volatile region could make the network's reputation.

Arnett was sent in to confirm CNN's commitment to the story. His coverage of the air campaign against Baghdad was among some of the most dramatic in the history of television journalism. His continued reporting from the city during the war also introduced him to a new generation of viewers. As in Vietnam his challenging of the carefully crafted official line inspired strong reactions. Since that war, however, the public had grown jaundiced about the press. No longer was it the crusading hero of Watergate. Instead, many Americans had little more trust in the integrity of the news media than they did in that of the government. With his stories tagged with a label advising viewers that the reports were "cleared by Iraqi censors," Arnett became known to many as "Baghdad Pete," a seeming tool of Saddam. Other Americans understood, however, that his pieces served as an important counterweight to the expertly stage-managed coverage allowed by the U.S. military.

From his reporting in Vietnam to his work as a CNN correspondent in Iraq, Arnett's career has illustrated journalism's potential to provide dramatic stories and powerful insights regarding U.S. diplomacy and military action. His personal story also demonstrates, however, the limitations that even the most dedicated reporter faces in trying to manage the complex relationships among the news media, the government, and the public that both claim to serve.

Notes

1. Peter Arnett, *Live from the Battlefield: From Vietnam to Baghdad, 35 Years in the World's War Zones* (New York: Simon and Schuster, 1994), 15.

2. Ibid., 17.

3. Ibid., 27.

4. Ibid., 29.

5. Ibid., 42.

6. Ibid., 70.

7. Ibid., 81.

8. Ibid., 80.

9. Ibid., 84.

10. Ibid., 86–87.

11. Ibid., 87.

12. Ibid., 90.

13. Ibid.

14. Dean Rusk to Frederick Nolting, February 20, 1962, Box 195, National Security File, John F. Kennedy Papers, John F. Kennedy Library, Boston, Massachusetts, cited in Clarence R. Wyatt, *Paper Soldiers: The American Press and the Vietnam War* (New York: Norton, 1993), 91–93.

15. Arnett, *Live from the Battlefield,* 92.

16. Wyatt, *Paper Soldiers,* 107.

17. Arnett, *Live from the Battlefield,* 98.

18. Ibid., 106.

19. Ibid., 128.

20. Ibid., 147.

21. Ibid., 163–64, 228, 255–56.

22. Ibid., 228.

23. Ibid., 232–33.

24. Ibid., 235.

25. Ibid., 169–70.

26. Wyatt, *Paper Soldiers,* 163.

27. Arnett, *Live from the Battlefield,* 249.

28. Ibid., 267–68.

29. Wyatt, *Paper Soldiers,* 189–90.

30. Arnett, *Live from the Battlefield,* 320–21.

31. Ibid., 323.

32. Ibid., 333.

Suggested Readings

In addition to the Arnett and Wyatt books cited in the notes, see Hedrick Smith, ed., *The Media and the Gulf War: The Press and Democracy in Wartime* (Washington, D.C.: Seven Locks Press, 1992), and Robert Wiener, *Live from Baghdad* (New York: Doubleday, 1992). These books discuss the Vietnam era legacy for the press working in the Gulf War. For more on media coverage of the Vietnam War, see William M. Hammond, *The U.S. Army in Vietnam: Public Affairs—The Military and the Media, 1962–1968* (Washington, D.C.: U.S. Army Center of Military History, 1988), and idem, *The U.S. Army in Vietnam: Public Affairs—The Military and the Media, 1968–1973* (Washington, D.C.: U.S. Army Center of Military History, 1996). David Halberstam, *The Powers That Be* (New York: Alfred A. Knopf, 1979), provides perspectives on the press by one of Arnett's well-known Vietnam colleagues.

Index